a celebration society

We have it in our power to begin the world over again.

~Thomas Paine

The world is very different now. For man holds in his mortal hands the power to abolish all forms of human poverty, and all forms of human life.

~John F. Kennedy

Notices

ISBN-13: 978-0692552391 (Inciti Publishing)
First print edition: December 1, 2015

Dedication

To my darling wife Jennifer, who gave me the title and so much more—without her love, belief, support, and tough editorship, this book would today remain only a disjointed set of notes.

To my father Philip, who taught me to write, and to Agora Financial, which taught me to write persuasively.

To Dr. Gerard O'Neill, who enrolled me into some big, possible visions—and led me to a key understanding.

To my Godson Sean Karlson, whose help with the permaculture section was invaluable.

To the many other teachers, seen and unseen, who have shown me pieces of the puzzle and how they fit together, and who continue to educate me.

Acknowledgements

I am grateful to several authors for shaping my own thinking: Gerard O'Neill, Marshall Brain, Ray Kurzweil, Stephen Belgin and Bernard Lietaer.

In addition, I credit Jacques Fresco, Peter Russell, Marshall Savage, Erik Brynjolfsson and Andrew McAfee, Peter Diamandis and Steven Kotler, Jonathon Porritt, Jerry Kaplan, Vivek Wadhwa, Tom Blees, Federico Pistono, and Jeremy Rifkin for creating foundation stones of this vision.

I wish to thank The Original 19, creators of *Café Lounge 19*, the interior title page font. To me, it embodies celebration.

I also thank the following persons whose timely reviews and critiques of this book provided constructive suggestions and improvements:

Robert W. Walter, Esq.

Alex Tabarrok, Ph.D.

Todd William

Eric Karlson

Rohit Sharma

Richard Maceyka, Esq.

Contents

A Different Future

Our public discourse is littered with dark and even apocalyptic visions of the future. While some of these are indeed plausible, focusing attention there does not avert them. Coherent alternatives are needed. As the saying goes, where light is needed it does little good to bemoan the darkness.

For vast multitudes of people, work may well be coming to an end. This will either become our greatest problem or our greatest opportunity. According to the Millennium Project, "The nature of work and political economic systems may have to change ... or else there could be massive long term unemployment. Avoiding this could lead to the beginnings of a new kind of self actualization economy in transition from issues of scarcity to issues of abundance."[1]

Solutions offered have been few and, even if possible, not politically viable or adequate. A real solution must be bold and extraordinary. It must be feasible and sustainable. It must captivate the attention not through fear but through great emotional appeal.

To draw us towards it, the future of which this solution is a part must sparkle with a translucent and kaleidoscopic beauty. Though visionary, it must be achievable within a reasonable window of time and be solidly based on known science and technology. The purpose of this book is to present such a future vision, contrast it with the dangerous path we are presently following, and show how such a future vision can be made real.

If this book succeeds for you, you are invited to join us in creating that different future.

---

[1] http://millennium-project.org/millennium/2015-SOF-ExecutiveSummary-English.pdf

Part I: Understanding the Problem

A problem well stated is a problem half solved.

~Charles Kettering

Standing at the Crossroads of Destiny

We are living at the most momentous juncture in human history. Our imminent choices are not just fundamental; they will create the foundation of the world to come. Consider the range of transformations happening right now:

- The nature of production is shifting in a way that may soon leave huge numbers of people both unemployed and unemployable. While manufacturing jobs have long been falling to increased automation, new artificially intelligent (AI) software is now taking over from human knowledge workers, the centerpiece of the "information economy".[2]

- We are in the process of developing AI with human-level capabilities, and possibly soon super-human capabilities.[3] This will either greatly liberate humanity or bring forth a dark reality as described in certain science fiction.

- Across the globe, nation states are becoming less stable yet with greater access to weapons of mass destruction.[4]

---

[2] http://www.telegraph.co.uk/technology/news/11123336/Meet-Amelia-the-computer-thats-after-your-job.html, http://www.ipsoft.com/

[3] http://www.scientificamerican.com/article/graphic-science-ibm-simulates-4-percent-human-brain-all-of-cat-brain/, http://www.kurzweilai.net/singularity-q-a

[4] http://www.theatlantic.com/magazine/archive/2014/11/chinas-dangerous-game/380789/

- We now can generate new forms of life based on existing genes, and even life that is based on different genes than any naturally occurring on Earth. Likewise, genetically modified organisms (GMO's) are emerging from laboratories, sometimes in uncontrolled ways. Beyond GMO's is "synthetic biology", offering the potential to create new life forms.[5] Such life may free us from disease and hunger or bring pandemic and ruin.
- We have the emerging capacity to expand terrestrial life into space and even to the stars, which could enable a far flung, wondrous and rich civilization or a new kind of dictatorship.
- We have nuclear technologies and engineered viruses capable of destroying human civilization but which can also provide power and medical cures. While nano-technologies will offer us the possibility of universal material abundance, there may also arise nano-weapons capable of extinguishing life itself.
- The nature of money is now undergoing a fundamental transformation.[6]
- Researchers are plunging deep into the nature of biology and aging, with some convinced that an end to age-related disease and decay is imminent.[7] This could further deplete scarce resources and strain social systems or provide a productive long life for all.

---

[5] http://www.theatlantic.com/technology/archive/2014/09/beyond-gmos-the-rise-of-synthetic-biology/380770/,
http://www.nytimes.com/2014/05/08/business/researchers-report-breakthrough-in-creating-artificial-genetic-code.html

[6] Later in this book, we will explore complementary currencies; a little known tool that is at least as powerful as the better-known crypto-currencies such as Bitcoin.

[7] http://sens.org/about/leadership/research-advisory-board

- Sensor devices are plummeting in cost and size with increasing mobility. Universal surveillance seems a certainty in the decades ahead.[8] The question is not so much whether it will happen but rather how it will operate and who will control it.
- The internet potentially offers everyone almost unlimited access to information. At the same time, governments are learning how to control and use it as a surveillance device.[9]
- The most successful 1% is rapidly increasing its share of wealth relative to the other 99%, with almost all of this gain going to the "1% of the 1%". Historically speaking this trend is likely to lead to social unrest.[10]
- We continue to implement ever-more clever and riskier tactics for extraction of hydrocarbon fuels even as radical and promising clean energy solutions often languish for lack of funding.[11]
- Asymmetric warfare, in which a small group such as those who hijack a plane can compel a government to respond with almost infinitely greater resources and expense, is becoming the norm—with ever greater destructive capabilities.
- With terrorism as the stated justification, governments that long enshrined the transparent rule of law and

---

[8] Edward Snowden asserted in *CitizenFour* that such surveillance is already here.

[9] http://www.theatlantic.com/international/archive/2015/02/government-censorship-21st-century-internet/385528/

[10] http://www.theatlantic.com/business/archive/2014/03/how-you-i-and-everyone-got-the-top-1-percent-all-wrong/359862/,
http://www.pbs.org/newshour/making-sense/wealthiest-getting-wealthier-lobbying-lot/

[11] http://www.theatlantic.com/national/archive/2014/12/the-alarming-research-behind-new-yorks-fracking-ban/383868/

personal liberty have rapidly receded from those values.[12]

- Climactic change is altering the acidity and temperatures of our oceans, shifting the terrains of species, and wiping out species whose importance we are only beginning to understand such as the coral reefs, upon which 25% of ocean life depends.[13]
- More broadly, scientists say that we have entered the Sixth Great Extinction of species. In 4.5 billion years, only five other extinctions of this magnitude have happened.[14]

Any one of these transformations is world-changing. Happening all together, their combined effects are unfathomable. In short, there can be little doubt that the world to come will be far different than anything ever before seen on Earth. Will it be a place where you would wish to live? Would you wish it for your children and grandchildren?

I have only touched upon some of the greatest challenges facing us now. Others exist, all with vigilant persons sounding the alarm.

One thing I have observed—and I am far from alone in this—is that most people of passion who wish to make a difference tend to identify a *particular* problem on the planet and focus their available resources on solving it. To the passionate person, nothing else seems as important. Such problems are legion, and they seem to be proliferating like the mythical hydra, especially right now. *Solving any one of them will not solve all of them.*

Less obvious, perhaps, is the fact that there are many solutions being offered; quite a few of them with real potential to make a profound difference. In many cases, I have observed that the creator and proponents are like the proverbial

---

12 http://www.theatlantic.com/international/archive/2014/11/british-liberty-under-threat-terrorism/382605/

13 http://wwf.panda.org/about_our_earth/blue_planet/coasts/coral_reefs/

14 http://news.stanford.edu/news/2014/july/sixth-mass-extinction-072414.html

carpenter: *every* problem looks to them like a nail needing to be driven by their particular hammer. However, such solutions are often incompatible with other proposed solutions or leave significant challenges unaddressed.

Something far more comprehensive is required, or else we will not make it through this century unscathed by devastating changes.

Grabbing the Problem by its Roots

The complexity of the modern world is staggering. Most of us struggle just to cope with and understand our little piece of it. The range of problems facing humanity seems overwhelming, and consequently many of us give up on trying to change the world.

In this book, I will argue that if we trace our myriad problems back to their genesis, methodically examining how they came to be and what might cure them, we will generally find a common origin, as if they were branches of one tree. I will argue that this origin lies in what I am calling the *Scarcity Game*, and in the kinds of decisions, practices, and beliefs that such a game leads people and societies to make, to pursue, and to hold.

If the common genesis of our major problems and crises lies in the Scarcity Game, what could possibly reach into the roots of such a vast and complex tree and shake it enough to effect fundamental change? It can only be something that reframes the entire game into something other than scarcity. I will make the case that we as a species stand at the threshold of a precious, epochal moment in which we can replace the Scarcity Game with an *Abundance Game*.

This book is neither the first nor the final word about an Abundance Game and how to achieve it. Others, some of whose work is discussed herein, have already begun such efforts and more will surely follow. This book will frame the problem in such a way that the need for an Abundance Game becomes clear, and it will offer as a vision one possible expression of an Abundance Game: a *Celebration Society*.

Other approaches to creating an Abundance Game are possible, though I doubt that any will offer us greater richness, joy and opportunities for fulfillment than a Celebration Society. I believe that such as society will be sustainable and satisfying for humanity and for life in general. A Celebration Society offers to us:

- Solutions to ecological and other crises based not on any single technology acting alone but rather an orchestra of technologies and social agreements, playing a beautiful concert together
- Solutions that will appeal not only to logic but also to the heart; to those who dare to dream of a society in which the elderly and the young are cherished while all are freed from deadening "work"
- A way to assure that the basic needs of everyone on Earth are met without coercive redistribution of wealth or reliance on an elusive carrot of "education" that will often recede when chased
- An entirely different way to characterize and organize a society based on:
    o Respecting the individual within a community of voluntary agreements
    o Integrating wisdom from great societies of the past with modern science and technology
    o Transforming the concept of citizenship and its relationship to governance
    o Understanding money in ways that are at once time-proven and revolutionary
    o Recognizing physical principles of production and abundance that are obvious once understood and which replace a need for endless growth
    o Shifting the role of people from workers into explorers, artists, students, creators, scientists, inventors, and gamers, and celebrating whatever they are passionate about

- o Using advanced technologies in a manner that minimizes their risks while embracing their potential for service in a sustainable society
- o Redesigning systems from the ground up to dynamically fuse resiliency with efficiency (including identifying and keeping legacy systems that work) in order to achieve sustainability
- A societal model that can be structured and deployed on a local basis within the next decade or so, not only being open source but actually designed to duplicate itself on a *pay it forward* model

This may sound idealistic, and perhaps it is. In a world where UN relief workers trade food for sex from desperate people and $500 million in Red Cross relief money yields 6 houses, it can be hard to remain idealistic.[15] But I intend to demonstrate that either we will soon move towards an Abundance Game vision, or we may well face a dark future together.

To many people—perhaps to you—notions such as a Celebration Society may seem preposterous. I can imagine some objections:

- That's impossible; it flies against human nature or the laws of nature
- Even if it were possible in theory, any such solution will upset so many vested interests that it could never be implemented in the real world
- It cannot be funded; who will pay for it?
- Where could it possibly happen?

I will address these objections, and I believe that a viable solution is at hand. This solution rests solidly on known science, emerging technologies, and understandings of human

---

[15] http://www.theatlantic.com/international/archive/2015/06/un-peacekeeping-transactional-sex-haiti/395654/

nature gleaned from cutting-edge research. For example, it is just as possible that humans evolved from cooperative primates similar to the bonobo as that we evolved from chimpanzee-like, more violent ones. Indeed, the recently discovered fossil record of *Ardipithecus ramidus* suggests a more bonobo-like origin for humanity.[16]

Parts of this solution will seem incredible to readers who are locked into a particular worldview. I feel for you: we all seek solace and comfort in certainty. I would simply ask that you look at the evidence and think for yourself. After examining this solution, you may remain persuaded that a Celebration Society is not viable or desirable, taken as a whole. However, given the magnitude of the crises we are facing, I hope you'll agree that implementing some portion of a Celebration Society is better than the alternative.

On the other hand, if you finish this book disturbed by the magnitude of the crises now roaring towards us at accelerating speed and convinced that conventional solutions will not be adequate; if you find yourself thinking that a Celebration Society *might* offer a viable solution and be worthy of a social experiment, then this book will have done its job. It will have sparked discussion of a different path.

Why this Book, Now?

Accelerating automation threatens to displace multitudes of workers. Here is a new solution. Thanks to the hard work of many others and some fortuitous life experiences, I am able to express it here.

If you find yourself shaking your head at the fanciful nature of such an idea; questioning whether it is worth your time to read further, then *please stop reading*. Instead, I would ask that you visit YouTube and watch the short video, *"Humans Need Not Apply"* by CGP Grey.

---

[16] http://greatergood.berkeley.edu/article/item/what_can_bonobos_tell_us_about_ourselves

This 15-minute video summarizes the single greatest threat to civilization now rapidly emerging in the world—a threat that will impact us far sooner than the potential impact of climate change. This development is being increasingly recognized as a problem in books and articles but so far no truly viable solutions have been proposed. It is a development that I can almost guarantee will seriously impact your life, or the lives of those you know, within just a few short years.

I am captivated by a vision. I fell in love with it in crude form half a century ago as a child, and have watched it follow a process of evolution and maturation in the decades since. I believe it to be a coherent vision that can successfully weave together solutions to many of the great problems and threats now facing humanity.

The remainder of this book explains that vision, and how it might be achieved in the form of a new model society. This society will be characterized by abundance, play, exploration, service—and celebration! In such a society, most if not all necessary work will be done by Artificial Intelligences (AI's) and robots using sensors that give them human-like perception, although people may of course provide such services for themselves or others as they mutually choose.

New institutions and systems of government may better serve those who dwell in such a new society than the old, scarcity-based ones. This book explores possibilities for such and discusses how these new models may address issues of non-representation, oligarchical tendencies, stagnation and disempowerment that prevail today.

Finally, this book will explore in depth one possible model society that can be implemented somewhere on Earth within a decade or so. It is characterized by open-source design, a reliance on science and technology in service to living beings and systems, a complete redefinition of the concepts of citizenship and security, and includes unique aspects such as a pay-it-forward feature.

If the ideas in this book provoke discussion, debate and action, it will have fulfilled its purpose.

The remainder of this Part I focuses on information that people may find upsetting and even depressing. It's necessary in order to understand the crisis at hand, and is followed by a detailed solution that is both hopeful and supported by research. If you feel that you already understand the problem, and agree with me that the conventional solutions being proposed are completely inadequate to our needs, then you are welcome to skip ahead to Part II. Part II begins to reframe the way we look at everything.

This Is *Your* Problem

What would you do if someone near and dear to you were to suddenly become unemployed and unemployable—or underemployed in such a way that they couldn't meet basic expenses? Would you take them into your home, offer them some money, or simply wish them well? Would you urge them to go back to school, to upgrade their skills? Yet with the increasing scope of automation, upgrading skills may prove to be a stopgap measure that merely defers the time when they are unemployable, draining resources both private and public in the process. Many lack even these resources, and face imminent disaster.

What if you were unemployed and unemployable?

There is an alternative to the stark future of mass unemployment that may soon be upon us. This alternative is bright, and it is beautiful. Much of this book is devoted to exploring the attainability of this future, and I fully expect further discussions to follow publication of this book. However, I do not know whether sufficient numbers of people will commit to this alternative before a darker path is taken by default.

This darker path is, sadly, a reasonable projection of what is to come unless we act now to shift the discussion and the paradigm. It is driven by the threat of an imminent massive wave of unemployment.

Job Loss

> AI will probably turf out whole regiments of white-
> collar workers...workers are doomed to dislocations.
>
> *~The Economist*

Most of us define who we are, in large part, by what we do—how we make money; our work. It is the central idea that defines our value to society as well as our ability to provide for ourselves and others. Work is so important to personal well-being that loss of livelihood is a significant risk factor for suicide.[17]

The stability of work is being shaken as never before. In recent decades, the concept of a job for life has gone by the wayside, even in nations such as Japan and corporations such as IBM where it was culturally entrenched.

In the US, "the percentage of economic output that's paid out in wages now stands at its lowest level since the government started keeping track in the mid-20th century... Loukas Karabarbounis and Brent Neiman, economists at the University of Chicago, have estimated that almost half of the decline is the result of businesses' replacing workers with computers and software."[18]

Not only jobs but whole professions are increasingly unstable and people are being forced to adapt. But what if this were only the leading edge of something far more disruptive?

---

[17] http://www.suicidepreventionlifeline.org/learn/riskfactors.aspx
[18] http://www.theatlantic.com/magazine/archive/2015/07/world-without-work/395294/

The Tsunami Approaches

Automation has already come to many forms of labor, but much more is coming. It is coming with a speed, scope and ferocity that few people understand or can imagine.[19]

Consider these facts. Computing power is now the primary driver of technological progress. Computing power (price/performance) has been doubling roughly every two years and the rate of this change is accelerating; a phenomenon known as the Law of Accelerating Returns; a case of exponential change.[20] (The significance of this law is perhaps best explained by the statement, "At this moment, the rate of technological change is the slowest you will ever experience for the rest of your life."[21])

Many forms of artificial intelligence are already here:

- Computers that recognize faces better than can people.[22]
- We converse with computers, in a more and more lifelike manner.
- A rule-based computer program named Deep Blue beat the highest-ranked human chess player, Garry Kasparov, in a match. More recently and more significantly, a newer program named Giraffe learned in a human-like manner to play at the International Master level in just 72 hours.[23]

---

[19] http://www.economist.com/news/briefing/21594264-previous-technological-innovation-has-always-delivered-more-long-run-employment-not-less

[20] http://www.kurzweilai.net/kurzweils-law-aka-the-law-of-accelerating-returns

[21] http://www.shellypalmer.com/2015/08/what-will-you-do-after-white-collar-work/

[22] http://www.ageekyworld.com/gaussianface-algorithm-beats-humans-at-recognizing-faces/

[23] http://www.technologyreview.com/view/541276/deep-learning-machine-teaches-itself-chess-in-72-hours-plays-at-international-master/

- While robots capable of fully performing nursing and other medical tasks are likely a decade or more away, health care workers and computer scientists are taking this seriously.[24]
- Robots are increasingly learning to do what people can do by being shown how to do something.[25]
- Drug discovery is becoming automated.[26]
- A number of Fortune 1000 companies are quietly moving their call centers from overseas outsourcing to automated call center AI's that understand emotional cues, communicate in a natural manner, and are capable of learning. ("Amelia" is discussed elsewhere.)
- Web site design, a very popular "new economy" job, may soon be largely automated. A new AI takes content in any format—words, pictures, or video—and builds a well-designed, responsive website.[27]
- Some of the best-paying high-education jobs are in IT and data science. However, these functions are starting to be automated.[28]
- Intelligent drone swarms are now entering military use, and will significantly reduce the need for human soldiers while providing superior protection.[29]

IBM and other organizations with formidable resources are plumbing the potential of AI. These include Google's Deep

---

[24] http://www.theatlantic.com/health/archive/2014/10/the-best-nurses-for-ebola-patients-might-be-robots/381884/

[25] http://www.technologyreview.com/news/541491/software-makes-robot-learning-like-childs-play/

[26] http://www.kurzweilai.net/robot-scientist-eve-could-speed-up-search-for-new-drugs

[27] https://thegrid.io/

[28] http://www.slideshare.net/IBM_BA/make-analytics-easier-with-ibm-watson-analytics

[29] http://www.theatlantic.com/technology/archive/2014/10/the-navys-future-fleet-of-swarming-boat-drones/381128/

Mind and others. Google's AI system has already learned how to recognize cats without ever being told about them; a huge advance in pattern recognition.[30] Another system called PANDA, "can accurately discern gender, hairstyles, clothing styles, and facial expressions from photos." Yet another can discern a concealed weapon. And now AI's have been developed that can not only discern objects within photos but even describe them in sentences.[31]

IBM's work deserves special mention. In a tour de force demonstration its AI program, Watson, trounced the two greatest human Jeopardy players of all time. Given that these two gentlemen had totally dominated their human competition and could legitimately be called "geniuses" of Jeopardy, one could say that this is the first demonstrated (albeit narrow) example of superhuman artificial intelligence.

Watson is now being repurposed to search for oil and to serve as an expert medical "assistant" in partnership with Cleveland Clinic/Case Western Reserve University. Its intended function and purpose is to enhance medical diagnosis.

Says IBM:

> Machine learning will enable cognitive systems to learn, reason and engage with us in a more natural and personalized way. These systems will get smarter and more customized through interactions with data, devices and people. They will help us take on what may have been seen as unsolvable problems by using all the information that surrounds us and bringing the right insight or suggestion to our fingertips

---

[30] http://www.motherjones.com/media/2014/09/deep-learning-artificial-intelligence-facebook-nsa

[31] http://www.kurzweilai.net/a-computer-vision-algorithm-that-can-describe-photos

right when it's most needed. Over the next five years, machine learning applications will lead to new breakthroughs that will amplify human abilities, assist us in making good choices, look out for us and help us navigate our world in powerful new ways.[32]

While IBM carefully avoids any suggestion that these applications of software could in any way displace or make obsolete human workers, it goes on to highlight five targeted fields for implementation before 2020: medicine, "sentient cities", education, retailing, and online security ("digital guardians").

Research is now establishing that the effects of this automation are pushing increasing numbers of workers down into less skilled positions or unemployment, thereby breeding ever-greater competitive employment pressures, under- and unemployment, and despair.[33]

According to Professors Frey and Osborne of Oxford University, "about 47% of total U.S. employment is in the 'high risk' category of being automated–meaning these gigs are likely to be automated in the next decade or two."[34] The Bank of England has predicted that 80 million US jobs and 15 million British jobs could be automated, in each case representing about half of the economy.[35]

Today, we shrug when the bank clerk or cashier at a supermarket is replaced by an ATM or by a self-serve checkout system. Tomorrow, we may shrug when our delivery person is replaced by a drone or by a robot that is transported within a

---

[32] http://research.ibm.com/cognitive-computing/machine-learning-applications/
[33] http://www.nytimes.com/2014/06/11/opinion/the-downward-ramp.html
[34] http://www.forbes.com/sites/elainepofeldt/2014/02/26/will-r2-d2-snag-your-job/
[35] http://www.cnbc.com/2015/11/13/robots-could-steal-80-million-us-jobs-bank-of-england.html

self-driving vehicle. Yet those represent millions of jobs that will disappear in America alone.

Says Prof. Vivek Wadhwa of Stanford, "Uber just hired away dozens of engineers from Carnegie Mellon University to build its own robotic cars. It will surely start replacing its human drivers as soon as its technology is ready—later in this decade."[36]

This is not theory. Google's self-driving vehicles have logged over 1 million miles of safe driving on roads alongside human-piloted vehicles. Twelve accidents have happened, none serious—and none due to the robotic vehicles.[37] Delivery robots are being developed in South Korea and elsewhere. Amazon is planning for drone delivery of parcels. Audi has a model A7 prototype vehicle that drives itself on roads.[38] Skilled jobs in factories are increasingly being automated as well.[39] So is the job of security guard.[40]

As horrific as working conditions are for many of those who labor in developing world sweatshops, those jobs are desperately needed by the families who rely upon them. However, such jobs will only exist until the capital investment and maintenance costs of equivalent AI/robotic systems are cheaper per unit of production than paying people to work.[41]

Says TechCast Global:

> Simple versions of mass-produced robots are being used for routine tasks, and more intel-

---

[36] http://www.huffingtonpost.com/vivek-wadhwa/yes-a-computer-will-take-your-job_b_7743914.html

[37] http://venturebeat.com/2015/06/03/googles-self-driving-cars-have-driven-over-1-million-miles/

[38] http://fortune.com/2015/01/28/audis-self-driving-car/

[39] http://www.nytimes.com/2012/08/19/business/new-wave-of-adept-robots-is-changing-global-industry.html

[40] http://www.theatlantic.com/technology/archive/2014/11/security-robot-watching-over-silicon-valley-is-less-robocop-and-more-r2d2/383078/

[41] *Smart Robots* by Colin Popell, *Techcast Global* 11/20/2014

ligent versions are rapidly being developed that walk and climb stairs, speak with humans, and perform complex tasks. As computer power, artificial intelligence, and other enabling technologies mature, smart robots are expected to create a new era of affordable and convenient robotic helpers. The Japanese and South Koreans, who lead the field, are even now gearing up to sell millions of robots to serve important roles in industrial work, home services, healthcare, military, and leisure activities. At the other end of the size spectrum, robotic bees could be pollinating agricultural crops in the foreseeable future.[42]

Household labor is becoming automated, in steps, over time.[43] The Roomba has automated routine vacuuming, and the concept is being improved upon by companies such as Dyson and Samsung. Robots can now learn to perform domestic tasks by watching them performed.[44] UC Berkeley researchers "have developed new algorithms that enable robots to learn motor tasks (such as assembling a toy airplane) by trial and error, using a process that more closely approximates the way humans learn."[45] While the researchers expect that generalized capabilities to do laundry and clean house may be a decade or more away, it is easy to extrapolate that once such capabilities exist mass production will commence, prices will plunge, and domestic service jobs will rapidly disappear.

---

[42] ibid.
[43] http://www.theatlantic.com/technology/archive/2014/06/your-dinner-table-soon-to-be-cleared-by-robots/373653/
[44] http://www.techtimes.com/articles/30166/20150201/darpa-trains-robots-to-cook-by-watching-youtube-videos-why-its-significant.htm
[45] http://www.kurzweilai.net/robots-master-skills-with-deep-learning-technique

Domestic helpers rarely have much of a voice, and are easily ignored. That is definitely not the case with professionals such as doctors, accountants and, especially, lawyers. There is a certain hubris that is common among professionals. It could be summarized as: I have a vast body of knowledge; it was hard-earned, and no machine will ever replace me. In the years ahead, this hubris will be shaken to the core.

With the exception of world-class experts, there is reason for concern that many and perhaps all of the professions may eventually fall to automation.[46] Today, routine legal research and medical diagnosis are being automated. As machine intelligence continues to rise at an accelerating rate, the range of skills that can be automated may well correspondingly rise.

A further concern comes from the new field of *clio-dynamics*. This is an academic effort to mathematically model history. Though its validity is open to debate, such research indicates that most civilizations go through two broad cycles, the shorter one roughly 50 years long. By these calculations, circa 2020 the US will experience a sharp spike in terrorism. "My model suggests that the next [peak in violence] will be worse than the one in 1970 because demographic variables such as wages, standards of living and a number of measures of intra-elite confrontation are all much worse this time," said founder Prof. Peter Turchin. Importantly, Turchin's model does not include automation, which will exacerbate the pressure, should his model prove correct.[47]

The social disruption caused by massive, sudden automation should not be underestimated. Says Prof. Wadhwa:

> Policy makers will have a big new problem to deal with: the disappearance of human jobs. Not only will there be fewer jobs for people doing

---

[46] *Rise of the Robots: Technology and the Threat of a Jobless Future*, Martin Ford

[47] http://www.livescience.com/22109-cycles-violence-2020.html

manual work, but the jobs of knowledge workers will also be replaced by computers. Almost every industry and profession will be impacted, and this will create a new set of social problems -- because most people can't adapt to such dramatic change.[48]

Anyone who doubts that corporations will drop managers and professionals as quickly as they do less skilled workers has not studied outsourcing. While some professional activities that humans perform uniquely well may remain, it appears that they will likely be far fewer than most of us imagine, and will require constant updating to avoid becoming obsolete. Similarly, humans may always be needed at the forefront of innovation, before processes become standardized, although that will account for just a small percentage of work.

Indeed, it is not necessary for automation to replace a profession; it need only make those few remaining workers far more efficient. When one worker does the work of 100, 99 workers' jobs are gone. We need only consider the history of farming in America to validate this understanding. Most of the knowledge that constitutes a "profession" is codified as facts and relationships between facts, with judgment based on probabilities and experience. Without in any way disrespecting the professions, there is no demonstrable reason why AI's cannot learn to do much or all of this, over time.

A Line in the Sand?

Many of those who write of the coming automation of jobs express confidence that it will not render vast numbers of humans permanently unemployed because, in their view, certain human abilities can never be automated. This argument holds, essentially, that there is a kind of "line in the

---

[48] http://www.huffingtonpost.com/vivek-wadhwa/yes-a-computer-will-take-your-job_b_7743914.html

sand" that AI's will not be able to cross. I believe this to be dangerously optimistic.

McAfee and Brynjolfsson cite "ideation, creativity, and innovation" as sustainable human advantages.[49] Others have suggested that intuition and intuitive forecasting are uniquely human gifts. However, even assuming that such thinking is correct, the argument made by McAfee and Brynjolfsson nevertheless acknowledges that the majority of normal work activities in a profession such as medicine will soon be automated, leaving only "special cases" for the humans. This is still a recipe for massive unemployment in medicine, and probably many other professions as well.

In *The Second Machine Age,* the authors write:

> Computers are... machines for generating answers, not posing interesting new questions.... Ideation, creativity, and innovation are often described as 'thinking outside the box,' and this characterization indicates another large and reasonably sustainable advantage of human over digital labor... While computer reasoning from predefined rules and inferences from existing examples can address a large share of cases, human diagnosticians will still be valuable even after Dr. Watson finishes its medical training because of the idiosyncrasies and special cases that inevitably arise.

The world's most successful political forecaster makes the same argument by way of describing the culture at what is arguably the world's most successful company; a company which makes extensive use of computer simulations. Said Nate Silver:

> What makes (Google) successful is the way it combines rigorous commitment to testing with its freewheeling creative culture. Google's

---

[49] *The Second Machine Age*, McAfee and Brynjolfsson

> people are given every inducement to do what people do much better than computers: come up with ideas, a *lot* of ideas. Google then harnesses its immense data to put these ideas to the test. The majority of them are discarded very quickly, but the best ones survive.[50]

While this obviously works extremely well at Google, it's worth noting that Google is known for hiring only geniuses and that geniuses, by definition, comprise a tiny fraction of the human population. Google may be a model for tomorrow's high-tech corporation, but it does not offer a solution to widespread unemployment. Until and unless we can figure out how to cultivate creative genius in the average person, the world cannot spawn vast numbers of Google-like companies to blanket all available goods and services.

Marc Andreessen is one of the world's most respected venture capitalists. In a blog he wrote, "... even when robots and AI are far more powerful, there will still be many things that people can do that robots and AI can't. For example: creativity, innovation, exploration, art, science, entertainment, and caring for others. We have no idea how to make machines do these."

Actually, however, we do.

Evidence of Artificial Creativity

AI's have invented "methods and apparatus" that were sufficiently creative (or in the words of the US Patent Office, "novel and non-obvious") to be awarded US patents.[51] They

---

[50] http://fivethirtyeight.com/features/rage-against-the-machines/
[51] http://www.ipwatchdog.com/2009/08/30/how-computer-automated-inventing-is-revolutionizing-law/id=5399/

have written short stories, news articles,[52] non-fiction books,[53] and poetry[54] that can be indistinguishable from human creations. They have created art, images[55] and musical compositions in the styles of human masters as well as in their own style that is at once non-human and yet beautiful.[56] They have discovered new mathematical proofs.[57]

As Ray Kurzweil has put it, "AI programs diagnose electrocardiograms with an accuracy rivaling doctors, evaluate medical images, fly and land airplanes, guide intelligent autonomous weapons, make automated investment decisions for over a trillion dollars of funds, and guide industrial processes."[58] An unspoken truth of the investment industry is that, in many cases, the people do not actually manage the money; software does. (For example, high-frequency trading—by its nature—must be done by software.)

Even science, to the extent that it is now a computational process of grinding through vast amounts of data, can be automated—though conceiving the great questions that become important falsifiable hypotheses does require a special kind of creativity.

Some will protest that this may be true for routine tasks but it will never be true for creative activities, and that those are as vital in business and science as in the arts.

Perhaps. Intuitive foresight is a growing field of research, and it is possible that certain human competencies will not be subject to automation. That said, the range of creative activities that can potentially be automated keeps expanding.

---

52 http://www.ft.com/cms/s/2/bb3ac0f6-2e15-11db-93ad-0000779e2340.html
53 http://singularityhub.com/2012/12/13/patented-book-writing-system-lets-one-professor-create-hundreds-of-thousands-of-amazon-books-and-counting/, http://news.bbc.co.uk/2/hi/programmes/click_online/9764416.stm
54 http://www.kurzweilcyberart.com/poetry/rkcp_poetry_samples.php
55 http://petapixel.com/2013/03/25/extremely-realistic-computer-generated-imagery-is-killing-photography-jobs/
56 http://www.theatlantic.com/entertainment/archive/2014/08/computers-that-compose/374916/
57 http://www.wired.com/2013/03/computers-and-math/
58 http://www.kurzweilai.net/singularity-q-a

Researchers have recently pioneered a technique for automating discovery in large data sets; a process that until now has required human involvement. To wit:

> The researchers... demonstrated this idea with data from real-world problems, including detection of anomalous cardiac activity from heart recordings and classification of astronomical objects from raw photometry. In all cases and without access to original domain knowledge, the researchers demonstrated that the performance of these general algorithms was on par with the accuracy of specialized algorithms and heuristics tweaked by experts to work."[59]

The realm of AI invention and discovery is not limited to data.[60] As of this writing, AI's have made at least one major scientific discovery. To wit:

> An artificial intelligence system has for the first time reverse-engineered the regeneration mechanism of planaria — the small worms whose extraordinary power to regrow body parts has made them a research model in human regenerative medicine...the discovery by Tufts University biologists presents the first model of regeneration discovered by a non-human intelligence and the first comprehensive model of planarian regeneration, which had

---

[59] http://www.kurzweilai.net/data-smashing-could-automate-discovery-untouched-by-human-hands

[60] https://www.newscientist.com/round-up/beyond-knowledge

eluded human scientists for more than 100 years.[61]

Even magic tricks, which most of us would assume to be uniquely human, are being performed by AI's.[62]

While most of our entertainment now remains the province of human performers and writers, there is nothing inherent in what we know about AI that allows us to state with certainty that human levels of creativity cannot be replicated. Examples of AI composers include David Cope's "Experiments in Musical Intelligence"[63] and Francois Pachet of Sony's Computer Science Lab,[64] among others.

AI-generated writings now have commercial value, though they have yet to demonstrate the capability to produce great or bestselling books. For example, Narrative Sciences' AI writes articles for 30 clients including *Forbes*.[65] (It is perhaps obvious that, by the same token, little of human writing qualifies as great.)

IBM's Watson, now being developed into thousands of applications by partner companies, is actually creating new and useful things by ignoring human biases. For example, it is inventing tasty food recipes that professional chefs thought to be impossible.[66]

Converging technologies are now enabling holographic representations of deceased musical performers, some of

---

[61] http://www.kurzweilai.net/planarian-regeneration-model-discovered-by-ai-algorithm; http://dx.doi.org/10.1371/journal.pcbi.1004295

[62] http://www.scientificamerican.com/article/artificial-intelligence-that-performs-real-magic-tricks-video/

[63] http://artsites.ucsc.edu/faculty/cope/music.htm

[64] http://francoispachet.fr/markovconstraints/audio/boulez_blues.mp3

[65] http://news.bbc.co.uk/2/hi/programmes/click_online/9764416.stm

[66] http://www.fastcompany.com/3049022/the-future-of-work/3-lessons-ibms-watson-can-teach-us-about-our-brains-biases

which may even perform songs that are newly created based on the style of the deceased person.[67]

As for caring for others, that depends what one means by this. Robotic nurses are already being seriously considered for disaster relief and more[68] and PARO, an animatronic seal, provides a convincing illusion of affection.[69] Preliminary research indicates that Watson can predict psychosis better than psychiatrists based on speech patterns.[70]

Exploration I will delightedly concede as being human, and if AI's ever develop an exploratory spirit, there is plenty of room in this vast universe for them to do so beside us rather than in replacement of us. (Exploration, expressions of caring and affection, learning, and the playing of games will remain forever available to humans—and if they have no economic utility in a Celebration Society, it will not matter.)

Another variation of this human uniqueness argument is raised by David Autor of MIT.[71] He says:

> machine learning will only ever 'get it right' on average while missing many of the most important and informative exceptions... interpersonal interaction, flexibility, adaptability and problem-solving.... [While] much contemporary economic pessimism attributes the labor market woes of the past decade to the adverse impacts of computerization, I remain skeptical of this inference.

---

[67] http://www.theatlantic.com/entertainment/archive/2015/04/the-inevitability-of-hologram-selena/390186/

[68] http://www.hsi.gatech.edu/hrl/project_nurse.shtml,
http://www.theatlantic.com/health/ archive/2014/10/the-best-nurses-for-ebola-patients-might-be-robots/381884/

[69] http://www.parorobots.com/

[70] http://www.kurzweilai.net/speech-analysis-program-is-better-at-predicting-psychosis-than-psychiatrists

[71] http://www.kansascityfed.org/publicat/sympos/2014/093014.pdf

There are several problems with his arguments, which are especially noteworthy in that they were presented by invitation to the Federal Reserve; arguably the most influential financial policymaking institution on the planet. First, Autor presumes that because machines have not demonstrated specific types of competency so far, they will not do so in the future, and that machines will remain limited to "brute force" learning. Recent advances in diverse aspects of AI—many of them dismissed as wishful thinking by many computer scientists until recently— should give pause. Second, he presumes that because a particular kind of work has been done in a particular manner in the past that it will continue to be done that way.[72]

In the latter part of the 20th century, stock brokerage was an established profession requiring good people skills. Today, the profession is much diminished, with most customers entirely happy to place orders directly via computer at lower cost. While Autor acknowledges that this has happened with stockbrokers, he expresses confidence that other professions will rise to replace the lost jobs. He cites as a growing profession, "the nurse practitioner occupation that increasingly performs diagnosing and prescribing tasks in lieu of physicians."

Ignoring for the moment that most stockbrokers would not be well suited to becoming nurse practitioners, what will happen when AI systems reliably perform such diagnoses faster and cheaper than people? The only constraint upon AI's writing prescriptions is regulation. While most of us alive today—myself included—may feel squeamish about taking AI-prescribed medicines, future generations are unlikely to share this prejudice.

Third, even if (as Autor says) computerization does not account for the recent reduction of job growth, this in no way precludes it from reducing job growth in the future.

---

[72] http://www.motherjones.com/media/2014/06/why-marc-andreesons-wrong-about-robot-economy

Wishful assumptions about lines that cannot be crossed are dangerous. Ask a historian about the impregnable Maginot Line.

The Vanishing Profession of Law

Already, professions long regarded as immune to automation are starting to feel the waters of the coming technological tsunami. Consider law, a profession that was until recently considered a strictly human province, and essentially an assured route to success. IBM has set its sights on this profession, starting with legal research. Said John Gordon, Vice President, IBM Watson Solutions:

> (These Watson-based processors) mimic the human nervous system, just as the latest "neural network" algorithm does. As a result, these "computers" can see, speak, listen, think and learn...Later this year, a small Canadian company is scheduled to introduce its "digital legal advisor" to the world's law firms... "You just ask it a question as you would ask another human being. (It) doesn't retrieve thousands of documents for you to sift through. It gives you an evidence-based response... IBM is looking for the right partners and institutions that will give Watson the best legal education. In the future, you can expect to see autonomous legal aides that go beyond just answering simple questions, digital paralegals that can actually help lawyers devise new strategies for their cases.[73]

---

[73] http://www.theatlantic.com/sponsored/ibm-transformation-of-business/watson-takes-the-stand/283/

According to IBM's partner company which is now releasing its Ross legal research app, "attorneys devote nearly a fifth of their working hours to legal research and law firms spend \$9.6 billion on research annually."[74]

IBM doesn't claim that Watson will replace attorneys; only those who support them. Yet it's obvious that a fifth of legal work is now at risk, and one can imagine Watson's scope being extended to other aspects of the legal profession.

What kind of market will then exist for lawyers in a world of AI legal services? It seems hard to imagine that there will be much use for human attorneys beyond the top graduates of the top law schools. I see three possible exceptions:

(1) <u>Serving as Human Faces</u>. In the short term, people will continue to desire human beings to deal with their important legal matters. The questions then become: how much skill will these people contribute, what will that be worth, and will the Millennials and later generations who are growing up comfortable conversing with machines care whether they are dealing with humans?

(2) <u>Litigation</u>. It will be decades before courts allow AI attorneys, probably using robotic housings, to argue cases—and given that both jurors and judges will be uncomfortable with them, they will first establish a beachhead in courts as "advisors" to human attorneys. But when the AI's make airtight arguments by pursuing lines of reasoning the humans missed, and performing more complete research into precedent, they will increasingly lead the humans.

(3) <u>New, personal legal services</u>. While it is clear that many people are under-represented with legal services, at least in the US with its adversarial system, it is unclear that those needs (which are often routine and rarely ground-breaking) cannot be better met by an AI

---

[74] http://www.wired.com/2015/08/voice-powered-app-lawyers-can-ask-legal-help/

attorney/paralegal team with a human front person, and perhaps a few human attorneys to check the work until at some point such checking becomes unnecessary.

The exceptions appear limited in both scope and duration. Generally speaking, when AI's become capable of dealing with work-related information and concepts as well as do the people in that profession, the days of significant human employment in that profession will be numbered. In software such as Watson and Amelia (discussed elsewhere), we now see the first waters lapping at the shore.

McAfee and Brynjolfsson argue in *The Second Machine Age* that non-routine jobs are more immune to rising AI and robotics than are other jobs. They say, "Routine clerical work like processing payments is easier to automate than handling customers' questions. At present, machines are not very good at walking up stairs, picking up a paperclip from the floor, or reading the emotional cues of a frustrated customer."

Just a few short years after *The Second Machine Age* was published, Amelia, an AI tool that handles customers' questions and relates to their emotional cues is, "... already being piloted within a number of Fortune 1000 companies"[75]. If even experts such as McAfee and Brynjolfsson can miss such developments, then clearly our greatest danger lies in underestimating what is coming.

Said Prof. Jerry Kaplan of Stanford, "Advances in information technology are already gutting industries and jobs at a furious clip, far faster than the labor markets can possibly adapt, and there's much worse to come."[76]

The Siamese Twin Problem

There is another aspect of all this that I have not seen addressed. I call it the Siamese Twin Problem. Directly or

---

[75] http://www.ipsoft.com/meet-amelia-new-artificial-intelligence-platform-interacts-like-a-human/

[76] *Humans Need Not Apply*, Jerry Kaplan

indirectly, all "B2C" (business to consumer) companies depend on a significant and growing number of consumers in order to thrive. While it is possible that, in future, the number of B2C companies could diminish and the relative share of B2B (business to business) vs. B2C sales could rise significantly, it is inescapable that *so long as businesses sell to consumers, such businesses must assure the existence of consumers.*

Put differently, if 50% or more of the workforce becomes unemployed in the decades ahead, then (without reflecting other factors) the revenues of B2C companies in aggregate will fall by the purchasing power of those 50%. The B2C companies will aggressively oppose such a development, and one particularly effective way to do so would be to get government to provide a permanent income to those consumers, probably under the guise of a politically palatable moniker such as "National Profit Sharing". While the B2B companies and private investors can be expected to fiercely oppose such measures, the likelihood of B2C support does make such measures politically plausible if still highly uncertain.

If such a tax were levied on all profits, the B2C companies would pay higher taxes—but so would the B2B companies and the investors. This would be a net gain from the B2C companies' perspective.

On this basis, it is possible that a kind of income redistribution will be enacted, at least in some countries, to provide for the permanently unemployed. However, it is extremely unlikely that such a tax will be universally adopted, and there is still the associated problem of companies that are taxed in this manner relocating to "friendlier" nations that do not enact such a tax, then exporting to those nations that do enact it.

Such employers, relocating to lower tax locales, will enjoy competitive cost advantages that it will be hard for their higher-taxed competitors to match. This is on top of the advantages of replacing people with automation.

Historically, raising taxes on corporations and the rich was a viable if arguably misguided way to increase government revenues. In the now emerging world where an ever-increasing percentage of assets are intangible, with globalization of business culture and skills, it is easy to relocate productive assets to no-tax or low-tax venues.

Such mobility effectively forces governments to compete with other governments for businesses. This is why governments offer enormous subsidies to attract and keep businesses, instead taxing their citizens more heavily or reducing services. There is no apparent way for governments to overcome this other than a worldwide treaty establishing and enforcing a common tax policy.

While Thomas Piketty and others advocate this, the practical difficulties are extreme. In particular, the more nations agree to such a tax the more attractive the remaining nations become as tax havens for both capital and industry. Right now, US and European enforcement efforts notwithstanding, tax havens abound. Within Europe, it has so far proven impractical to integrate the different national tax systems. In the US, the desire for a new tax system is almost universal yet the IRS remains a byzantine mess. Multiple administrations have promised to implement a new tax system. None ever has. Why would a global wealth tax be any different?

Not only is there no good way for governments to hold major corporations captive, but there are growing competitive pressures for corporations to eliminate whatever jobs may remain.

Advantages AI/Robotic Systems Offer to Employers

Robots are increasingly learning to do what people do by observation and trial and error. This eliminates the need to program a particular manual skill set. Currently, this is limited to simple tasks, but exponential progress assures us that these skills will progress rapidly.[77]

---

[77] http://www.wired.com/2015/05/remaking-google-facebook-deep-learning-tackles-robotics/

Once one robot knows how to do something, other identical robots can be given the same skills. Robots do not tire or require breaks, except for occasional maintenance. The replication of the human senses of touch, sight, and hearing is proceeding rapidly.[78] Few jobs require a refined sense of smell or taste, and there can be no assurance that those will not, over time, be replicated as well.

Also, as IBM's Watson and other systems now being deployed indicate, AI computers will soon have the ability to absorb vast troves of human knowledge, sift through it to discern useful patterns (AKA meaning), never forget, think with a precision and speed far in excess of an ordinary human—and quickly share what they have learned with additional computer systems. When they make mistakes, those particular mistakes (AKA bugs) once corrected will not be repeated. All of these are significant competitive advantages.

Robots can be guided by such AI's, either embedded within the robots or operating at a distance.

Once an artificial system has human-equivalent or better sight, hearing and touch,[79] coupled with robotic reliability and the intellectual competency to replicate a human job function, only one question remains: what do the financial aspects look like? Employers will focus on the capital investment, training and maintenance costs of the artificial system relative to the hiring, training and "maintenance" costs of comparable human workers.

---

[78] http://www.engadget.com/2013/04/26/artificial-sense-of-touch-gets-smarter-lets-robots-really-feel/, http://www.scientificamerican.com/article/new-software-gives-robots-gift-hearing/, https://www.qut.edu.au/news/news?news-id=70136, http://www.kurzweilai.net/short-probabilistic-programming-machine-learning-code-replaces-complex-programs-for-computer-vision-tasks

[79] http://www.theatlantic.com/technology/archive/2015/01/meet-the-robot-champion-of-beer-pong/384285/

When the employer's financial analysts compute that the net present value[80] of the artificial system is superior to that of the human, the human will be replaced. If some companies resist or some nations legislate against this, they will lose the competitive edge to companies or nations with no such scruples, much as outsourcing has rewarded the low-cost provider. In a sense, this is the ultimate in outsourcing.

Robots are already demonstrating capability to improve productivity over people. A Chinese factory recently replaced 90% of its workers with robots, and production soared.[81] Leaders in the automotive industry are projecting that automation will soon replace those jobs *en masse*.[82] While it is clear enough that a robot performing a set of manual tasks can outperform a person, there is no reason to presume this is limited to factories. In the future, professional services firms aided by AI's may attain unprecedented levels of efficiency, reliability, and low costs coupled with very high profits. Whatever it takes to achieve this, whether "moral" or not, is fully consistent with the "11th Commandment" taught to MBA's worldwide: maximize shareholder value. In the vast majority of corporations, any executive who does not treat this as a top responsibility will be summarily fired.

This cost efficiency will become possible because these firms will largely be reduced to sets of AI's that perform much of the back-office work, as well as research, administration, and other support services with very little human involvement. Top management, which is accountable only to the owners, will not hesitate to terminate lower-level managers and executives as soon as reliable replacements are found—whether human or not. Again, outsourcing demonstrates this. Within decades, I expect that humans in such firms as well as many

---

[80] Net present value (NPV) reduces to a single number all of the expected cash flows and risk factors of an investment, including relevant uncertainties

[81] http://www.techrepublic.com/article/chinese-factory-replaces-90-of-humans-with-robots-production-soars/

[82] http://www.reuters.com/article/2015/09/20/us-autoshow-frankfurt-magna-idUSKCN0RK0YC20150920

manufacturing firms will largely be reduced to serving as public faces, with the need for very few technical persons, managers and executives.

In our present Scarcity Game, there will be unrelenting pressures on those remaining workers to work ever harder and more efficiently, until replaced.

Work Addiction Is No Solution

It is understandable if sad that, in order to survive, less skilled, lowly paid workers often must work multiple jobs, which can have serious health and relationship consequences.[83] However, it is perplexing to note that many highly paid professionals do a similar thing. Today, there is cultural cachet among professionals and "serious" businesspeople to working long hours.

For example, investment bankers—who earn extraordinary compensation measured on an hourly basis—also work some of the longest hours of anyone, often clocking in at 17 hours a day with few days off. Likewise, top attorneys and doctors may do the same. Yet such overwork is destructive in many ways. Beyond a certain point, hours worked can become counterproductive without the worker realizing it, and the loss of balance in life has destructive impacts on health, families and, by extension, societies.[84]

Regardless of its merits or deficiencies, such a work ethic offers no job security against the rise of the machines.

Further, this addiction to work is dangerously combined for many with a sense of identity and self-worth derived from their jobs. When demand for their professional services shrinks, it is likely that such professionals will experience

---

[83] http://www.theatlantic.com/health/archive/2014/09/when-you-cant-afford-sleep/380128/

[84] http://www.theatlantic.com/business/archive/2014/08/to-work-better-work-less/375763/2/

profound stress from the mixture of shrinking wages, reduced job opportunities and shattered self-esteem. This has enormous social implications. It seems reasonable to expect significant increases in suicides and other health problems such as alcoholism.[85]

The Dark Underside of Automation

Those who expect that a proliferation of new jobs will counter the losses of jobs to automation are counting on a rapid broadening of the economy into new sectors—an effect spawned by coming technological breakthroughs. While I agree with the broadening of the economy and the breakthroughs, there are three reasons for being skeptical that any of this will lead to large numbers of new jobs:

1. As the costs of expressing AI into software and then equipping it with robotic extensions including human-level touch, hearing, and sight plunge, more and more forms of labor will be automated. This will reduce the number of existing jobs for humans, offsetting new job creation.
2. The AI's will evolve and be duplicable into many such emerging niches faster than most humans can adapt or learn. Further, even if the automation is slower than anticipated, the humans will eventually be displaced yet again.
3. The social support required for many millions of displaced human workers will either cripple new (and existing) businesses or not be provided at all, stunting economic growth across the board.

Such displacement has long been accepted for "menial labor", and dismissed with a shrug, as if those people don't matter. After all, the argument goes, if they had "drive and determination" they'd get an education or start a business. Those who don't do so, or who try and fail, are presumed to be

[85] http://www.huffingtonpost.com/2014/10/03/suicide-unemployment_n_5926056.html

somehow morally defective, inferior and unworthy of the better things in life.

One might think it would be harder to make this argument when vast numbers of successful professionals are displaced all at once, but our human capacity for willful blindness is large. We need only look back at what happened when the US space program was effectively shut down following the Apollo Program. Huge numbers of engineers were cast adrift. Sadly, amongst those not directly affected, there was a collective shrug.

Moving forward, it is vitally important that we distinguish antiquated notions from facts. Public policy based on illusions or fantasies will lead to increasingly dire consequences. The next displacements of professionals are unlikely to be few or temporary.

The so-called "jobless recovery" of recent years may be the first warning of the tsunami to come. US jobs have recently failed to keep pace with what is needed, especially since many of the new jobs are lowly paid. In particular, among the generation now emerging into the workforce, some stark trends are showing:

> The Economic Policy Institute has found that entry-level hourly wages fell on average for both female and male college graduates from 2000 to 2013—8.1 percent among women and 6.7 percent among men. And the unemployment rate for 20- to 24-year-olds remains exceedingly high, at 11.4 percent (compared with 5.9 percent overall).

Note that these numbers are artificially low, as they ignore those who have stopped looking for work. One consequence is that parents are caring for their children until later in life. But at what cost?[86]

---

[86] http://www.theatlantic.com/business/archive/2014/10/25-is-the-new-21/381421/2/

Even people whose families are not directly affected will nevertheless be indirectly affected because there are almost always others who could perform one's job and, as automation removes more and more jobs from the workplace, desperate people will work ever more cheaply at whatever work remains in order to survive.

Economists have some curious notions about this. In *The Second Machine Age*, after acknowledging that advances in AI and robotics could drive down wages, the authors wrote:

> Economic theory also holds open the possibility that the remaining workers would see an increase in pay. In particular, if their work complements the technology, then demand for their services will increase. In addition, as technical advances increase labor productivity, employers can afford to pay more for each worker.

Yes, employers can *afford* to do this. But what evidence is there that they will do so rather than pay higher dividends to owners or higher bonuses to management? Corporations are profit-maximizing entities.

What will we say to these displaced workers? What do we say to them, right now? I have met talented men, trained as engineers, who were laid off as their industries shifted and moved abroad. Some sprung back; others wound up flipping burgers or the equivalent. Some committed suicide, unable to stand watching everything they loved crumble around them as their professional and social status plunged them into poverty.

Is anyone so hard-hearted that not an ounce of compassion comes out for such a person, or such a family? Regardless of our feelings, even a cold-blooded analysis reveals that, on a broader scale, such events, repeated again and again, are corrosive to a community. A state. A nation. A planet.

Awareness of this crisis is rising, thanks largely to books such as *The Second Machine Age*. But the solutions are generally few, stale and inadequate. They amount to advocacy of greater educational opportunities and new taxes or redistribution of incomes. They are not sufficient to the need of the time—if they are even feasible or desirable.

Research is showing that the "American Dream" of upward mobility for everyone is rarely realistic, and automation will only compound the problem as it becomes harder to convert labor into capital.[87] Further, Americans—and presumably people in other economies as well—are well aware that it's becoming harder to succeed. Indeed, in America "78 percent of adults agreed that 'compared to earlier generations ... it is currently harder' for young people today 'to get started in life'."[88]

Apparently, environment is a dominant factor in social mobility. Simply moving poor kids to a better environment improves their chances for success.[89] A key finding is that, "the policies that would address the situation are even more extreme—and more politically unfeasible" than previously thought.[90]

Some thinkers, such as Bill Curry, are creatively looking at new ways of organizing work and production via cooperatives to save people from desperate unemployment.[91] Such efforts may help us while we transition to a new kind of system. However, if humans will eventually be unable to economically compete with machines in most productive activities, then such efforts must ultimately fail.

Among a group of 1,900 professionals who have studied AI and thought about this problem, there is a sharp division

---

[87] http://www.theatlantic.com/magazine/archive/2014/07/whats-in-a-name-everything/372271/

[88] http://www.theatlantic.com/business/archive/2015/06/even-baby-boomers-think-its-harder-to-get-started-than-it-used-to-be/395609/

[89] http://www.theatlantic.com/business/archive/2015/07/rich-people-raise-kids-family-wealth/399809/

[90] http://www.theatlantic.com/business/archive/2015/07/america-social-mobility-parents-income/399311/

[91] http://www.salon.com/2015/04/29/neoliberals_are_killing_us_the_ted_talk_techno_utopian_thomas_friedman_economy_is_a_lie/

between the roughly half who are expecting a massive loss of jobs by 2025 and the other half who believe that, "human ingenuity will create new jobs, industries, and ways to make a living, just as it has been doing since the dawn of the Industrial Revolution."[92]

Bill Gates is surely one of the most astute persons at understanding the implications of broad technological change. Said he, "Software substitution, whether it's for drivers or waiters or nurses... it's progressing.... Technology over time will reduce demand for jobs, particularly at the lower end of skill set.... 20 years from now, labor demand for lots of skill sets will be substantially lower."[93]

The more optimistic view is based on the presumption that certain core forces which have propelled progress for centuries will continue to do so. It would be helpful for some economist to develop a "job proliferation index" that measures the rate of emergence of new professions and, critically, the trends of change in that rate. For practical impact, it should also be translated into the number of jobs created. I would predict that if the rate has not already slowed down it will soon do so.

Writing in *The Wealth of Nations*, Adam Smith identified specialization as a primary driver of progress, and these arguments presume that specialization will continue to allow humans to add ever greater economic value through advanced education and technical training. The need of the time, from this point of view, is for a populace that is better-educated in technical fields.

Among the more articulate proponents of this view are professors McAfee and Brynjolfsson, authors of *Race against the Machine* and *The Second Machine Age*. While I am very much in agreement with much of their argument, in my view they give short shrift to the chasm of disruption that looms for the vast majority of workers.

---

[92] http://www.theatlantic.com/technology/archive/2014/08/the-robots-are-coming-but-are-they-really-taking-our-jobs/375655/, http://www.pewinternet.org/files/2014/08/Future-of-AI-Robotics-and-Jobs.pdf
[93] http://www.businessinsider.com/bill-gates-bots-are-taking-away-jobs-2014-3

Heedless of the social cost, capitalist enterprises will relentlessly squeeze human workers into ever lesser-paid and more demanding positions as the economic advantages of AI and robotics come to justify such change. International outsourcing of jobs has provided a glimpse of what is to come. This new wave of change will affect not only many remaining first-world workers but also those in less-developed nations who recently found jobs due to outsourcing.

Education and Taxation are Inadequate Answers

Those who acknowledge the threats posed by automation seem to invariably conclude that the damage can be contained through education, or by tax policies to provide a guaranteed income for all. This is doubtful. Already, we are seeing evidence that education—at least of the non-technical sort—does not guarantee employment. Indeed, the belief in education to provide for employment has resulted in, "a system that has produced an entire generation of over-credentialed, underemployed, and deeply indebted young people."[94]

People are being encouraged to go back to school and learn new, technical occupations. But what happens when those occupations are automated—as is now happening with web design, to cite just one example? Will they return to school again and again, each time incurring more student loan debt, greater frustration and, eventually, despair? What of those who cannot qualify for such loans or training? The promise of education as a solution to automation-driven unemployment is like the proverbial carrot that, attached to its nose, lures the horse forward. Eventually the horse tires and abandons its efforts.

Also, today's employers increasingly view the hiring of employees as a last resort, to be done only when equipment

---

[94] http://www.theatlantic.com/features/archive/2014/08/the-law-school-scam/375069/

(such as automation) or outsourcing is inadequate. There is little indication that employers are eager to invest in re-training. Therefore, even when re-schooling makes a person employable for immediate job needs, when those needs shift again that person will get dumped once again for people (or equipment) who can meet those needs.[95]

What of a guaranteed minimum income? This has been advocated by Nobel Laureate economists across the spectrum including Paul Krugman, Milton Friedman, F. A. Hayek, Herbert A. Simon, and Robert Solow.[96] Switzerland recently voted to consider this option.

A guaranteed income for all will be expensive. Who will pay the new taxes? Large enterprises have many options to avoid taxes—especially as their assets are increasingly intangible and portable. If possible, they will use their lobbyists to kill such taxes or make them toothless and, failing that, move operations to lower-tax nations which eagerly welcome new businesses.

The taxes could in theory be paid by smaller businesses that cannot relocate, such as those providing local services. These taxes will then be passed on to customers as higher prices, indirectly taxing them in a hidden manner.

Politicians will talk about taxing upper income earners, but those persons will often find ways to shelter their income by gaming the system; relying on creative tax accountants' and lawyers' manipulation of the byzantine tax code. The trend in recent decades has been towards lower rather than higher tax rates for the wealthy; for example, the "carried interest" tax rate of 20% for hedge fund managers treats their income differently than others' income.[97]

---

[95] http://www.theatlantic.com/business/archive/2015/09/whos-responsible-for-erasing-americas-shortage-of-skilled-workers/406474/

[96] https://en.wikipedia.org/wiki/Basic_income

[97] http://www.slate.com/articles/business/moneybox/2014/06/taxation_of_carried_interest_the_loophole_for_hedge_fund_managers_could.html

Our tax systems remain absurdly complex, and at least in the US there is no evidence that any politician or party can fundamentally change them, although presidents from Carter through Bush II have tried.[98] Given that fact, the idea of permanently raising taxes on the wealthy will likely remain a fantasy, though modest adjustments to laws and regulations may give the temporary appearance of change.

The likely reality, then, is that middle income workers will be taxed heavily to pay for a guaranteed income. However, the pressure upon these workers (and smaller businesses) to pay may exceed their willingness or capacity to do so. Were that to happen, social instability could result.

Even presuming that the adoption of a guaranteed minimum income proves to be politically feasible, there is no assurance that those receiving it will have the continuing vigilance and clout to defend it against the ravages of inflation or the clever tax avoidance schemes that are endlessly propagated by the politically well-connected wealthy.

McAfee and Brynjolfsson believe that the coming pervasive availability of technological tools to billions of poorer persons through smartphones and, probably, other means such as so-called Sixth Sense technology will enable huge networks of collaboration and creativity, spawning a flourishing "utopian"[99] era of productivity and progress. However, I note that only a tiny fraction of humanity creates the truly game-changing innovations that lead to new industries, and that most of us—at least so far—have displayed no such profound creative capabilities.

Disruptive mass unemployment needs to be dealt with via a solution which can actually be implemented[100] that provides for the basic needs of everyone—and quickly. There can be no certainty that an aggressive campaign for education will solve this problem, nor that any massive redistribution of wealth

---

[98]   President Carter called the income tax system, "a disgrace to the human race".

[99]   McAfee's word choice. I consider it a misleading and dangerous term, as utopias are generally envisioned as perfect and static.

[100]   *Rise of the Machines: Downfall of the Economy?* Roubini's Edge 12/8/14

can (or even should) be implemented. Humanity does not have the luxury of counting on such solutions that may, with hindsight, prove inadequate or illusory.

Millions of Startups?

If people can't rely upon work for incomes and government-paid incomes are not going to be available in most countries, what is left?

One other solution is being proposed. It is that the unemployed, underemployed, and others should become entrepreneurs who start businesses that provide incomes for themselves, their families, and those whom they employ. Sramana Mitra has even developed for this purpose a virtual incubator system called One Million by One Million.

While this is romantically appealing and will work for some, I see five reasons to believe that its impact will be far less than what is hoped.

First, new companies that succeed will have the same view of employees as do more mature companies. Once those functions can be automated, the jobs will disappear—or never be created at all.

Second, successfully starting a business requires that one be able to pay the basic expenses of living while doing so. Often—especially with high-tech startups—it takes years for cash flow to turn positive. While many entrepreneurs are ingenious in cutting expenses, there are limits to this. (The oft-told story of the entrepreneur who eats ramen noodles and lives in a tiny apartment/office is generally told about someone who is young and single.)

Third, when startups fail, many such entrepreneurs will have drained their resources and will not be able to start again, at least not right away. Their sustenance will then come from government handouts, private charity or jobs.

Fourth, research has found that success in entrepreneurship requires a skill set that is partially trainable and partly character-based. For example, "grit" has been identified as such a characteristic.[101] It is not clear that all people can develop the needed characteristics.

Fifth, the success rate of startups amongst those who have previously built a company from start to successful exit isn't higher than that of others.[102] Since such persons presumably know what they are doing and still face a high risk of failure, failure is a major and inevitable risk associated with startups.

Most people, I expect, will lack the resources or personal characteristics necessary to start a company. Those whose startups fail will still need food, shelter and so on. While we may get one million startups from Mitra's and others' efforts, and this may yield thousands of new services to humanity, this does not broadly assure people's incomes.

Coming Soon: a Wrenching Transitional Period

The transformational changes now manifesting faster and faster in the world are being driven by doublings in computer power (as measured by price/performance) that are happening roughly every two years.

This *Law of Accelerating Returns* was formulated by Ray Kurzweil, Google's Director of Engineering. It has often been confused with *Moore's Law*, which states that the number of transistors on a computer chip doubles every two years. According to Intel, the rate at which transistor densities are doubling has recently slowed from 24 months to 30 months[103],

---

[101] http://www.businessinsider.com/how-to-develop-grit-an-important-success-trait-2014-10

[102] https://hbr.org/2014/02/research-serial-entrepreneurs-arent-any-more-likely-to-succeed/

[103] http://www.ft.com/intl/cms/s/0/36b722bc-2b49-11e5-8613-e7aedbb7bdb7.html#axzz3iR9fojmu

and Gordon Moore himself recently stated that these doublings will eventually halt.

This highlights the differences in the two "laws", since doublings in computer power can happen without doublings of transistor densities. Ray Kurzweil insists this will continue for decades, and is based on the exponential progress of technology in multiple dimensions of measurement.[104]

Regarding computer power, while miniaturization has driven most of the advances so far, large leaps forward have also accompanied new architectures. For example, Intel's Quad Core was a significant advance over previous designs without size being the issue. Supercomputer speeds continue to advance rapidly. Likewise, researchers are now developing 3D and optical designs that are expected to significantly impact speed.

Researchers at IBM and elsewhere may be closing in on the "holy grail" known as quantum computing, which will radically increase processing speeds for important classes of problems.[105] In addition, novel approaches to AI now being developed at IBM, Google, and elsewhere may substitute for more power.

Based on computer power continuing to double every two years, the displacement of massive numbers of people from their jobs is likely to come within the next 10 – 20 years. By 2034, there will thus be twelve such doublings representing an astonishing *4,096-fold increase* in computer power.

I think it is reasonable to assume that, somewhere before the twelfth doubling, important new computer capabilities will manifest. As co-founder of an early computer speech recognition startup, I recall the confidence of our technologists that more computing power was not an adequate solution to achieving human-level speech recognition. We were wrong, and I see no reason to presume that other seemingly unique

---

[104] http://www.kurzweilai.net/kurzweils-law-aka-the-law-of-accelerating-returns
[105] http://www.kurzweilai.net/optical-chip-allows-for-reprogramming-quantum-computer-in-seconds

human abilities will not also fall to a massive increase in computing power.

Some AI experts argue that we have yet to surmount the gap between "narrow" (specialized) AI and a "general" AI and may never do so. However, every time an AI is developed that performs a key support function within a profession, as IBM is now doing with legal research and medical diagnosis, huge numbers of jobs within that profession disappear. With many "narrow" AI systems performing in concert there will be far less need for people in most professions, and it may not matter for most practical purposes whether or not we ever achieve general AI.

Serious scholars are raising the alarm that nearly all jobs are in the crosshairs of automation:

> With advances in artificial intelligence, any job that requires the analysis of information can be done better by computers. This includes the jobs of physicians, lawyers, accountants and stock brokers. We will still need some humans to interact with the ones who prefer human contact, but the grunt work will disappear. The machines will need very few humans to help them.[106]

At some point, the ratio of employed to unemployed persons within a society becomes unsustainable—especially as increasing automation will press wages downward for those fortunate enough to remain employed. Since neither humanity as a whole nor any society has ever faced this situation, we can only guess where that breaking point will occur. We mustn't learn the answer.

Assuming that the rich will continue to effectively oppose any significant mandatory redistribution of their wealth, this will lead to a situation in which vast numbers of people are unemployed with no way to provide for themselves in the

---

[106] http://www.huffingtonpost.com/vivek-wadhwa/yes-a-computer-will-take-your-job_b_7743914.html

conventional economy. How, then, will these people be provided for until a new economy is implemented that does not rely on jobs?

Policy makers may choose to rely on faith that we will somehow muddle through this tsunami as we have all previous crises. However, I submit that faith—at least, faith that runs counter to empirical evidence—is a very poor basis for public policy. It could lead us to mass unemployment, social degradation, and even societal ruin.

We need something more fundamental than new educational initiatives, new taxes on capital, or faith in undefined new solutions. We need a solution that upends our fundamental conceptions of production and social organization.

Part II: Vision, Work and the Games We Play

The supreme accomplishment is to blur the line
between work and play.

~Arnold J. Toynbee

Whether the domain is politics, business and money, environmental stewardship, jobs, or personal relationships, one bumper sticker has captured the mood of the time. It seems to be true regardless of one's political persuasion. It reads, *if you're not outraged, you're not paying attention.*

Outrage is not enough. In the US, political outrage of both left and right has resulted in a decade of finger-pointing, name-calling and legislative gridlock. We need something positive to align upon, something that transcends the current divisions and offers a real, attainable way forward out of our present quagmire. We need a new vision.

Vision is not merely the province of starry-eyed idealists. For better or worse, it has directed the lives of countless men and women throughout the ages; men and women who have been either compelled or enrolled to participate in the visions held by great leaders. Such leaders are as influential today as at any other time in history; perhaps more so given the greater speed with which infectious ideas (memes) can now spread.

Vladimir Putin is motivated in part by a vision of a Russia restored to prominence in the world as a cultural bulwark against Western decadence. Xi Jinping envisions a "Chinese Dream...to build a moderately prosperous society and realize national rejuvenation."[107] Narendra Modi, perhaps the most electrifying and divisive leader in Indian history, has his own

---

[107] http://www.chinadaily.com.cn/china/Chinese-dream.html

vision of a Hindu-centric state, free of corruption and prosperous.

Looking at visions historically held, Ronald Reagan saw "the magic of the marketplace" leading America to become a "shining city on the hill".[108] Churchill articulated a vision of a Britain that would rise to any challenge and withstand any test. His vision carried the British people through the hell of World War II.

Pope Francis appears to be motivated by a vision of a Catholic Church that focuses on pastoral service to the poor and leads through acceptance of human nature, as he sees it.

On the other hand, Torquemada was motivated by a vision of religious purity in service of which any torture was acceptable, as were many of the other fanatics and brutes of history. (Whether these leaders really believed what they espoused or merely used their particular vision as a tool to accumulate personal power is another question.) Without any apparent religious underpinning, Hitler envisioned what he viewed as a pure, Aryan race of humans leading the world to 10,000 years of glory.

I could go on, but these examples serve to make a point. Many, if not all, of the most powerful people in history have been directed by their particular vision to lead masses in new directions.

What of this book, then? I know myself far too well to consider myself "great" by any stretch of the imagination. I am merely an ordinary person who has been captivated by an extraordinary vision. Further, I do not propose that my vision offered in this book is *the* vision. That is the way of fanatics, and too often leads to bleached bones stretching across vast expanses of land; bones of men, women and children sacrificed on the altar of some conception of righteous wrath. What I propose is instead *a* vision; one that can include within a new paradigm all of the other visions that are willing to coexist.

---

[108] Originally attributed to John Winthrop.

The vision I am offering is not truly mine. I am a steward of it. It has been informed by the great service of many others; I have simply brought the elements together in a new way. I have given it a name. This vision stands outside of our current divides of religion and politics. It has as much to offer to a devout believer who is willing to accept differing beliefs as to an atheist; as much to a socialist as to a capitalist. It can do all of this because it reframes the present paradigm that divides us. I will demonstrate that it offers most—though not all—of us a viable way to fulfill our personal needs and our personal visions in the decades ahead, without the need for further warring amongst visions.

It strikes at the very heart of a construct that is silently governing us and artificially dividing us. This hidden structure is, perhaps, best seen as a game.

The Game of Our Lives

We are all playing a *Scarcity Game* and we have been playing it for a very long time. We play it so intensely and thoroughly that few of us even recognize it as a game. Yet it is the game of our lives.

The Scarcity Game preoccupies us. It shows up most clearly in a never-ending quest for more "money," a peculiar thing that is at once a mental construct and its physical expression; both inherently artificial and artificially (and unnecessarily) scarce. Human productive activities revolve around money, and nearly all of us react to it with either fear or desire.

Money serves as a proxy for winning the game, though a brief reflection reveals that it offers no permanent victory even for the billionaires; they wind up in the dust the same as do the paupers—at least for now. And, in the future, should they be so fortunate as to become immortal billionaires living in a world of desperate hordes, they will either be forever looking over their shoulder or live within a kind of totalitarianism that would have given George Orwell cold shivers—as certain recent Hollywood productions depict.

For most of us on this planet today, money equates to survival. The lack of it may mean fear, privation and even agony or death. Money usually dictates our career choices and even our most intimate relationships, since money issues are the leading cause of divorce. In short, it permeates our lives.

We can choose, in this generation and for the very first time in recorded history, to begin playing an entirely different game as a species: an *Abundance Game*. (As will be discussed later, some "primitive" societies have achieved and sustained localized models of abundance that we can recreate and far surpass.)

We will enjoy the other game far more; it will be richer in that which supports and enables a high quality of life. This is as true of those who are winners in the current Game as it is true of today's losers. It is my intention to enroll you into my conviction that the Abundance Game is both preferable and feasible.

The Scarcity Game is based on certain "self-evident" assumptions about the nature of reality; assumptions shared across the spectrum of religious and political beliefs. Centuries ago, I doubt very much whether the flat Earth was considered a Christian, Jewish, Muslim, Hindu, Confucian, Shinto or Buddhist belief. It was just the self-evident truth. That is the nature of beliefs within a paradigm, until they fall away as the new paradigm takes hold.

The central assumption within the Scarcity Game is that of scarcity itself. We assume that there is not enough to go around of what is wanted, and so some must do without in order that others can have what they want. Indeed, economics is called the "dismal science" because of its assumption that desires will always outstrip production.

We assume all manner of physical limitations that are either false right now or else will soon become false, thanks to certain demonstrable facts about technology. The Scarcity Game includes what some have called a dominator worldview rather than a partnership one, with competition over-shadowing cooperation rather than the two working together in a dynamic balance.

We also assume that there are "limits to growth" either because of perceived physical limitations or very valid concerns about sustainability and despoliation of the environment. Each of these limiting assumptions has consequences, some of them highly destructive.

I will demonstrate that, from a physical perspective, we can achieve in the 21st century universal abundance, rapid creation of material objects on an as-needed basis, and far more sustainable, rich, and rewarding living environments in harmony with nature's ecosystems—and with ecosystems we will create elsewhere—enhanced by and entwined with supportive technology.

We really can have it all, and we had better recognize this fact sooner than later if we are to avoid wrenching, potentially catastrophic change as we shift from the current Scarcity Game to what comes next. Time is running out for us to make this change gracefully. Says the Millennium Project, "new economic mechanisms have to be seriously considered now— because it may take a generation or two to make such changes."[109]

In addition to technological advances, there is also inner work to transform scarcity beliefs, and some of the most successful people I know will argue that, for them and for others who so choose, there is abundance even today. They manifest this to an extent in their own lives, and in many ways they set an example for the rest of us. However, even their abundance is a mere fraction of what they and others like them could enjoy later in this century.

Regardless, if we can create a society in which all have their basic needs met, attaining an enduring condition of fundamental safety for all, without it seriously inconveniencing anyone, then I believe we should do so. Untold generations to come will thank us, as they will be playing a very different game than that of survival. They will be playing an Abundance Game.

---

[109] http://millennium-project.org/millennium/2015-SOF-ExecutiveSummary-English.pdf

What is a Game?

> People like playing games because they know the rules
> and the score... when we don't know the score we tend
> not to want to play, or we play safe.

> *~The Game of Work*

The word "game" can be a noun, a verb or an adjective. For purposes of this book, I am using it as a noun. Game the noun is defined by Google as:

1. A FORM OF PLAY OR SPORT, ESP. A COMPETITIVE ONE PLAYED ACCORDING TO RULES AND DECIDED BY SKILL, STRENGTH, OR LUCK.
2. A TYPE OF ACTIVITY OR BUSINESS, ESP. WHEN REGARDED AS A GAME.

Game, in this second meaning, is a far broader term with deeper significance than, perhaps, most have considered. I am reminded of a conversation I once witnessed between a spiritual teacher and a man in his audience.

Man: Is there any evidence that God cares about us?
Teacher: Do you like games?
Man: Yes.
Teacher: Which one do you like best?
Man: Chess.
Teacher: When is it a fun game of chess?
Man: When the opponents are well matched.
Teacher: When is it a good game of chess?
Man: When there is a serious chance of losing.
Teacher: And when is it a great game?
Man: (silence)
Teacher: It is a great game when we forget that it is a game. This universe is a huge amusement park. We are the rides. And if it is not amusing for you, then it is so for someone else.

Some, such as this teacher, argue that we are living in a great game right now. The game seems real, yet upon completion of our life we remember or discover the truth. Others would argue for their preferred religious belief which, while not viewing this life as a game, does contain rules and both a win condition and a lose condition.

For purposes of creating a Celebration Society, it doesn't matter how we view religious beliefs or which religious beliefs (if any) we hold. Instead, what matters is how we choose to express our beliefs in our social agreements and in our actions. One of the most fundamental of these social agreements is work.

Some New Understandings about Work

For most people, work is a necessity. It is the focus of their lives. If satisfaction is found in doing work, that is a bonus. Few undertake work with the primary intention of enjoying it.

The phrase, "I'm going to work" doesn't usually evoke an image of a person with a huge smile and excitement so palpable that she is bouncing on her feet. Work connotes other things to most people. Among these are:

- Duty
- Effort
- Discipline
- Struggle
- Competition
- Survival

None of these words sounds like happiness to me, though some can bring deep satisfaction when pursued freely of one's own choice. People who define work in the above way, and they are most of us, regard it as basically about survival. "If you don't work, you won't eat" will get most readers' heads nodding. For most people, this has been true for all of humanity's existence.

And yet, some interesting things are changing. For example, as Henry Ford knew a century ago, it now appears that paying workers higher wages than necessary can actually be profitable.

Prof. Zeynep Ton of MIT has spent a decade falsifying the traditional assumption that raising wages for lowly paid clerical workers cuts corporate profits. As "profit maximizing" entities, corporations are required to cut costs where this increases profits, and executives who fail to go along are penalized. It's an assumption about the system that's been nearly universal for a long time, and yet it's increasingly coming into question.[110]

Dr. Ton's research only makes sense if we view people as having feelings and motivation—which can be evoked or dulled. By recognizing employees' attitudes as having a direct impact on a company's bottom line, it's clear that responsible employers should do what they can to make their workers happy in their jobs.

According to research by the Gallup organization, the majority of employees in the world today give the appearance of working hard while, in fact, working little or not at all. Even worse, according to a 2013 Gallup report:[111]

> 13 percent of employees from 142 countries are 'engaged' in their jobs. However, twice as many are 'actively disengaged'—they're negative and potentially hostile to their organizations. The majority of workers, though, are simply 'checked out,' the report says.[112]

Gallup concludes, "Right now, the bleak reality is that 63% of the world's employees have essentially checked out, and an additional 24% are acting out their unhappiness and under-

---

[110] http://www.forbes.com/sites/forbesleadershipforum/2014/07/01/why-companies-that-pay-above-the-minimum-wage-come-out-ahead/

[111] http://www.ihrim.org/Pubonline/Wire/Dec13/GlobalWorkplaceReport_2013.pdf

[112] http://www.theatlantic.com/business/archive/2014/11/the-art-of-not-working-at-work/382121/

mining the accomplishments of the 13% who are committed to innovation and organizational progress." The fact that the majority of workers worldwide are so thoroughly detached from their jobs cries out for a better system of production.

COSTCO shows us how to more effectively run a traditional "brick and mortar" retail operation. The average COSTCO employee earns $21/hour and COSTCO's stock price appreciation—the gold standard for capitalist success—has greatly surpassed that of WalMart, the employer known for making its workers dependent on government assistance. COSTCO has also shown rising profits, over time.

The CEO of COSTCO sets an example on pay scale by taking total compensation of "only" 139 times that of its most lowly paid worker, as contrasted to the American average CEO pay of 354 times the lowest worker, with other advanced nations having lower ratios.[113] We are proud to spend our money in a place that offers a decent life to those who serve us, and where top executives are not far removed from and indeed generally rise from within the ranks of the lowest paid workers. This has cultural effects, not only inside the company but also among the much larger body of its customers.

A System Rotting from the Inside

If what I have said about work has failed to convince you that it will be a good idea to end this anachronism—something I fully expect to happen regardless of our preferences—then perhaps looking at it from a different angle will suffice.

Work is incredibly nonproductive.

Much of the "work" performed is of questionable value or even deleterious. For example, about 200,000 people work in the US tax system. Few seem to feel loved by their fellow citizens, and some whom I've met feel guilty about how they make

---

[113] http://seattletimes.com/html/businesstechnology/2021235266_biztaltoncol23xml.html

an income. All of this revenue could be generated by a simple, flat 17% national sales tax with a fraction of the workers and almost none of the aggravation imposed upon the rest of us.[114]

Since ending such "work" would save the rest of us a lot of money and aggravation, this begs the question: why not put these people on permanent, paid vacation? (The answer, "that would be unfair to the rest of us", in turn begs for *celebrationism*, a new system which I will explain shortly.) Such permanent paid vacation, at least for those whose work is actively destructive per the above-mentioned Gallup research, might be a good first step in certain countries.

To sum up, 87% of the world's "workers" are essentially either shuffling papers or actively destructive to their employers. As incredible as this statistic may be, perhaps even more so is the implication that almost all of the world's productive improvements results from just 13% of its people. The rest of the workers are either destructive or automatons. In effect, we have already eliminated most jobs—only the shells remain.

Playful Work and Serious Play

> The strict distinction between work and play or input and output that economists make is not always so clear. The billions of (zero wage and zero price) hours that people spend uploading, tagging, and commenting on photos on social media sites like Facebook unquestionably creates value.
>
> ~*The Second Machine Age*

Almost everyone loves games. I say this without fear of contradiction. Just look at any healthy child. He or she plays with abandon; freely, joyfully. This is not only true of humans but mammals in general.

---

[114] http://www.nber.org/digest/aug97/w5885.html

Some say that childhood's play is rehearsal for adulthood. This may be so but even if true it misses a key point. Play is hard-wired into us; the desire does not disappear with maturity. Most of us play or at least watch games as adults unless our responsibilities become crushing. There is now even a National Institute for Play that studies the science and the opportunities for social advancement through a fuller understanding of play and its value.[115]

Who among us does not know someone who lives for the next football, baseball or soccer game; their weekly poker match or some other gaming pursuit? I submit that this passion for games is healthy and normal, and—as we shall see—much of what looks like high-performance work can best be understood as games in masquerade form.

Further, by converting tasks that some consider unpleasant into games, they often stop being unpleasant. Many people find learning a second language to be difficult. Yet the app DuoLingo turns it into a game that one can play against oneself and even against others. Likewise, the app Epic Win turns household chores into "quests" with experience points that allow leveling up for rewards. The Land of Venn turns the learning of geometry into a game of monsters and potions.[116]

The most popular Youtube channel is all about games,[117] and Amazon just paid $1.1 billion for Twitch, a service that streams game competitions with live commentary. Said Michael Frazzini, vice president for Amazon Games, "I think it's fairly safe to say at this point that on anything with a screen, games are the No. 1 or 2 activity."[118]

Even some of the great challenges in life may best be addressed by turning them into games.[119] For example, the

---

[115] http://www.nifplay.org/
[116] http://www.thelandofvenn.com/
[117] https://www.yahoo.com/tech/pewdiepie-truly-why-96476190194.html
[118] http://www.nytimes.com/2014/09/01/business/media/amazons-bet-on-content-in-a-hub-for-gamers.html
[119] https://www.psychologytoday.com/articles/201508/it-s-time-think-gamer

bane of many a planner's existence, procrastination, may fall to gamification:

> Procrastinators are more likely to complete a piece of work if they're persuaded that it's not actually work. In one study ... students were asked to complete a puzzle, but first they were given a few minutes to play Tetris. Chronic procrastinators only delayed practice on the puzzle when it was described as a cognitive evaluation...When scientists described the puzzle as a game, they were just as likely to practice as anybody else.[120]

What is the difference between work and play? Is there some line that divides the two? My wife, echoing a common sentiment, encapsulated it as, "work is what someone or something makes you do and play is what you choose to do."

When I grow tomatoes and other things to eat in my garden I hardly consider it work. It is play; it is pleasurable. I choose to do it without any pressure, and it will cost me more money than buying the same produce in the grocery store. When someone else does the same thing because they need to grow food to eat or to sell for an income, the activity is perceived as work.

The example I just gave regarding gardening also applies to many other human activities. Among them: art, investing, hunting, fishing, knitting, pottery, game design, game playing, working on vehicles, writing, and so forth. Essentially, any activity can be done either playfully or as work, and it may be impossible for the outside observer to tell the difference on casual inspection.

I know an attorney who works as an oil/gas trader, and he helps people with their wills and other legal matters for fun. He likes being of service. Many other people volunteer their time and skills for similar reasons. For example, Burning Man

---

[120] http://www.theatlantic.com/business/archive/2014/08/the-procrastination-loop-and-how-to-break-it/379142/2/

is one of the most intense and immersive "vacation" experiences in the world. People come together for a week in the Nevada desert, literally creating from nothing a small city (Black Rock City; population 50,000+) in one day.

Many "Burners" spend weeks or even months preparing for this annual experience and invest hundreds or even thousands of dollars as well. How, then to explain those who then spend much of their week volunteering their services in the Bicycle Repair Shop or other service venues such as massage tents? (Bicycles are the primary means of transportation other than walking.) Why do people assume that needed human contributions would wither and disappear in a society without monetary motivation?

There is an emerging field called *Serious Games*. Specialists in this field develop games to inculcate knowledge and skills that were previously inculcated in a less pleasant manner. They have clients including Fortune 1000 companies.

Most of us consider business a "serious" matter. However, its practices and business itself are increasingly being looked at as games. "We have a tendency to be dismissive about games, but what we're learning is that games in general are wonderfully powerful tools that can be applied in all sorts of serious contexts," said Kevin Werbach of the Wharton School.[121]

Likewise, according to Jesse Schell of Carnegie Mellon, "game ideas are creeping into every nook and cranny of everything because reward systems are satisfying. Our affluence has allowed us to move to a place where we tend to make things pleasurable, as opposed to efficient."[122]

Few would think of a billionaire businessperson as someone playing a game. After all, making that kind of money is a

---

[121] http://www.nytimes.com/2012/12/24/technology/all-the-worlds-a-game-and-business-is-a-player.html
[122] ibid.

serious business, isn't it? Yet consider: few such persons actually spend a large percentage of their wealth on personal pursuits. While most do enjoy significant perks, they could stop making money far earlier and yet enjoy the full spectrum of pleasures. Why did Ray Dalio, multi-billionaire founder of the world's most successful hedge fund, say, "Treat your life like a game."[123] Why does someone such as Bill Gates amass a fortune exceeding $50 billion, then spend the rest of his life giving it away? Why does Warren Buffet continue to live in the same home he purchased for $31.5K in 1958?[124] Could it be that *possessions* per se are not what motivates them?

Said angel investor David Rose on Quora, "My father, who received the E&Y Entrepreneur of the Year Award a few years ago (he's now 85!) says that for him, being a real estate developer is like getting to play Monopoly with real money. I come from a family in which no one ever retires; they just keep working until they pass away... and every one of them does it because they WANT to. For all of us, working at what we love to do is the most fun one could possibly have!" Said Donald Trump, "Money was never a big motivation for me, except as a way to keep score. The real excitement is playing the game."[125]

A close friend of mine is herself close friends with a self-made billionaire. He built from scratch one of the most successful office supply companies, and now buys and sells huge companies and owns a television network. This same man lives in a mountain home without running water or indoor plumbing. Obviously, this is a choice. Equally obviously, he is not engaged with material objects in the same way that most of us are—or in the way most of us would expect him to be. What keeps him going? What motivates him? It certainly isn't a lavish lifestyle.

Some wealthy businesspeople may genuinely desire to amass a fortune as the first step in changing the world. Others

---

[123] http://www.brainyquote.com/quotes/authors/r/ray_dalio_2.html

[124] http://time.com/money/3843188/this-is-how-much-it-costs-to-live-next-to-warren-buffett/

[125] *The Art of the Deal*, Donald Trump

simply continue to increase the pile of wealth and superficial trappings such as luxury homes and beautiful partners until they die or retire, without taking up any evident social causes beyond what is expected of them. Their financial accumulation far exceeds their spending. The only apparent reason that they continue is that they are not working; they are playing a game. When asked their reasons for making so much money, many will answer, "He who dies with the most toys wins."

Great scientists often compete to win Nobel, Lasker, Field, and other prestigious prizes. It's not the monetary aspect that motivates these thinkers and researchers; most could make far more in industry. No, they seek the satisfaction of making contributions, and the recognition of their peers for "winning" discoveries and creations.

Top sports figures who continue to lead their fields year after year are clearly no longer motivated by money, if indeed they ever were. Yet they continue rigorous physical training and punishing exertion in their continuing quest to win at their chosen game.

The Coming of Replications

Currently, one way that the wealthy distinguish themselves from others is through the collection of rare objects. In a Celebration Society, to own an "original" of something will remain significant. However, barring a desire to prevent others from enjoying the experience, it will become possible to have perfect replicas of all manner of objects including paintings and sculptures.

There will still be pride of ownership in the original. Others will be able to fully enjoy the "same" piece as well.

When we think of art reproduction, we think of prints or paintings—something that looks strikingly like the original from a viewing distance, but is clearly not the same. Other forms of reproduction include artists who copy the works of great masters. This has a long history of both "legitimate" reproduction and forgeries.

There is an entire village in China named Dafen, which is devoted to assembly line art.[126] Similar operations on a smaller scale exist in Thailand and Taiwan. Most create reproductions of famous art.

Recently, a radically different technology has come into existence and deployment. The Metropolitan Museum of Modern Art has an art replicator system. It takes a molecular signature of the piece, capturing every pigment type and the precise three-dimensional attributes of the piece. Then the digital data is used to create a replication of the original piece down to every brushstroke. Replications are so close to originals that specific errors are embedded as a "signature" that this is not the original.

While a general purpose replicator based on nanotechnology is many years away, already we have 3D printers capable of making:

- A gun that fires
- Food
- Machine parts
- Prototypes
- Buildings
- Commemorative statues of online role playing characters
- Even living tissues, potentially including organs[127]
- Clear and colored glass[128]

I am sure that this list, extraordinary as it is, is only partial—and only a beginning of what will rapidly increase in scope. 3D printers are becoming ever more popular, useful in a wide variety of applications and situations.

Molecular manufacturing techniques continue to advance. Biological organisms are being engineered capable of pro-

---

[126] http://xiaoshuang198911.wordpress.com/2014/02/26/dafen-oil-painting-village/
[127] http://www.nature.com/nbt/journal/v32/n8/full/nbt.2958.html,
http://www.theguardian.com/science/2014/jul/04/3d-printed-organs-step-closer
[128] http://www.kurzweilai.net/mit-researchers-invent-process-for-3d-printing-complex-transparent-glass-forms

ducing all manner of products, from oils for energy to high-protein foodstuffs. Soon, I expect that scientific permaculture (discussed elswhere in this book) will afford humanity all manner of ingenious ways to work with nature to restore harmony and balance.

Morality and Work

Since it is clear that work is ending for many people, the question of whether this should be celebrated or opposed becomes important. Many people believe that work is necessary to character development and virtuous life. These beliefs are sincerely held, often with a religious basis, and as the tsunami of AI and robot-generated unemployment rises we can expect fierce advocacy of "make-work" programs from those holding this viewpoint.

Is "work" for the sole purpose of employment really necessary to character development? Or is doing something meaningful, which actually benefits society even if not "work" per se, more likely to lead to a virtuous life?

The Moralistic Argument for Work

Assuming that there will be an opportunity for people to continue working in the future, some think this to be a good idea. Since I have elsewhere argued that "work" is what one does because one must, while the same activity undertaken for pleasure is play, I call this the moralistic argument in favor of the continuance of work.

In my view, this is due to a cultural bias that crosses the divides of religion and politics. The bias is that work is somehow necessary to human well-being. It is a bias rooted in the Scarcity Game. There is a distinction between work and productivity.

Advocates of the moralistic argument may well agree with Voltaire, who said, "Work saves a man from three great evils: boredom, vice, and need." I would respond that in an age when minimum-wage pay can require a person to work two or even three jobs merely to survive, work no longer saves one from

73

need. The necessities of life often require minimum wage workers to work multiple jobs and regularly lose sleep. With many such persons living with as little as 4 hours of sleep a night, they are apparently suffering permanent brain damage and other health issues.[129] Likewise self-expression and engagement with community, friends, and family are needs not necessarily met by work.

Voltaire's statement that work reduces boredom is similarly disproved in modern society. One need only look at minimum wage workers at mall stores, data entry clerks or assembly line workers to see that in many instances work actually induces boredom.

According to Benjamin Hunnicutt of the University of Iowa, "American society has an irrational belief in work for work's sake...if a cashier's work were a video game—grab an item, find the bar code, scan it, slide the item onward, and repeat—critics of video games might call it mindless. But when it's a job, politicians praise its intrinsic dignity."[130]

If work reduces vice, then one would expect those with the most secure and respected work positions to exhibit less vice than others. Few have more secure or respected jobs than federal elected officials such as members of Congress. Congressmen enjoy extraordinarily high salaries as compared to average Americans and also receive important job-related perks such as a "cadillac" health plan far beyond what ordinary people enjoy—not to mention the sinecures such as board seats, consulting contracts and lobbying positions that typically chase them. Despite these extraordinary benefits and having a job that essentially lacks supervision or risk of firing except at election time, Congressmen actually have worse

---

[129] http://www.theatlantic.com/health/archive/2014/09/when-you-cant-afford-sleep/380128/2/

[130] http://www.theatlantic.com/magazine/archive/2015/07/world-without-work/395294/

criminal records and (apparently) worse ethical standards than average people.[131]

According to the US Substance Abuse and Mental Heath Services Administration, roughly ¾ of substance abusers are workers. Specifically, "... of the 20.3 million adults in the U.S. classified as having substance use disorders in 2008 — the latest year for which figures are available — 15.8 million were employed either full or part-time."[132] If work reduces rather than increases substance abuse, it is not particularly effective at doing so.

Economists across the political spectrum have advocated that a cash income be paid to every citizen.[133] Analyses have been done showing that ceasing to administer various government assistance programs (AKA welfare), instead consolidating them all into one single payment, would reduce fraud, waste, and government intrusion. This would be a simple way to assure that needs are met with minimal bureaucracy. The immediate source of this income would be redirected taxation to pay for the consolidated programs until, in the future, the income can be based upon machine production.

As to boredom, one can have purposeful activity without it being work, and one can have work without it being purposeful activity. Understanding this distinction will enable a Celebration Society to avoid the problems of boredom.

How many retired persons enjoy maintaining a garden, traveling, volunteering their time, gourmet cooking, watching television programs or documentaries, reading books and magazines, or meeting with friends for games and other social activities? Why would younger people, freed from the oppression of forced work, not do the same?

While it would be absurd to argue that a Celebration Society will be a utopia free of human failings, it is nevertheless reasonable to project that certain vices will diminish.

---

[131] http://harpers.org/blog/2007/09/congress-the-most-dangerous-neighborhood-in-america/, http://www.citizensforethics.org/

[132] http://fortune.com/2011/02/03/drug-use-at-work-higher-than-we-thought/

[133] https://en.wikipedia.org/wiki/Basic_income

Vices that are based upon a need to escape an unpleasant environment, such as the abuse of sex or drugs, will lose their hold in an environment that is more pleasing than the escape. Likewise, greed, envy, and other vices dependent upon the prospect of material gain or loss should fade away along with the significance of such gain or loss. Consider snobbery:

> snobbery, generally speaking, flows from social insecurity and only two groups are free of it. The one is the tiny group of aristocrats at the top who feel that no matter what they do, they cannot lose their social position. The other is the group of men at the bottom who have no social position to lose.[134]

In a Celebration Society, one's social position will depend upon others' perceptions of one's actual contributions rather than the warped proxy for contributions we call money. Also, static social classes should cease to exist.

The notion of placing billions of people on an unearned, permanent vacation will strike many people as immoral. However, those who hold work to be sacred will find themselves free to structure societies which include work for themselves and other like-minded persons. (They will be like the Amish and Mennonites who shun certain advanced technology, thereby necessitating more work by people.) They will be limited only by their inability to impose work upon the rest of us.

Ultimately, it is not a question of whether work is a "good idea" or "moral" but simply the fact that inexorable forces of supply and demand coupled with the accelerating power of technology will make a lot of work and workers noncompetitive. Societies that force non-productive work upon people on moral grounds will fall behind societies that encourage meaningful non-work activity. Such "moralistic" societies will, in effect, be tying a hand behind their backs.

----

[134] http://www.theatlantic.com/magazine/archive/1948/04/ive-kept-my-name/306256/

John Henry lost to the steam engine, and many if not most of us—as productive units—shall lose to the intelligence engines. But we can win by redefining ourselves into something grander than productive units.

Is Joblessness a Moral Failing?

In assessing the moral aspects of providing for those unable to work, one important question is surely whether their inability to work is of their own making. Permit me a personal anecdote.

My wife worked at IBM for 22 years. During that time, she held positions in software development, sales, customer support, technical writing, and website development/support. She received numerous awards for her contributions. She had entered Rensselaer Polytechnic Institute (RPI) at age 17 on a scholarship and was later awarded a full fellowship to attend graduate school, in part because of her perfect score on the math analytical section of the Graduate Records Exam. She earned an M.S. degree in artificial intelligence in only one year and has authored over a dozen published books.

I say this not to brag but rather to make a point. Laid off from IBM in 2011, my wife aggressively sought work for 2 years. Repeatedly a finalist for positions, never was a single job offered to her in two years of consistent searching.

If such a person, well qualified by both experience and training, was not employable then what hope is there for the less talented and less accomplished; i.e. the vast majority of us? I see little such hope, especially with less and less earned income as a percentage of the whole production system as we move forward.[135] The great question then becomes: what quality of life will those who are placed on permanent vacation enjoy—or be forced to suffer?

What shall we offer to the displaced? Shall it be harsh moral judgments, based on particular interpretations of moral codes dating to antiquity? Shall they be condemned to

---

[135] *Capital in the 21ˢᵗ Century*, Thomas Piketty

homelessness, or to meager warehousing in small box-like apartments, with barely adequate food and endless passive entertainment, as some have foreseen? Or shall it be a welcoming attitude, of persons who have perhaps shown us only a fraction of who they really are because so much of their life's time and attention was focused on simply surviving? What untold Picassos, Mozarts, Gausses, and Newtons await us once they are freed from deadening work?

Michael Faraday, inventor of the electrical motor and generator, grew up impoverished and was trained as a bookbinder. Had a lucky break not given him a job as scientific assistant, his world-changing discoveries would have been delayed; perhaps for a long time. One of the greatest mathematicians of all time, Srinivasa Ramanujan, was a self-taught Indian. His greatness was recognized only when the mathematician G.H. Hardy paid attention to Ramanujan's correspondence. Einstein worked as a patent examiner until recognized, and Adam Smith worked in a customs office.

Recently, as an experiment, a free course in AI was taught online by two Stanford computer scientists and offered to the world. In evaluating the results, the professors were struck by the fact that the top performing students in the class were not enrolled at Stanford, but were unknown students from other countries. Specifically:

> Rather than set a limit on class size, the AI Class simply let everybody join. Out of 160,000 who enrolled, 23,000 obtained a Certificate of Completion. While the 14% completion rate started the ongoing controversy of MOOC's retention rate, (professor) Sebastian Thrun focused on the fact that 23,000 people from all around the world passed a class with the same criteria as Stanford students (none of which were even in the top 100). [136]

---

[136] http://www.thegoodmooc.com/2013/05/a-review-of-stanford-ai-class.html

Given that Stanford is one of the world's most elite universities, this indicates that there is a large pool of unknown talent in the world. That talent is waiting to be tapped, needing only the right environment to manifest.

Some will call such expectations optimistic. They perceive a human tendency to laziness, to idleness, and think this to be a common characteristic of the majority. I submit that this is more a matter of the *type of activity* available to people (not to mention a natural conservation of energy for those who do not get enough food) than any inherent lack of interest in doing something more.

If you doubt this, look at any healthy newborn child. Look at the child's curiosity, playfulness, energy, and enthusiasm. Whether this child is inherently gifted in some conventional way or not, there can hardly be doubt that—given a nourishing and stimulating environment—this child will flourish in some way.

I have no children. The closest I may come is the raising of our Siberian kitten, LK. LK is a healthy, energetic, and happy animal. She is almost always exploring, chasing things, or playfully wrestling with our older Siberian (whom we adopted as an adult cat). LK is highly intelligent, having learned how to open doors with her paws and (apparently) communicate with other animals.

Excepting a medical emergency, she has never known anything truly dangerous, nor has she known privation. She has never been struck in punishment. She has been surrounded by feline and human "pack" during her entire short life,[137] and when the "big cats" deprive her of something that she desires, her purring suggests that she can feel the caring in their actions, for Siberians are empathic cats. I call LK an original celebrationist because she has no experience of scarcity, and I intend that she never will.

---

[137] Unlike other housecats, hypoallergenic Siberians are pack animals, like dogs. Most greatly enjoy playing together. Uncles in the wild have been known to help raise kittens.

What would it be like to raise humans like this? What would a world of such humans be like? I don't know, and I very much look forward to finding out!

In our present world, many people who are unemployed or retired withdraw into passive pursuits such as television watching and internet browsing instead of socializing in-person or taking up new activities. Critics of what some are calling a post-work society worry that this sort of behavior will then become much more widespread.[138]

This argument derives from certain context-dependent assumptions. In particular, in a Scarcity Game society where work is held as a primary source of self-esteem and social respect, one who cannot work is viewed as a lesser person than a worker. Not working is not an acceptable choice; the poor who do not work are often viewed as parasites and even among the rich, the idle playboy or socialite is viewed with contempt albeit sometimes tinged with envy.

In a Celebration Society, where uncompensated service to others is viewed as the highest form of good, not working will carry no opprobrium if the person gives something back to society. Indeed, some of the most respected persons may do nothing at all to make money. Instead, they may happily accept the support of friends and family or an income from the General Welfare Fund. Their contribution will still be appreciated. Say critics:

> Research has shown that it is harder to recover from a long bout of joblessness than from losing a loved one or suffering a life-altering injury. The very things that help many people recover from other emotional traumas—a routine, an absorbing distraction, a daily purpose—are not readily available to the unemployed.[139]

---

[138] http://www.theatlantic.com/magazine/archive/2015/07/world-without-work/395294/

[139] ibid.

In a Celebration Society, there will be many "distractions" available to residents without cost. Further, a purpose that does not relate to work but rather to service will change the social dynamic so fundamentally as to turn it upside down. Currently, the lack of a job implies that one has been judged and found wanting by one's fellow members of society—or is too picky or lazy to accept what is offered. (Else, one would surely have work, the thinking goes.) Both causes of unemployment, though increasingly suspect and just wrong as the automation tsunami comes on ever stronger, are pejorative.

In a world without work, there would literally be no one to offer or withdraw jobs; only projects needing people to collaborate and help out as they may wish to do. No coercion would be needed, and no judgment would be involved except insofar as a person is invited to play with others or not. Those who do not play well with others, or who do not like the games/projects being offered, will be free to create their own games/projects and invite others to join them, or simply to play alone.

I will concede that in a Celebration Society there could well be "couch potatoes" who simply "veg out" endlessly, immersed in virtual worlds. So what? If it harms no one else, coming at no one else's expense, does it really matter? If we care about them, we may seek to engage them more in life with their fellow people. But, ultimately, is their fate really worse than the elderly and infirm who are today discarded and warehoused like society's dross? I think their fate is much better. At least they will be free to re-engage at any time, perhaps rejuvenating themselves and rejoining the human race.

Further, recent developments in gaming are making this stereotype of the isolated, antisocial (usually male) gamer more questionable. According to the Guardian, "The whole meaning and purpose of video games has shifted: for many players, they have become venues for social interaction rather than solitary confinement."[140]

---

[140] http://www.theguardian.com/technology/2015/may/11/the-cliche-of-lone-male-gamer-needs-to-be-destroyed

A Different View of the Morality of Work and Poverty

Based on a recent Gallup poll, 20% of Americans believe in reincarnation[141] and, of course, the numbers are much higher in certain other cultures. Among some groups in India, this has been used as a "moral" basis for arguing that the poor deserve their fate. But, to such believers I ask: would it not then be our "karmic" duty to uplift them if we can? To others who do not believe in reincarnation, I simply say: there can be no moral basis for leaving children to suffer when we can uplift them, especially when it is without personal cost.

It is easy for one who grew up in some abundance or one who, through a rare combination of personal characteristics, managed to overcome harsh poverty, to say that people deserve their fates. Such a person may greatly underestimate how narrow and precarious is the path from poverty to their present circumstances. It is much easier to adopt such attitudes and beliefs when one grows up in a household and society where there is a plentiful supply of food, clean water, sanitation, clothing, reliable medical care, full educational opportunities, physical safety, and loving relationships.

As Warren Buffett once put it, he is a winner of the genetic lottery. Said he, "Having the investing gene wouldn't do much good if I were in Africa running from lions, screaming (that) I allocate capital!"

I would challenge what seems to many a self-evident tenet of capitalism: the idea that competency somehow connotes value to society. One may ask, how could this idea be challenged? After all, if the ability to do something in a superior way is to have any economic impact, it must show up in higher value.

This is rooted in Scarcity Game thinking. In a world of scarcity, one's productive capacity is primary, since it is the only way to claim a "piece of the pie" unless one happens to be blessed with good fortune such as inherited wealth. Those who

---

[141] http://www.gallup.com/poll/16915/three-four-americans-believe-paranormal.aspx

have worked hard and succeeded naturally assume that others can do the same and, failing that, that they are lazy—or otherwise incapable.

A common yet often unspoken assumption among all capitalists, whether they call themselves liberal, conservative, or something else, is that greater ability and effort should confer greater rewards. Persons who have earned a lot of success for themselves seem to consistently believe this, and economic theory holds that only systems hewing to such a correlation can effectively produce growth over time. Yet, as the outsourcing of jobs in the late 20th century showed, being superior at something was generally not valued as much as being inexpensively adequate.

Currently, we are experiencing what has been called the "winner take all economy". Capital is increasingly rewarded more than labor and, among the share afforded to labor, superstars dominate their fields of expertise as never before. This is due to the effects of certain individuals and groups leveraging their productive assets and skills, as never before, with technology. We could see a future in which almost all rewards flow to capital owners and superstars.

However, in a society of automated abundance one's productive capabilities will be irrelevant, except insofar as one can voluntarily serve and delight one's fellow citizens. The delight might come in the form of new scientific discoveries or inventions, dance, music, art, mathematics, poetry, systems, theater, sculpture, oratory, or innumerable other activities and pastimes. It is amazing to me how many people, when asked what they'd love to do if money were no concern, light up and mention an artistic activity. Are most of us merely frustrated artists? If so, we can look forward to a future in which we all freely express and create—with a mind-boggling variety of creations to enjoy.

In addition, there is clearly an unlimited number of games to be created and played. Anyone who doubts this should visit one of the thousands of board gaming groups that meet in large cities around the world every week. Many of these players own and play hundreds of different board games, and there are over 72,000 such games in existence as of 2014,[142] with many more developed, tested, published and played every year.

Even this number doesn't include card games or computer/app games, of which there are tens if not hundreds of thousands as well. Now consider that this staggering number of games has been created by a tiny fraction of humanity. What if everyone with an inclination to create such games were set free to do so, and everyone with an inclination to spend significant time playing them were also set free?[143]

Finally, consider that VR games will soon exist that offer all of the enjoyment of the above games and much more, in fully immersive and realistic environments.[144] (Also, as discussed elsewhere, many "serious" activities are being gamified as researchers are finding that games can elicit desirable results.)

Such abundance may seem impossible or pointless. Further, it may seem that a system of production cannot exist based primarily on the creation of art and the playing of games. The crucial confusion here arises from this fact: incentives and rewards are necessary for capitalism to work, and capitalism is today generally regarded as the only viable system of production. Incentives and rewards are indeed necessary to all of the historical systems of production, which are without exception rooted in the allocation of scarcity. They are not, however, necessary for celebrationism.

Names, Symbols, "Isms", and Movements

There are solutions to our most pressing problems, solutions that are today within the grasp of an informed and motivated citizenry. It is a matter of awareness and will.

---

[142] http://boardgamegeek.com/

[143] http://www.theatlantic.com/entertainment/archive/2014/11/board-game-bars/382828/

[144] http://www.cnet.com/news/zero-latency-vr-entertainment-revolution-begins-melbourne-australia/

Thanks to the previous efforts of many others, this book can offer the awareness. It will then be up to those who care to sustain the will.

In order for this to happen, that will must be expressed and sustained in an effective manner. Proper packaging for the message is part of this.

Names and images have power. They can arouse emotions, crystallize ideas and align people for a common purpose. In this way, they can move us toward transformations. The Nazi swastika[145] still evokes strong emotion, as do the Confederate flag of the Southern USA and the symbols of all major religions.

"Isms" are sets of beliefs that motivate those who share them. Examples include not only religions (e.g. Catholicism) and political movements (e.g. communism) but also causes such as environmentalism. The most memorable isms of history have often come to us with imagery and banners. Such symbols express a great deal succinctly.

Isms offer solutions—whether real or illusory—to actual scarcity. When they offer such solutions compellingly, they can succeed in becoming movements. Superficially, isms have been the source of much of human conflict. To those with oratorical skills, isms offer a highly seductive tool to manipulate and control masses. New isms tend to most succeed when scarcity, ever unsettling, moves to become truly terrifying.

Terrifying scarcity is what caused an economically decimated Post WWI German populace to elect Adolf Hitler. It is what causes many of those now seeking solace from economic and social upheaval to join Golden Dawn in Greece, Jobbik in Hungary, ISIS in the Middle East and the other nationalistic movements offering salvation through a simple program of "us vs. them", blaming "the other" for wrongs suffered and seizing what is "rightfully ours."

Such movements are never far from home. Desperate people will grasp at any solution that sounds compelling and

---

[145] The Nazi symbol is a physical inversion of the ancient Indian Sanskrit symbol for *swasta*, or "health". It therefore could be interpreted to mean, "disease".

quick. Neither the Republicans nor the Democrats need be the beneficiaries of what might soon appear in the United States, as Ross Perot's brief ascendancy before he withdrew from the 1992 presidential race suggests. The end of the Dollar's status as global reserve currency may well be approaching, with consequences that can perhaps best be appreciated by looking at the British Pound's earlier displacement.

In my view, then, the root cause of much of human misery and conflict is our antiquated system of Scarcity Game-based production, which today essentially consists of capitalism, the other isms having fallen aside as one after another has conspicuously failed. However, there are fundamental structural issues with capitalism that are not easily addressed.

Problems with Capitalism

Capitalism is the dominant economic paradigm on the planet today. That said, it is never practiced in pure form, but always with elements of socialism or oligarchy.

Capitalism has taken us from feudal pre-industrial systems into the modern era. It has rewarded innovation, especially technological innovation, and thereby given humanity unprecedented economic progress and wealth. It has created more opportunities for more people than any other system. That said, capitalism is increasingly beset with problems, some of which may be terminal.

While some speak of the death of capitalism, I prefer to speak of its completion. Capitalism has taken us to the frontier of an entirely new approach to production and distribution, which is discussed in the next section. In the decades ahead, I expect capitalism to increasingly transition into this new system.

If the proponents and beneficiaries of capitalism see the benefits of the new system as being greater for themselves than those of capitalism, the transition can be a graceful one. Otherwise, I fear that it will involve serious social disruption as the rapidly increasing ranks of the unemployed become a burden upon societies everywhere. In the remainder of this section, I will explore the problems of capitalism in order that we can then see how a new system can successfully address these.

Capitalism originated in a time when external effects of production such as pollution were unknown and disregarded. Today, there is widespread awareness even amongst Fortune 1000 companies that these effects can no longer be ignored, as environmental degradation becomes ever more dramatic, costly, and potentially devastating.

While the market mechanisms inherent to capitalism will tend to price resources in a manner that assures their continued availability, this does not always work. For example, while there is a general consensus that rising CO_2 levels threaten the oceans, vested interests have managed to confuse the discussion and prevent the stringent regulations (or, less intrusively, pricing of pollution) necessary to incentivize reduced emissions.

Capitalism favors disposable products over enduring ones. If a company were to produce a product that met its customers' needs for life and never needed replacement, that product would eventually no longer produce revenues.[146]

Like other scarcity-based isms, capitalism treats people, other living beings, and natural resources as inputs to production; replaceable or disposable. This naturally rewards sociopathic behavior: the executive who is comfortable treating everyone and everything as disposable and consumable without regard to their welfare has an advantage over other executives who are conflicted about such decisions.[147] Even

---

[146] It might be possible for such a product to be leased rather than sold. Tesla automobiles are being designed for very long life and upgrades, and might well in future be transacted this way.

[147] Harvard professor Martha Stout, author of *The Sociopath Next Door,* estimates that sociopaths constitute about 4% of the general population but a higher percentage of executives. Further, recent research indicates that the percentage may be higher than standard tests have suggested, because intelligent

those who find this abhorrent begrudgingly accept capitalism in the absence of an alternative.

Capitalism requires endless growth to reward the cost and risk of capital. Also, the growth that it requires has no regard for sustainability or social conscience, unless owners, customers or governments demand it. Adam Smith warned us of this in strident language over 200 years ago, and it remains true today. Said Pope Francis, "An economic system centered on the god of money needs to plunder nature to sustain the frenetic rhythm of consumption that is inherent to it."[148]

As discussed elsewhere, the War on Drugs was originally motivated by capitalist interests seeking a financial advantage, and that remains true today with asset forfeiture and other financial rewards generated from keeping drugs illegal. While economists can disagree as to the relative influence of unions and for-profit prison corporations, the fact is that in America imprisonment has become a parasitic growth industry, with far higher per capita incarceration rates than other nations. Lobbying campaigns have led to new and harsher laws being passed yielding new "criminals".[149] These have increased inmate populations and therefore revenues for such corporations, heedless of the ravaging effects of this incarceration on families and communities.

Destructive industries such as armaments are among the most profitable, in part because they create their own demand. *War is a Racket*, by US Marine Corps Major General and two time Medal of Honor winner Smedley Butler, views war as an

---

sociopaths can and will "game" most tests, though they may not be able to "game" fMRI brain tests.
(http://www.sciencedaily.com/releases/2014/09/140908120716.htm)

[148] http://www.nationalreview.com/article/395779/pope-francis-climate-and-leftism-dennis-prager

[149] http://www.americanbar.org/publications/human_rights_magazine_home/human_rights_vol38_2011/human_rights_summer11/prisons_for_profit_incarceration_for_sale.html

industry and gives weight to President and five-star general Eisenhower's generally ignored admonition to beware the rise of a military industrial complex. While national defense is a basic necessity, it is hard to understand why the USA needs to spend more on defense than the next 9 nations combined.[150] (Analysts point to the job-creating influence of military contracts, including contracts for projects unwanted by the military itself.)[151]

In capitalist societies, everything in society is viewed through the lens of money. Many people make major life decisions such as profession and marriage largely based on monetary considerations. Wealthier people are generally treated as superior, regardless of how they attained their wealth.

The mythos of capitalism is that anyone can become rich through hard work. This mythos is especially prized in America. However, serious academic research now shows that the prized American notion of upward mobility is grossly overestimated, and that for the vast majority it is illusory.[152]

Some would argue that capitalism will eventually spawn the solutions to our environmental crisis by incentivizing those solutions. Though plausible in theory, this ignores the real risk that such solutions may come too late. Already, we are in the Sixth Great Extinction of species. Historically, it has been estimated that 25% of our medicines have come from the rainforests. What remains to be discovered there, yet will be lost before it is ever found? And what of the corals, a unique and diverse form of life now rapidly being decimated?

Even as we are now living in the era of undisputed dominance by capitalism; what some might call its "golden age", new problems are arising with its intellectual foundation.

---

[150] http://www.janes.com/article/40083/analysis-us-no-longer-spends-more-on-defense-than-next-10-biggest-countries-combined

[151] http://www.mccain.senate.gov/public/index.cfm/floor-statements?ID=42987243-f045-7da7-6952-e32c98949a64

[152] http://www.theatlantic.com/politics/archive/2014/02/the-end-of-american-exceptionalism/283540/

In particular, a new type of "natural monopoly" is rapidly emerging.

Governments have long understood that monopolies are bad (except regarding money, where they have a blind spot) and laws exist to prevent or regulate them. However, it now appears that monopolies may be a natural outcome in much of the emerging digital marketplace.

When a product is difficult to develop but, once developed, free to make in unlimited quantity then it becomes, over time, very difficult for any but the best manufacturer to survive, *especially if this type of product is offered for free.* Consider the example of Waze, the free, intelligent, crowdsourced and adaptive GPS-based traffic routing program. When Google purchased Waze for $1 billion, Waze already dominated its market niche. With Google's resources behind it, what room exists for a competitor to displace Waze from its niche?

Google and other tech giants appear to be systematically acquiring such leading startups in many diverse fields. While the synergies between some of these may be hard to discern at present, a futurist can imagine quite a few of them. Google may be on course to become the world's dominant company, with defacto monopolies in many markets. What then? Will they adhere to their charming corporate motto of, "Don't Be Evil"? If so, how will they interpret that? Will there be any accountability? Already, their search algorithm decisions cause businesses that are dependent on Google's rankings to rise and fall.

It becomes possible to envision a future in which new product and service niches emerge as new discoveries make them possible, followed by a flurry of competitors creating and entering such niches. However, after a few years, one competitor would come to dominate each such niche and that would, in most cases, be the end of competition in that niche. (An alternate business model may sometimes be put forward to capture a niche, the way Facebook overtook Myspace and Ello is attempting to overtake Facebook. However, this is rare.) Occasionally, such a niche-dominating company will remain independent and grow into a giant. In most cases, however, they will be acquired by a Google or another future-oriented technology company.

In *The Second Machine Age,* this is one aspect of what is called a winner-take-all economy, the other being people with world-class expertise. They provide a detailed argument as to why this is happening, with the "free" economy being one major element. In addition, they talk about proliferating telecommunications and particularly the internet as forces breaking down barriers that used to protect small, local producers, and which make it easy for consumers to weed out all but the best value provider. Finally, they talk about the network effects (scaling) that essentially mean: the more who use a particular type of online service, the more valuable that service becomes and the greater the challenge of offering a competitive service.

The prospect of a world in which competition exists only in the early stages of a product is likely to trouble many proponents of capitalism. It is, however, fully compatible with a system (introduced below) in which product competition is viewed as a game or as a way to stimulate early innovation prior to product maturity, with no further productive advantage.

The shift to a winner-take-all economy is not the only problem with capitalism.

Capitalism is an essentially amoral (neither good nor evil) system for effectively allocating resources to favor growth. Strangely, it does have a particular ethic. "Maximize share-holder value" is the so-called 11th Commandment taught in business schools. Under this principle, an executive could actually be accused of dereliction of fiduciary duty for deciding to remove a dangerous product from market if the lost profits would exceed the expected legal liability.

Though some companies commit themselves to a so-called "triple bottom line" and other principles designed to encourage ethical behavior, these are add-ons and not central to capitalism. Capitalism as an economic model is not suited for a social system in which people are more important than profits—a criticism often leveled but without a specific viable alternative being offered.

Perhaps the greatest challenge leveled against capitalism is that it will ultimately self-destruct. Capitalism encourages and indeed lavishes wealth upon those who are busily eliminating jobs. Said prolific Quora social commentator Jeff Ronne,

> The trend of technology replacing virtually every worker destroys the model of capitalism. Capitalism assumes that economic production chiefly employees (sic) people not machines. Workers derive personal wealth from employment. When the majority of goods and services are produced by machines without human labor then the capitalist model falls completely apart.[153]

Scholars and other leaders are now calling for a "new capitalism".[154] However, unless there is a counter to the above analysis based on something other than wishful thinking or dogma, and I am not aware of any, we as a species must find a viable successor system to capitalism, and soon.

---

[153] http://www.quora.com/Bill-Gates-says-software-bots-will-eventually-take-jobs-away-in-20-years-What-do-you-think
[154] http://www.washingtonpost.com/news/innovations/wp/2015/07/20/we-need-a-new-version-of-capitalism-for-the-jobless-future/

Part III: A Celebration Society

> Perhaps the 20th century will strike future historians as
> an aberration, with its religious devotion to overwork
> in a time of prosperity, its attenuations of family in
> service to job opportunity, its conflation of income
> with self-worth.
>
> ~*Derek Thompson*

I dream of a world without work, but not the default world toward which capitalism is careening—a world in which ever more outsourced, downsized, laid off, "surplused," terminated and otherwise desperate people scramble for the scraps from a tiny elite's bountiful table.

Instead, I envision a world in which everyone is set free upon a kind of permanent vacation. I see lives of endless exploration, play, learning, inquiry, research, invention, artistic contribution, mutual service and, of course, celebration! (Those who wish to work may do so. We will call it having a hobby.)

In such a world, the wealthy elites will have even more of what they desire than today. They will still be fabulous winners, but at a different game—unless they prefer to retreat to enclaves where they continue to play their current game.

What is Celebrationism?

Celebrationism is the name I have given to the system of production and philosophy of government that I expect to enable and empower Celebration Societies. It is a fresh word; without the baggage or expectations existing systems entail. It harbors no political agendas nor any moral judgments. Yet, because of what it enables, it offers us a vehicle for unrestricted progress.

In its fullest implementation, I expect celebrationism to have two aspects. The first is as a system of people-centered automation. The second is as a philosophy of societal design that elevates service as its highest value.

Celebration as the Focus of a Society

Google's online dictionary defines *celebration* as "the action of marking one's pleasure at an important event or occasion by engaging in enjoyable, typically social, activity."

While the notion of a society focused on celebration may seem absurd, much of the purposeful human activity in advanced nations is already focused on celebrations. Indeed, it could be argued that many of us live for the opportunity to participate in celebrations.

A celebration is not a *what* so much as a *why*. Permit me an anecdote. For years, my wife celebrated her birthday by visiting an amusement park with friends. She also enjoyed visiting amusement parks at other times. The act of going to an amusement park is not in and of itself a celebration. Sharing the activity with friends to mark a special occasion makes it a celebration.

Consider the elaborate preparation along with considerable investment of money many people invest into destination trips such as Disneyland, Venice, and Las Vegas, or into ocean cruises—often to celebrate occasions such as holidays and anniversaries. Parents may spend a month planning a child's birthday party. The average US wedding now costs $30,000.[155]

People enthusiastically share in others' celebrations. Who has not enjoyed a St. Patrick's Day parade, wearing something green, even if they're not Irish? Many American bars celebrate Cinco de Mayo, and gay pride parades include many non-gay people.

Corporations and groups of people with shared interests will rent ballrooms and hire entertainment to celebrate major events, often engaging the services of an event planner. Even

---

[155] http://money.cnn.com/2014/03/28/pf/average-wedding-cost/

the New York Stock Exchange, that staid bastion of capitalism, has a kind of coming out celebration for newly listed companies. On the day trading begins, the CEO of that company gets to ring the opening bell.

A new societal design has to be very appealing to overcome the inertia of present-day approaches. I can think of nothing more appealing than frequent celebration.

Principles of Celebrationism

Centuries ago, writing in their respective books, *The Descent of Man* and what is today called *The Wealth of Nations*, Charles Darwin and Adam Smith foresaw a future world in which a cooperative human society (Darwin) and "universal opulence" (Smith) would reign. We now stand at the doorway to that world.

Said Darwin, "Moral qualities are advanced, either directly or indirectly, much more through the effects of habit, by our reasoning powers, by instruction, by religion, etc., than through natural selection."[156] In his writings, Darwin actually mentions "survival of the fittest" only twice, and the second of those times was to apologize for exaggerating its importance in *The Origin of Species.*[157]

Smith believed that an opulent future would be achieved in well-governed societies based on specialization of labor.[158] It is precisely this specialization, combined with technology, which has brought us to this historic juncture.

By focusing on celebrations with attendant honorifics such as awards, prizes and certificates, a society will inspire ever more creations of all sorts that add value to humanity. Even when an award is competitive, as they often will be, the celebration of that award is by its nature a cooperative act. Cooperation and competition will find a natural balance.

---

[156] *The Descent of Man;* Charles Darwin's lesser-known book.

[157] *Darwin's Lost Theory of Love,* David Loye

[158] http://www.econlib.org/library/Smith/smWN1.html#B.I, Ch.1, Of the Division of Labor

Celebrationism is a system that recognizes and embraces, rather than ignores or opposes, the advent of automated methods of production for all necessary goods and services, and eventually for most luxuries as well. It is designed to answer the question, what can vast numbers of unemployed people do to enjoy a high quality of life?

Realizing that celebrationism is an audacious proposal, I have been careful to collect evidence supportive of its viability. With the promise that most of this evidence will be provided elsewhere, here, then, are key understandings of celebrationism as a system of automated production:

- All material wealth is always and without exception the confluence of three factors in some configuration. These factors are energy, matter and organizing intelligence.
- The law of supply and demand states that when supply of something is greater than the demand for it, the price of that something falls.
- The supply of energy, matter and organizing intelligence will soon increase so dramatically that they will far outstrip any conceivable demand by humanity in the near future.
- The FREE! culture that has been emerging rapidly in software will soon spill out into the physical environment as more and more physical products become, in essence, replicable information applied to inexpensive matter.[159]
- Most services will be provided by robots and AI's, including food production and preparation, cleaning, construction, manufacturing, and even personal services. Eventually, we can have a world wherein all necessities of life become ubiquitous and free.
- When money is not needed for one's well-being, its distorting effects on society will gradually disappear as people adjust to a new reality.

---

[159] *The Zero Marginal Cost Society*, Jeremy Rifkin

- Enough jobs will cease to exist that having jobs as the basis for an economy will no longer be viable, and the ripple effects will be experienced everywhere.

- A deep new understanding of play and of games will inform us as a society, and people will come to realize that those who act from love of what they do in a spirit of service do so not only as a particular form of play but that this play can actually replace work. (Some of us will prefer that people do certain things for us, even when AI's and robots can do those things quite well.)

- People will meet their needs for social recognition and sense of contribution via their gifts to society: creations, shared discoveries and acts of service.

- Celebration will be a frequent occurrence, and serve not only to uplift participants and build community bonds but also encourage more of whatever is being celebrated.

- A Celebration Society will be a scientific society. Though revealed knowledge will be respected as a personal experience, it will not be given credence as a basis for societal design. Instead, the scientific method (falsifiable hypotheses, rigorously tested through repeated and controlled experiments) will be prized. While science never gives us "absolute" truth, it does something more practical: it leads to ever-improving understanding, and avoids much of the dogma and institutionalized falsehoods that have so damaged past societies.[160]

- A dazzling array of emerging technologies, some with great power for both help and harm, will be brought together in a balanced way within a Celebration Society to enable and rapidly generate this vision.

---

[160] Science already has a solid role in diplomacy. Its role in government could be greater still. (http://www.theatlantic.com/science/archive/2015/09/science-diplomacy/407455/)

These points will be discussed in more detail later. Likewise, celebrationism as a philosophy of government will be discussed, as will the matter of transitioning from capitalism to celebrationism.

Celebrationism is not at odds with any existing system of social organization, except to the extent that such a system seeks to monopolize the world or to enslave people. Provided that any system allows its residents the freedom to leave, that system can function more effectively than it presently does by using celebrationist production. This is so because celebrationism will provide for the basic needs of everyone, thereby eliminating a major future source of social unrest and instability.

Making Assumptions and Testing Beliefs

Back in a previous life, I was a technical writer. One of our favorite sayings was "a-s-s-u-m-e, makes an ass of you and me". It was a cautionary note, reminding us to make sure of the ground upon which we stood. In fact, we cannot live without assumptions and faith. Take a step; you assume and have faith that the floor below you will not open up.

Life is full of assumptions. Many of them are as vital as that one and as unquestioned. The difficulty is that some of our assumptions, including vital ones for our lives and for the future of the planet, are also unquestioned—and, as I will demonstrate, wrong.

Our beliefs rest on assumptions. Beliefs govern much of human history, past, present and future. Therefore, when assumptions are wrong there can be serious consequences.

Have you ever realized that you were wrong about something that you had previously been certain was true? I have. It's quite an uncomfortable experience.

There were times in history when people generally believed that the Earth was flat; that it was the center of the universe, and other things that few, if any, today still believe. I find it interesting and timely that the Millennials seem to value work less than any previous generation.

Many commonly held beliefs of today are being proven wrong or at least subject to serious challenge. Here are some examples.

- Autism is viewed as a form of mental retardation. However, researchers are finding that overstimulation drives autistic behaviors and that the autistic brain is actually hyper-functional with hidden advantages.[161]
- The "Cyclic Universe" theory apparently fits the data as well as does the Big Bang theory, and is described as an "alternative theory that turns the cosmic history topsy-turvy...."[162]
- Research may be establishing that life can only originate in specific dry chemical conditions. The alternative suggested by this research is equally radical: that another, unknown reproductive molecule preceded RNA.[163]
- Scientists have found what they thought to be impossible: real dinosaur blood inside a bog-standard fossil bone, and they now believe that cells extracted from better preserved fossils may contain complete dinosaur DNA.[164]

The Advantage of a Scientific Approach to Knowledge

The crucial point for this discussion is that even when essentially the whole scientific community has resolved that a theory is correct, it may still be superseded by a better one, so we should keep some humility about our beliefs. Testability is,

---

[161] http://www.kurzweilai.net/autistic-brain-is-hyper-functional-needs-predictable-paced-environments-study-finds,
http://www.theatlantic.com/health/archive/2015/09/autism-hidden-advantages/406180/

[162] Paul Steinhardt, Albert Einstein Professor of Science at Princeton University, writing in http://edge.org/3rd_culture/steinhardt02/steinhardt02_index.html.

[163] https://www.newscientist.com/article/mg22229650.300-no-more-primal-soup-creating-life-without-water

[164] http://www.newscientist.com/article/dn27687-dinosaur-blood-cells-extracted-from-75millionyearold-fossil.html#.VXce6c9Viko

in essence, why a scientific approach to societal design is superior to one based on revealed knowledge or other fixed beliefs.

Unlike revealed knowledge, science is a process of progressive unfoldment of truth. It offers little comfort to those who seek immediate certainty, but unlike revealed knowledge it offers a testable and repeatable basis for societal design decisions. Science is and will always be, imperfect. That said, its imperfections are far easier to work with in every practical sense than revealed knowledge, which differs from person to person in such extreme ways as to often be incompatible with other revealed knowledge. (Those who harbor revealed knowledge that they know *must* be true will often fight opposing ideas.)

Without making judgment, I observe that most of the world's population believes in religious doctrines based on a book. It is not, however, the same book. Since there are in addition widely different doctrines that arise from the various readings of these books, it is obvious that they cannot all be right. These are some of our most cherished beliefs. I have mine; you have yours.

Religion is considered a belief system precisely because there is no empirical way to test the fundamental theses. Where certain behaviors are called for by religious doctrine, those behaviors can be empirically modeled and tested to determine their usefulness in societal design. That is entirely valid in a Celebration Society. The underlying doctrine, however, has no place in societal design, at least for the common principles of all Celebration Societies.

That said, a group of persons sharing a set of religious beliefs and wanting to live by its rules could create a successful Celebration Society. The key understanding is that they would do so voluntarily, without coercing others.

Another belief that is commonly held today is that our present civilization embodies the most advanced social systems in history. This is not only unfounded, it is dangerous because it deprives us of precious knowledge.

A Great Lost Civilization

In the 20th century, especially its last decade, scholars made some astonishing discoveries about a major lost civilization. While we know little about other lost civilizations submerged under water near the coastline of India[165] and possibly near Cuba,[166] this one flourished inland in Europe almost 1,000 years ago and left significant records now being unearthed and understood.

A detailed and colorful description of this historic period, written for the lay person's comprehension and enjoyment, is to be found in the book *New Money for a New World*, which I edited. For those who lack the time or interest in reading another book, I offer the following synopsis of some key points.

From about 1,050 to 1,300 AD, a civilization known as the Central Middle Ages (CMA) flourished in Europe, especially in the Languedoc region of what is today France. This was such a flourishing and dynamic culture that scholars have now labeled it "The First Modernization", "European Takeoff", and even "The True Renaissance".[167]

The first universities were founded in Europe during this period, and significant mathematical and other intellectual advances occurred as well, centuries before what has been called The Renaissance.[168] While scholars are still piecing together a fuller picture of this time, certain conclusions are already becoming mainstream. According to Guy Bois, "This at the very least is now generally accepted: Europe experienced a period of economic growth of an exceptional scale and length."[169]

---

[165] http://news.bbc.co.uk/2/hi/south_asia/1768109.stm

[166] http://news.nationalgeographic.com/news/2002/05/0528_020528_sunkencities. html, http://news.co.cr/lost-city-found-beneath-cuban-waters/15221/

[167] *La Grande Dépression Médiévale*, Guy Bois

[168] *The Twelfth Century—Renaissance or Proto-Renaissance?*, Eva Matthews Sanford

[169] *La Grande Dépression Médiévale*, Guy Bois

For much of human history, caloric intake has served as a good marker for the health of a civilization. (Malnutrition, which may be characterized as eating enough calories but in forms with harmful side effects or lacking beneficial nutrients, is a separate issue.) The average daily caloric intake in the CMA was approximately 3,500 – 4,000, a number exceeding the average of 3,000 in developed nations today.[170]

The average workday was 6 hours, with two days of rest each week. Workers enjoyed 3 - 4 meals daily. There were no fewer than 90 official holidays, and in some areas far more.[171]

Urbanization, commonly believed to have started in the 1700s, actually began during this period.[172] An important enabling factor for this quality of life was reliance on technology. For example, at the start of the 12th century in France alone, "(there were in operation at least) 20,000 water mills, which represented the energy of 600,000 workers. Such technologies liberated massive amounts of labor."[173] Further, "ordinary life is revolutionized: coal is used for heating, candles for lighting, eyeglasses for reading, glass is used more and more commonly, paper is manufactured on an industrial scale."[174]

Europe's population doubled during the CMA; an unprecedented rate of increase.[175] Likewise, the average productivity of cultivated land doubled.[176]

The rate of change was phenomenal. Said one scholar, "One can only be impressed by the extraordinary vitality and power of the changes that occurred during those three

---

[170] *La Vie au Moyen Âge*, Robert Delort
[171] ibid.
[172] *Cathedral, Forges and Waterwheel: Technology and Invention in the Middle Ages*, Frances and Joseph Gies
[173] *L'Énergie au Moyen Age*, R. Philippe
[174] *La Tradition cachée des cathedrals*, Jean-Pierre Bayard
[175] *Les Oeuvriers des cathédrales*, François Icher
[176] *Histoire économique de l'Occident médiéval*, Guy Fourquin

centuries.... One will have to wait five hundred years to live another wave of transformation of that scale: the capitalist Industrial Revolution."[177]

Several scholars' observations are illustrative: "[CMA] growth isn't limited to a demographic explosion combined with a strong agricultural expansion. A flourishing commercial expansion was its third dimension."[178]

> There was...a growing manufacture of textiles, pottery, leather goods, and many other things. The list of articles manufactured gets longer and longer...the products get better and better. Prices go down in terms of man hours because of more efficient management, improvement in tools and machinery, and better transport and distribution.[179]

CMA residents enjoyed abundance. They invested resources not needed for present purposes into physical works that improved life for present and future generations. They built waterworks, mills, and other infrastructure to better the community. They built the Great Cathedrals (originally purposed as tourist attractions; the Church acquired them later).[180] In addition, they built hundreds of lesser cathedrals and many other structures.[181] Said one historian, "It was the greatest period of building activity that there has ever been, and no mere catalog of names and places can convey any idea of the strength and quality of its products."[182]

---

[177] *La Grande Dépression Médiévale*, Guy Bois
[178] ibid.
[179] *Europe Emerges: Transition Toward an Industrial Worldwide Society*, R. L. Reynolds
[180] *A Prix d'Or: le Financement des Cathédrales*, H. Kraus
[181] *La Vie au Moyen Âge*, Robert Delort
[182] *The Gothick North: A Study of Medieval Life, Art and Thought*, Sacheverell Sitwell

This was not a patriarchal society; women could assume the same roles as men. There was equality of the sexes in both education and trade.[183] Women could own property and had an equal voice in community affairs.[184]

The immense prosperity and growth of the CMA is well documented. Missing from nearly all analyses is a mechanism to explain why this historical period had results so superior to those of the centuries that followed it.

The answer apparently lies in its *dual currency system*.[185] This consisted of national money functioning alongside a network of local currencies that complemented the national money (hence the term, *complementary currencies*).[186]

CMA people used the national money for long distance transactions, savings, and paying taxes. Their uses of that national money resembled modern uses of national money.[187]

The local type of currency had some unusual design features. Notably, it apparently included *demurrage*, a kind of carrying charge that decreases the value of money over time. It thereby discourages the saving of this type of money while encouraging transactions, which economists call *velocity of money*. This, in turn, increased local trade and, once basic needs were met, investment of the surplus into infrastructure.[188]

We can infer that the use of demurrage-based local money alongside national money apparently offered certain benefits that may explain the CMA's success:

- By increasing economic resiliency, the system reduced the shocks and wasteful dislocations commonplace in a monetary monoculture

---

[183] *La femme au temps des cathédrales*, Régine Pernoud
[184] *The Year 1000: What Life Was Like at the Turn of the First Millennium*, Lacey and Danziger
[185] *New Money for a New World*, Belgin and Lietaer
[186] http://www.cluboffrome.org/cms/wp-content/uploads/2012/05/Money-and-Sustainability-the-missing-link-Executive-Summary.pdf
[187] *Mysterium Geld*, Bernard Lietaer
[188] ibid.

- By encouraging local transactions, it strengthened community bonds
- By incentivizing velocity of money, it shifted thinking from the saving of money to other uses. Local money that exceeded present needs was therefore naturally deployed for the construction of productive assets
- By building a strong middle class, there was no great divide of income inequality

The CMA ended when the French King made local currencies illegal and he embarked upon a program of debasement of the national money in preparation for war. The economy then collapsed. A 150 year "Greatest Depression", far more extreme than the Great Depression of the 1930's, ensued.[189] Half a century into it, with sewage uncollected and decay everywhere, rats brought the Black Death, one of the great plagues of history.[190] In desperation, people devolved to cannibalism and other grotesqueries.[191]

It is little wonder that the intervening centuries until the (Second) Renaissance are remembered as dark years. We are only now beginning to comprehend the magnitude of the loss that this tragedy represented for humanity.

When resources effectively address needs, there is not only a dynamic balance but also a sense of well-being that spreads across the community. People feel safer and so they are more willing to share, to support public works and to plan and act for the future. Such a society clearly has much worth emulating.

A New Advanced Civilization

Though we can learn from it, we are actually in a much better position than the CMA. Our technology is far in advance of theirs. By marrying 21st century technology to the informed

---

[189] *La Grande Dépression Médiévale*, Guy Bois
[190] *The Central Middle Ages*, Daniel Power
[191] *The Great European Famine of 1315 – 1316*, Henry S. Lucas

social structures of the CMA and to other wisdom, we may yet attain a golden age surpassing all ages that have gone before it.

Imagine a world with a CMA culture, supplemented by the great lessons from the Venetian Republic that thrived for centuries, the American Constitutional system, successful parliamentary democracies such as Iceland's 1,000 year unbroken experiment, and others. Imagine such a world, suffused with sustainable technologies, such that every human community enhances the natural beauty and harmony permeating and surrounding it.

Importantly, we do not need to transform the whole world at once. We need only transform it enclave by enclave. If just one such enclave adopts Celebration Society principles, then steps forward to sponsor and mentor two more enclaves, it all progresses without coercion and at the expense of no one.

A world where people have their basic needs met, both internally and externally, will be a far more cooperative world. Competition will exist primarily for fun, not for survival.

One of the more encouraging developments of recent years that supports the feasibility of such a world has been the rise online of what Jeremy Rifkin calls the *collaborative commons*. Open source architecture products and services such as Firefox and Wikipedia have become competitive or even dominant in their markets despite the fact that they essentially rely on part-time volunteers for their development, maintenance and evolution.

Clay Shirky has defined this emerging collaborative resource as, "cognitive surplus". This is, "the ability of the world's population to volunteer and to contribute and to collaborate on large, sometimes global, projects."[192] He further points out that the creation of Wikipedia took 100 million hours of volunteer time. Given that American television viewing alone consumes an estimated 200 billion hours per year, the potential for planetary collaboration is staggering, if

---

[192] www.ted.com/talks/clay_shirky_how_cognitive_surplus_will_change_the_ world/transcript

people are sufficiently motivated and supplied with the right tools (essentially, collaboration-enhancing software and a personal computer with broadband access).

To even more fully appreciate the potential of this, consider that people already do this to such a standard as Wikipedia and Mozilla (among others) in a world where there are terrific competitive pressures to make money. (Already, according to *The Second Machine Age,* 6 of the 10 most popular websites rely on user-generated content.) How many more such enterprises and projects will flourish in a Celebration Society, where everyone who chooses will be free to devote themselves to such endeavors rather than to work? I expect that the results will far surpass present levels of volunteerism.

If work is to no longer be a significant part of the economy, a possibility we must now entertain, this leaves us with fundamental questions about the production and distribution of goods and services.

Production, Distribution and Consumption

As is becoming evident from diverse fields of technology, the capacity to automatically produce everything required for the basic needs of everyone on Earth is either real today or will become real soon.

Climate change could slash agricultural production and turn desperate populations into refugees, thereby leading to wars and destabilizing many governments. However, emerging technologies discussed elsewhere can enable the production of as much clean, salt-free water as may be required, and allow for the indoor growing of crops where adequate arable land is not available or the climate is inhospitable. Likewise, as we shall see, new technologies show the potential to rapidly reverse CO_2 levels to pre-industrial levels in a controllable manner.

Enclosed monoculture and permaculture food production facilities capable of withstanding extreme weather conditions and providing for local needs can be built in multiple climactic regions from fast-growing guadua bamboo. Guadua is comparable in strength to steel yet flexible enough to withstand a hurricane, and can grow as much as 3 feet in a day.[193]

As discussed elsewhere in this book, hemp farming and permaculture systems can remediate poor soil in diverse environments, thereby increasing fertility and food production and even transforming ecosystems.

With full deployment of known and emerging technologies, production need not be an issue. That leaves distribution and consumption as potential problems.

Economists have pointed out that great disparity between the wealthiest members of society and the others historically leads to social instability.[194] Yet the disparity between "haves" and "have nots" is not so much a matter of possessions as it is the benefits of those possessions.

For example, in a society where mass transit is lacking, the difference between owning a luxury car and owning an ordinary car is far less significant than the difference between owning the ordinary car and having no car. Also, there may be no functional difference between owning the ordinary car and having a driverless vehicle show up whenever needed for transportation.

Everyone must consume. Consumption is part of life. Breathing, drinking water, and eating are all forms of consumption. However, not everyone need enjoy luxuries. Peoples' desire for luxuries is much of what drives capitalist progress, acknowledging the argument that marketing often persuades people that luxuries are actually necessities.

Ignoring for the moment conspicuous consumption, wherein luxuries are not wanted for their inherent benefits so much as for the status they connote, yesterday's luxuries have in many cases become today's necessities by common understanding (e.g., a toilet was once deemed a luxury), and the same evolution can be expected going forward. For example, while the personal computer may still seem a luxury, the fact that many public schools are now requiring that

---

[193] www.BambooLiving.com
[194] Capital in the 21st Century, Thomas Piketty

papers be written on them suggests that in future they may become necessities.

A key understanding is that there is no bright line separating necessities from luxuries, and the only way to create such a line would be through centralized control. This approach to economic planning has been historically discredited and would, if implemented once again subject people to the decisions and rule of a tiny elite and, eventually, the rule of their AI or AI's.

Between an unfettered free market—were such to ever truly exist—and totalitarian control lie various degrees of centralized control. All such centralized control rests upon control of the means of production. Under capitalism, this is an endless competitive struggle.

There is constant pressure of large corporations within industries to figure out how to circumvent antitrust laws and manipulate the system to their advantage. Lobbying can be one of the most lucrative uses of capital. Particular industries, notably defense, pharmaceutical, and investment management have done this especially well. They spend millions in lobbying and campaign contributions in order to earn billions in contracts and favorable laws and regulations. The more this happens, the more the system shifts from capitalism to corporatism or, as Fed Chair Janet Yellen has mused, oligarchy.[195]

While people can debate how oligarchical the US system is, research has recently determined that the global financial system is more tightly interwoven than most had suspected. According to analysts at the Swiss Federal Institute of Technology in Zurich, who sought to untangle the web of ownership amongst trans-national corporations, "...much of it tracked back to a 'super-entity' of 147 ... that controlled 40 per cent of the total wealth in the network. In effect, less than 1 per cent

---

[195] http://www.huffingtonpost.com/2014/05/09/janet-yellen-oligarchy_n_5296399.html

of the companies were able to control 40 per cent of the entire network".[196]

Given that market-based economies depend on consumers, that those consumers depend on work in order to afford what they consume, and that work is likely ending for many if not most of us, I see no future for capitalism beyond the 21st century. Either we will see a great increase in centralized control or we will see an Abundance Game. I see no third possibility for humanity.

A centrally controlled oligarchical or totalitarian world will be run by AI's which might be instructed to dole out some basic stipend to everyone except the tiny elite who "own" those AI's (for so long as the AI's cooperate). While it will be clear that the technology is capable of providing abundance to all, due to customs, egos and prejudice the distribution of that abundance will in this scenario be tightly restricted. (This will be justified on moral and/or practical grounds, all based upon selective assumptions and interpretations of data.)

Likewise, in a Celebration Society everyone's basic needs will be met through automated production. However, the definition of "needs" will be a matter of consensus within a community whose membership is voluntary. Further, as technology rapidly advances in capabilities, this automated production will rapidly expand its scope to include luxuries, and I expect that the distinction between necessities and luxuries will fade away. It is, ultimately, only a meaningful comparison within the Scarcity Game.

Ethics of Celebrationism

There are a few guiding principles I would propose for a society.

---

[196] http://www.globalresearch.ca/revealed-the-capitalist-network-that-runs-the-world/27191

It has been said that morality is absolute, while ethics are contextual. Assuming this to be true, a rational political system will have a foundation in well-defined ethics.[197] The issue of ethics cannot be avoided. Even the least intrusive government—as idealized by libertarians—provides for common defense, protection of individual rights and enforcement of honest, non-coercive contracts. These, in turn, depend upon concepts of property and the definition of rights, and there it gets muddy.

For example, in ancient Rome a father literally owned his children. Parents could kill their children if they so chose. While no significant society presently sanctions such a viewpoint, modern societies specify rules by which parents can physically modify their children (e.g. circumcision), strike or otherwise discipline them, as well as rules regarding parental responsibilities to children (education or lack thereof, proper food and medical care, etc.) and rules regarding the transition of those children to adult status. A society that gave children full autonomy as soon as they were old enough to demand it would have large numbers of two-year olds wandering and endangered. (As a practical matter, I cannot imagine parents consenting to such.)

This is but one example of how ethical values of a society become expressed as law. It therefore behooves those of us contemplating the creation of a Celebration Society to reflect upon, discuss and debate the kinds of ethical values and system we wish to enshrine. This, in my view, is the most sacred duty of such founders.

Here are a few ethical guidelines that I would advocate, along with my thoughts on how they should be codified:

- A Celebration Society is guided by its Charter. This is the highest law of the land, never subject to override by any other law. The Charter is an expression of ethics

---

[197] "the branch of philosophy that involves systematizing, defending, and recommending concepts of right and wrong conduct." (http://en.wikipedia.org/wiki/Ethics)

intended to bind people into a cohesive society by virtue of being commonly cherished.

- As part of the citizenship process, Citizens demonstrate a commitment to living by the Charter. This includes a duty to contribute to the society's legislative and judicial processes.
- In addition to common constitutional principles and provisions found elsewhere, the Charter makes explicit a set of values all Citizens are expected to share. Chief amongst these is a commitment to service as a way of life.
- Government operations are as transparent as possible amongst Citizens.
- The legal system is based on the minimum number of laws required to peacefully prevent or resolve disputes, protect the society (and especially those without competent adult capacity), enforce honest contracts, and provide for the general welfare in a non-coercive manner. All laws are unambiguous, publicly published and with the number of words not exceeding a predetermined threshold.
- Justice is impartial, swift, rational and primarily restorative and preventative rather than punitive in intent.
- No consensual act between adults or solely involving one's own adult body is criminal, with the caveat that prior to any irrevocable act or commitment those persons who care may call for a competency hearing.
- Acts coercive of others, including fraud, are prohibited. Voluntary, honest contracts between competent adults are enforced by the legal system.
- The production of necessities is based upon creating abundant, sustainable sources and systems of matter, energy, and organizing intelligence. This is a societal responsibility.
- Regulations are replaced, whenever practicable, by systematized incentives including complementary currencies (discussed elsewhere).

- A culture is fostered in which it is recognized that happiness does not depend on chasing "the best" of something but rather in finding what is "good enough" to meet one's needs and desires.[198] Excellence is pursued as a matter of personal choice.
- The society provides for the common defense in a manner open and transparent to the Citizens.
- Everyone has access to advanced AI-generated "virtual worlds". Some of this blends with their reality, creating *augmented* environments. Beyond that, all manner of experiences that are considered too dangerous, immoral, impractical, or even impossible in the real world will be available to people in VR.

Encouraging Behavior

In general, whatever behaviors are favored by consensus as expressed in the Charter should be encouraged rather than required, except as necessary. Required behaviors, however well-intentioned, risk calcification of the system and great limitations on freedom, happiness, health, and even life itself.

In changing a culture, it is generally less effective to coerce behavior than to encourage it. Consider the difference between taxation and tithing. Also, in cultures that support it such as the USA, tipping is almost universal without any coercive mechanism.

Encouragement can have surprising power. Consider how widespread is the behavior of cutting back on sleep—a physiological necessity—in favor of being more "productive." In the US, it apparently began with Thomas Edison.[199]

---

[198] http://www.theatlantic.com/health/archive/2015/03/the-power-of-good-enough/387388/

[199] http://www.theatlantic.com/health/archive/2014/05/thomas-edison-and-the-cult-of-sleep-deprivation/370824/2/

Regulations and laws often carry unintended consequences, which are harder to correct once something is legally
codified. Cass Sunstein has insights in this regard and,
thanks to the power of what he calls "nudges" (including the
deliberate adoption of cultural norms)[200] just a few activities
apparently need be prohibited in a Celebration Society. Here,
as I see it, are those few that need to be prohibited:

- Anything which poses an existential threat to the
  Society must be prohibited, taking full account of then-
  contemporary meanings of the phrase, "existential
  threat"
- Any coercion of a Citizen, resident, or visitor, excepting
  actions by Peace Officers acting under administrative or
  judicial authority
- In general, any public behavior that violates the common sense of decency, understanding that this changes
  with time and place
- Any private behavior that involves children, animals, or
  incapacitated adults in a manner that the common
  sense of decency regards as inappropriate

Complementary currencies, discussed elsewhere, can be
viewed as a new kind of nudging mechanism; stronger than a
recommendation such as a Recommended Daily Allowance yet
weaker than regulation or law. People need not use a
complementary currency even if it is popular within their
community, yet it becomes a conscious decision and so
behavior is influenced.

The guiding principle I would advocate is that anything
which is consensual among or by consenting adults is permissible in private, while anything that is consistent with the
Charter and evolving community standards is permissible in
public. Each adult would have sovereignty over his or her own
body, with suitable protection for children and the incapacitated. Outside the Celebration Society, when visiting other

---

[200] http://www.macleans.ca/news/world/mr-moneyball-goes-to-washington/

nations, each Citizen or resident would be responsible to obey the local prevailing laws, without any expectation of assistance from the society for actual violations of same.

A New Paradigm

When a new paradigm successfully emerges, it transcends and includes the previous paradigm. It does so by more completely explaining the data; by integrating anomalous yet repeatable elements that the previous paradigm could not explain. It constitutes a change of worldview, and is therefore much more comprehensive in its influence than an ordinary scientific advance.[201]

Said philosopher Christian de Quincey, author of the Wisdom Academy, "Paradigms have great potency. They are, in effect, the framework of beliefs and assumptions that shape our understanding of reality and how we fit in. This potency is amplified because for the most part the beliefs we inherit from the paradigm are unconscious."

Paradigm shifts are messy. They happen when the number or significance of anomalies become sufficient to throw the prevailing worldview into a state of crisis. The shift includes an intellectual battle between proponents of the old and new views.[202] Notable paradigm shifts in science include those from Ptolemaic to Copernican astronomy, and from Newtonian mechanics to relativity.

Previous paradigms may be seen as special cases within the new paradigms that supplant them. Though wrong in demonstrable ways, they still work in limited contexts. Just as Newtonian mechanics works fine for all of our everyday experiences, people successfully used the apparent motion of the Sun around the Earth to plan agriculture.

A Celebration Society (or other Abundance Game-based social system) will support within itself all manner of other

---

[201] *The Structure of Scientific Revolutions*, Thomas Kuhn
[202] ibid.

social systems. Much as the human body supports beneficial bacteria and other organisms that were formerly independent but less successful existing apart from each other, a Celebration Society will support enclaves of capitalist, socialist, fascist, fundamentalist, and such other systems as people may choose to create. These enclaves will be ethically limited in particular ways, notably protection of all individuals from coercion and of their right to emigrate, thereby preserving the rights of all individuals within such an enclave to fundamental self-determination. No system within celebrationism will own a person's mind or body.

In a Celebration Society, failure takes on a very different meaning. It is like losing at a game of chess, cards or ball. While one may have invested great effort, passion and time in the project, loss or failure will never be a matter of life and death. It will not even threaten one's basic welfare, since the necessities of life will be available to all as byproducts of the great Celebration Society productive system.

Play, Reconsidered

One of the strangest conversations I ever had about a Celebration Society was on a transcontinental flight. I was seated with three beautiful young women. They could have been in entertainment or modeling, but they were all recent graduates from the same Ivy League school, with degrees in aerospace engineering. My impression was that they had the world before them, and it was remarkable to meet not one but three such women at once.

In learning of their plans for the future, I was struck (as I often am) by how little people know of the material in this book. I thought it might help them with their planning, so I gave them a bird's eye view. All recoiled from the idea. One asked, "What would I do in such a society? Sit around and watch TV? Play games?" Another chimed in with, "Stuff my face and get fat!"

Clearly, these young women—potential superstars in a capitalist economy—were convinced that their motivation to produce was external. If they did not need to earn an income, they believed that they would do nothing productive.

I have since come to appreciate that many people share the fear that they will become the equivalent of human vegetables; the cruise ship passengers of *Wall-E.* This is a serious consideration, and I regard it as one of the more substantial criticisms of a Celebration Society.

But is this true?

People whose basic needs are met may be more motivated to act productively, not less. Pilot studies by Guy Standing, professor of development studies at the University of London, have led him to conclude: "When people stop working out of fear, they become more productive."[203]

Other research has found that, "Achievement motivation can be defined as the need for success or the attainment of excellence. Individuals will satisfy their needs through different means, and are driven to succeed for varying reasons both internal and external.... All of our behaviors, actions, thoughts, and beliefs are influenced by our inner drive to succeed."[204] If we observe someone sitting around and playing games for an extended period of time, what does this tell us? It depends, like so much else, on context.

If the person recently completed an exhausting project, they may be recovering from burnout. Or, they may be escaping from an intolerable situation—much like addicts use substances, gambling, and so forth to escape. On the other hand, perhaps they are studying the game(s) for purposes of developing their own game or developing the skills necessary to master something. The military has found that games can offer excellent training for soldiers.[205]

Dr. Standing's findings are supported by Gallup Organization global research (discussed elsewhere) that only a tiny minority of "workers" are actually productive. Further,

---

[203] http://www.guystanding.com/files/documents/Basic_Income_Pilots_in_ India_note_for_ inaugural.pdf

[204] http://www.personalityresearch.org/papers/rabideau.html

[205] http://www.livescience.com/10022-military-video-games.html

evidence from the historical record supports the idea that people can be valued members of society even when they are not deemed to be productive.

Throughout human history, production by humans has been necessary for survival. Those who did not produce generally did not survive. There is evidence, both historical and modern, of cultures that have dealt harshly with deformities. And yet, fossils also show that children who sustained severe, debilitating injuries were cared for and supported for many years by their societies with no hope or expectation that they would ever be productive.[206] In particular, "It is now becoming clear that the Neanderthals had cultures and social organizations developed to the point that community members unable to provide for themselves were fed and cared for."[207]

These discoveries suggest that long-term care might have been a more common practice in prehistory than has been imagined. In a future Celebration Society where all production of necessities is done by machines and human work ceases to matter for survival, where service is the highest value, I expect that compassion and care for others will become much-admired forms of human expression.

We can also find clues that work is not synonymous with productivity by studying the behavior of two seemingly very different classes of people, babies and superstar performers. Babies, for the most part, live in a temporary cocoon that resembles a Celebration Society. Assuming a family is able to meet its needs, the baby has everything provided without cost or care. What do babies do with this freedom? They play. They explore. They learn. They take joy in creating, even if it's moving a pile of sand.

Now consider another class of people, superstars.

In diverse fields of excellence, whether it be business, art, science, sport, and more, where there is competition there is a

---

[206] http://news.nationalgeographic.com/news/2009/03/090330-deformed-child-fossil.html

[207] http://anthro.palomar.edu/homo2/mod_homo_3.htm

game. Superstars spend a lot of their time, energy and often money playing their particular game to win.

Most people think of business as being about money, and in a sense it is. But where lesser lights struggle for a living, or perhaps for a few million dollars, billionaires often talk differently. When asked why they pursue more money, they may respond that it's a way of keeping score, or that he who dies with the most chips wins. Said Larry Ellison, Founder of Oracle, "Whatever money is, it's just a method of keeping score now. I mean, I certainly don't need more money." Most great achievers in business, at least the self-made ones, set out to do something that excited them. The money was a side effect.

Some of them have said things like, "I never worked a day in my life",[208] which sounds preposterous except when stated by a master gamesman. After all, this is almost certainly someone who lives, eats, and breathes his or her particular obsession. They have passion for what they do, apart from the money. Said Warren Buffett, "Without passion, you don't have energy. Without energy, you have nothing." Some even expressly call what they do a game. Said multi-billionaire John Malone, "I have earned so much money that money doesn't interest me. Now it is only the love of the game that drives me."[209]

An increasing number of the wealthy are starting to take the viewpoint of persons such as Bill Gates, Peter Thiel, Peter Diamandis, Craig Venter, Elon Musk, and Jeffrey Skoll, among others, and use their fortunes for something much greater than further winning at the game they have already mastered. They are using their resources, both personal capital and relationships, to back truly world-changing projects. They have defined a new game for themselves.

---

[208] Thomas Edison
[209] http://www.independent.co.uk/news/people/profiles/john-malone-the-man-who-shook-up-murdoch-6158230.html

In the sciences, Nobel prizes and other such honors are coveted. They signify great accomplishment amongst one's peers. They can be viewed as recognition for a game well played. Says Colin Milburn, "Science is most successful when it abandons method and opens itself to play... games motivated by childish curiosity have long informed cultural narratives about science and its practitioners."[210]

In reality much of the research that wins these prizes might never have happened if the winner had instead followed a more lucrative but conventional path. How many astounding discoveries have we lost because budding physicists and other scientists have been lured by huge corporate paychecks? We'll never know, but the fact remains that quite a few stay in research.

Sports figures often keep going back to the well, seeking another victory, another trophy or award, even when their own finances are set for life. They may be in love with the game, or they may be driven to be "the best." Regardless, they are not working as most of us understand work.

Just as play amongst baby mammals fascinates and delights us, even as it prepares them for successful lives as adults, so too we ought to respect the playful impulses of children. As I will show elsewhere in this book, play can guide us to unimagined heights of accomplishment.

Permit me a personal anecdote. When I was 6, I already disliked school. I viewed it as stifling; a prison to which I had been sentenced. Yet I loved dinosaurs. I asked my parents for library books about dinosaurs. As I plowed through the easier ones suitable for 6 year olds, I realized that I couldn't read well enough to enjoy the others. A dictionary became my friend and companion, not due to any pressure except my innate curiosity and desire for the tools to support my exploration.

Within a year I was reading at a 6th grade level, and was invited to lecture on dinosaurs to the 6th graders. This was quite an experience! Unfortunately, I soon thereafter reached

---

[210] *Mondo Nano: Fun and Games in the World of Digital Matter*, Colin Milburn

a level where I needed to understand scientific disciplines to progress further in my study of dinosaurs yet no one competent was there to help me. My interest and passion died.

This, I submit, is the common experience of children everywhere, with the only difference being that few are privileged to have been given, as I was, a taste of learning as a delightful entre to wonder. This is why we equate "work" with productivity. We have forgotten, or perhaps never known, that prodigious human productivity comes hand in hand with harnessing a drive to explore, understand and to share that is innate in the human spirit.

Some critics wonder, "In a post-work society, the financial rewards of education and training won't be as obvious. This is a singular challenge of imagining a flourishing post-work society: How will people discover their talents, or the rewards that come from expertise, if they don't see much incentive to develop either?"[211]

The problem with this view is that it is rooted in a Scarcity Game context. As stated above, incentive may be created either externally or internally. External incentive comes from the need to overcome scarcity by working, from social pressure, or both. Critics correctly note that much of such incentives will disappear along with work. However, internally generated incentive is also real when one feels safe to explore, create, and achieve based on one's own preferences. It can, as the many superstar performers show us, enable people to be far more productive than we had imagined.

Soon, that productivity may be awakened in many for whom it now lies dormant; directed away from work and towards other pursuits as a mighty new productive paradigm emerges. To begin the transition to celebrationism, we need to understand certain fundamental principles. These principles cause us to look at economics and production in a new way.

---

[211] http://www.theatlantic.com/magazine/archive/2015/07/world-without-work/395294/

Part IV: Three Pillars Supporting Abundance

There's this vast universe of limitless energy and
limitless resources. I look at wars fought over access to
resources. That could be a thing of the past, once
space becomes our backyard.

~Neil deGrasse Tyson

All discussion of a Celebration Society will remain theoretical unless we can deliver viable, resilient, and duplicable systems for generating such a society. Perhaps the most important of these systems are technologies for creating abundance.

Adam Smith, writing in his book known as *The Wealth of Nations*, upon which the whole field of economics is founded, asserted that wealth arises from land, labor and capital. Smith looked at what was known of production at the time and quite reasonably inferred that every product of value was made via labor from raw materials provided by land, enhanced by capital in the form of specific improvements (to property) or general improvements (as inventions).

He saw labor as an ever-specializing body of skills, expressed through ever-more highly trained workers who would, by virtue of their higher productivity, thereby reap a larger amount of production for each hour worked as their value-added rose. He expected this to lead humanity to universal opulence.

To my knowledge, until the advent of Ray Kurzweil's Law of Accelerating Returns, no social thinkers or futurists understood the exponential nature of technological progress. They thought this progress to be linear and, in fact, exponential change does appear linear until its later, explosive stages.

With the benefit of fuller understanding, we can see that the concepts of land, labor, and capital as the basis for wealth are antiquated and spongy. Let's consider each in turn.

What is capital? Capital can be symbolically represented by monetary instruments (bonds, notes, bills, etc.) and electronic bookkeeping but, while suitable for finance, this is removed from the physical world where actual value resides. Paper (or electronic) capital has no intrinsic value—a person stranded on a desert island and dying of thirst will gladly trade any amount of currency or bank accounts for water. In the form of money, capital is symbolic. Such symbols have real and precise utility, but it is non-physical. None of it is intrinsic.

In the world of actual, physical value that humans want and need, capital can be viewed as the expression of labor into objects with inherent utility, objects capable of extending production beyond labor alone. (In this regard, capital is distinct from consumer products.) By this definition, a factory system for making a particular product in huge quantities is capital. But what happens when that system is made obsolete by a computerized, much smaller 3D printer capable of making that same product on demand, in a customized manner, at equal or lower cost per unit?

This is not just some abstract notion. Today, we have huge companies that make modular housing and components for home construction. We are also seeing the emergence of 3D printers capable of building homes with far more variation and customization than industrial processes can offer, and faster as well. Will the 3D printers displace the housing manufacturers? This is but one of many such industries whose long-term viability is now being called into question.

With advancing technology, physical capital becomes less and less valuable and eventually obsolete and worthless except as scrap. You've probably seen this in your own life when computers purchased for hundreds or thousands of dollars couldn't even be given away five or ten years later.

Given that technology is advancing at an exponentially accelerating rate, we can expect this process of obsolescence to be accelerating as well. But if paper capital has no inherent real-world value and physical capital is valuable only in the context of a time and place, how can one be certain that any particular form of capital has lasting value? We cannot.

What is labor? Smith defined it as work that is useful to the laborer or to others. But what does "useful" mean, in reality?

Most would agree that the thousands of hours invested in a startup without pay by optimistic and passionate founders are labor. But how useful are those efforts if the startup fails, they are never paid, and no viable product ever results?

My point is that certain forms of what appear to be labor, including some that are arguably quite valuable to society, can be utterly without economic value—and that oftentimes this can only be determined with hindsight. The labor that created Intel was indisputably invaluable. The labor that created Failco, a startup with great promise that crashed and burned having created no valuable assets, was not useful in any productive sense.

What of land? In an age where production was closely tied to material objects, land capable of producing agriculture, timber, oil, and valuable minerals was crucial to production. What, I wonder, would Adam Smith have made of Silicon Valley, where some of the most valuable production in the world happens with little if any connection to the physical place (or, increasingly, anything physical at all) other than the human relationships it enables.

Taking this further, software is a completely non-tangible product that nevertheless represents a vast and growing part of the valuable production in the world. It has laws entirely different from physical products. (As has been said, the first copy of a program requires huge investments; additional copies are free to make.) As physical production increasingly becomes a function of software thanks to 3D printers, relying in the physical sense only on inexpensive inputs of plastic, organic compounds and metal, we can expect production to almost completely decouple from land in the decades ahead.

So, the modern world's productive system can no longer be properly understood in terms of land, labor and capital. What, then, replaces those components?

Modern economists define production in terms of money. They use Gross National Product (GNP) and Gross Domestic Product (GDP) as ways to measure this. However, these do not necessarily measure *useful* production. For example, building a prison increases GDP—and so does subsequently tearing it down.

The most extreme example of useless production designed to boost GNP/GDP may be the "ghost cities" being built in China. Said *Forbes*, "hundreds of new cities in China are largely empty. And yet more cities are still being built...."[212] Each contributes massively to GDP/GNP without providing any physical benefit. (While some will no doubt eventually be occupied, at present they represent only an accounting mirage.)

Clearly, GDP and GNP are poor measures for abundance. Numbers also miss the importance of favors, services within families and between friends and other non-quantifiable aspects of a system of production. Abundance will be better measured by quality of life measurements, which has already started.[213]

Going forward, production can be understood as the confluence of three factors: raw materials, energy and organizing intelligence. To my knowledge, Eric Beinhocker, writing in *The Origin of Wealth*, was the first to publish this idea in 2006. I independently came to the same understanding in 1975 based on insights gleaned from reading *The High Frontier* by Gerard O'Neill.

The crucial insight is that, when these three factors are all in ample supply, abundance can prevail. (While not all useful molecules can yet be generated in production quantities, we do not need all of them to meet the basic needs and most of the wants of humanity.) As I will show, such ample supply of all three of these factors is now within reach. I therefore call energy, matter and organizing intelligence the three pillars of celebrationism.

---

[212] http://www.forbes.com/sites/kenrapoza/2015/07/20/what-will-become-of-chinas-ghost-cities/

[213] http://www.economist.com/media/pdf/QUALITY_OF_LIFE.pdf

The First Pillar: Abundant, Clean Energy

Though you would not know it from the endless drumbeat of doom and gloom about dwindling energy supplies, real and sustainable solutions to our energy shortages—and sources of effectively unlimited clean energy—are at hand.

It has been argued that there has been a systematic process by which certain elements have worked to maintain energy shortages. Whether true or not, most people understand in the abstract that fossil fuel interests control or influence much of the world's policy. Consider, for example, that former Fed Chair Alan Greenspan publicly declared that the Second Gulf War was about oil.[214]

Some have said that abundant clean energy can solve all other problems. I believe that this is not far from the truth, given that the energy is used to intelligently transform matter.

Abundant clean energy solves a staggeringly wide range of problems. First and arguably foremost, it enables humanity to produce abundant clean, salt-free water. (To be clear: there has never been a shortage of water on Earth. The shortage is of clean water.) As discussed in *Abundance: the Future is Better than You Think*, abundant clean water itself solves a vast number of problems, including much of the world's death, disease and attendant loss of productive capability. It also addresses hunger, poverty and much ecological damage.

The water can be produced through several technologies, but reverse osmosis (RO) is generally considered the most mature such technology. RO is already viable but expensive. Reducing the cost of energy will reduce the cost of operation. Further, nanotechnology is making the RO filtration process far more efficient. Holey graphene nanosheets offer a particularly promising approach.[215] (Other solutions for producing abundant clean water are discussed elsewhere in this book.)

---

[214] http://www.theguardian.com/world/2007/sep/16/iraq.iraqtimeline
[215] http://pubs.rsc.org/en/content/articlelanding/2014/nr/c4nr03104k#!divAbstract

Here are some additional benefits of abundant, clean, renewable energy:

- Clean air (elimination of sources of pollution)
- Expansion of habitable land
- Production of artificial, natural sunlight enables dense production of healthier food inside robotically tended multi-level closed-loop food forests. This will effectively increase arable land, eliminate need for fertilizers and produce food that is closer to point of consumption, more nutritious and fresher, in turn leading to:
  - Reduction of fertilizer runoff into rivers and coastal areas (preserving corals and fisheries)
  - Removal of pressure upon rainforests and oceans

Any massive increase of energy production on Earth will lead to thermal pollution (excess heat), as physicist and Intel co-founder Robert Noyce pointed out to me. However, much of that problem can be addressed by moving energy-intensive production into space, away from Earth. In space, the disposal of excess heat is trivial. Products manufactured in space can be transported to Earth via carefully controlled use of gravity. Once on Earth, products that have reached the end of their useful life cycle can be re-used and recycled.

Here are some technologies and production systems poised to help create abundant, clean energy.

Solar Cells, Panels and Batteries

Although oil prices rise and fall dramatically, solar power is now becoming cost competitive. Solar cell prices are expected to continue plunging, and the efficiency of solar cell power capture is rising as well. Financial institutions in major oil producing states are acknowledging that solar will replace oil for energy generation.[216] Even $10/barrel oil won't be

---

[216] http://cleantechnica.com/2015/03/04/deutsche-bank-solar-will-be-dominant-global-electricity-source-by-2030

competitive, they state.[217] *Energy Darwinism II*, a report by Citibank concurs, stating that when the costs are leveled wind is already sometimes cheaper than fossil fuels and solar is rapidly becoming cheaper as well.[218]

There remains one great challenge with making solar power a primary power source, and that is storage. When the Sun sets or is blocked, the power turns off. The obvious solution is to capture the Sun's energy for later use. However, this has not been easy to do efficiently. Two well-established technologies, electrolysis and fuel cells, are now allowing hydrogen to serve this crucial role. Other emerging technologies are also being proposed as potential solutions.[219]

The game changer here may be Tesla Energy's Powerwall (home) and Powerpack (industrial), a mass-produced, intelligently controlled and networked battery system which could make storage efficient, reliable, and easy for the end user. Tesla's "Gigafactory" is scheduled to produce 50 gigawatts of battery storage capacity annually by 2020, with each year's production capable of powering ½ million electric cars. These batteries will come with a 10 year renewable warranty.

Of course, some areas do not receive abundant sunlight year round. Given that arrays of solar panels can also be placed in deserts, alongside roads and in other such places where land is not otherwise being used, this opportunity to store the power for later use makes the connection of such arrays to the grid a sensible way to meet power needs in less sunny areas. Tesla's Powerpack is designed for such mammoth applications, being fully scalable. In short, solar appears finally about to begin replacing fossil fuel for power generation.

---

[217] http://cleantechnica.com/2015/03/04/oil-cant-match-solar-on-cost-even-at-10barrel/

[218] https://www.citivelocity.com/citigps/ReportSeries.action

[219] http://www.kurzweilai.net/how-to-store-solar-energy-more-cost-effectively-for-use-at-night, http://spectrum.ieee.org/energy/renewables/hydrostor-wants-to-stash-energy-in-underwater-bags

Tesla is open-sourcing its patents and structuring the Gigafactory as a kind of huge product; itself reproducible. Creation of multiple factories could enable a solar/battery based energy economy. According to Tesla CEO Elon Musk, the goal of producing 2 billion of these battery packs powered by solar panels is achievable and will yield enough steady power to meet humanity's needs.[220]

Further, two major materials science discoveries at MIT seems likely to greatly enhance the efficacy of solar power capture and storage systems. The first is a material that captures all of the usable frequencies of sunlight, resists high temperatures such as those in large solar concentrator mirror arrays, and requires no tracking of the Sun. It can apparently be made inexpensively in large quantities from various metals.[221]

The second discovery is of a design for, "(an) almost perfect battery, solving most of the remaining issues (of battery lifetime, safety, and cost)." The new battery design utilizes a solid rather than liquid lithium storage medium, will hold 20 – 30% more power than an equivalent liquid battery and can be recharged for "hundreds of thousands of cycles."[222]

Finally, it is significant that improvements keep coming in this space; multiple times per year. For example, Stanford engineers recently developed a special semi-transparent material. It allows all of the frequencies of sunlight that are useful sources of power for existing solar cells to pass through, while reflecting infrared (heat) energy back into space. (Excess heat degrades solar cell performance.) In particular:

> Experiments showed that the overlay allowed visible light to pass through to the solar cells, but that the pattern also cooled the underlying absorber by as much as 23 degrees Fahrenheit.

---

[220] http://www.theguardian.com/technology/2015/may/01/tesla-announces-low-cost-solar-batteries-elon-musk

[221] http://www.kurzweilai.net/mit-researchers-design-perfect-solar-absorber

[222] http://www.kurzweilai.net/rechargeable-batteries-with-almost-infinite-lifetimes-coming-say-mit-samsung-engineers

For a typical crystalline silicon solar cell with an efficiency of 20 percent, 23 F of cooling would improve absolute cell efficiency by more than 1 percent, a figure that represents a significant gain in energy production.

The researchers said the new transparent thermal overlays work best in dry, clear environments, which are also preferred sites for large solar arrays. They believe they can scale things up so that commercial and industrial applications are feasible....[223]

It will be interesting to see how this material works alongside the above-mentioned MIT material.

Hemp Biomass and Hemp Oil

Hemp oil, pressed from the *cannabis sativa* seed, is essentially ready to burn as biodiesel.[224] (The remaining part of the seed is an almost perfect food source.) Compared to oil extracted from the ground, it requires little if any refining.[225]

Although biodiesel hemp does introduce some byproducts of burning into the atmosphere (as do all carbon-based fuels), unlike the extraction industries this source requires no fracking that may cause earthquakes or drilling that may decimate whole ecosystems, such as the Deep Horizon disaster in the Gulf of Mexico. In fact, it actually remediates depleted soils, and the process of growing hemp removes CO_2 from the air, so the cycle as a whole is carbon neutral.

---

[223] http://www.kurzweilai.net/transparent-photonic-coating-cools-solar-cells-to-boost-efficiency

[224] http://today.uconn.edu/blog/2010/10/hemp-produces-viable-biodiesel-uconn-study-finds

[225] *Hemp Makes Comeback as Biofuels Feedstock in 43-acre California* Trial, Biofuels Digest, August 24, 2009, and *Hemp Biodiesel: When the Smoke Clears,* H. Jessen, Biodiesel Magazine, February 2007 (Source: Congressional Research Service, *Hemp as an Agricultural Commodity* December 18, 2012 http://naihc.org/images/NAIHC/crs_report_2012.pdf)

It is not clear as of this writing whether hemp oil can be refined into a gasoline substitute. However, hemp biomass can be used to produce electricity which can power electric vehicles, and diesel powers the trucks that are used for industrial transportation. These together would significantly reduce demand for gasoline—and diesel passenger vehicles could once again be manufactured, if necessary. Hemp biomass can also be made into ethanol at higher productivity per acre than corn—with numerous other uses for the plant matter not converted into ethanol.

Hemp can also enable more ecologically safe burning of coal, working synergistically to meet regulatory requirements while improving public health.[226]

Here are key points from the University of Connecticut's Biofuel Consortium regarding hemp:

- The plant's ability to grow in infertile soils reduces the need to grow it on primary croplands (unlike some other biodiesel plants, which displace food production for energy production)
- The plant's ability to grow "like a weed," means that it doesn't require huge amounts of water, fertilizers, or high-grade inputs to flourish
- Hemp biodiesel showed a high efficiency of conversion – 97 percent of the hemp oil was converted to biodiesel – and it passed all the laboratory's tests, even showing properties that suggest it could be used at lower temperatures than other biodiesel[227]

It seems clear that hemp offers a superior way to produce biodiesel relative to crops such as soybeans and corn. Depending on the process selected, hemp can produce up to

---

[226] http://www.patriotbioenergy.com/data/uploads/whitepaper/whitepaper_an-energy-crop-to-transform-kentucky-and-west-virginia.pdf

[227] http://biodiesel.engr.uconn.edu/research.html

270 gallons/acre of premium biodiesel in addition to significant quantities of ethanol, methane, or synthetic gasoline.[228]

The amount of biomass produced per acre approximately correlates to the potential for generating fuel. In the case of hemp, "...farmers' dry stem yields ranged from 2 tons/acre to 12.5 tons/acre, but averaged 5 tons/acre under good conditions."[229] By way of contrast, production of corn stover, the residual biomass of corn, "would range from 3 to 4.5 dry tons per acre."[230]

Algae Biodiesel

To produce carbon-neutral biodiesel efficiently, algae farms appear to offer a far more promising route than conventional crops. Not even hemp approaches the enormous potential of algae, where the production may approach 15,000 gallons per acre.[231]

Significant progress has been made in algae-to-fuel-oil efforts recently. US Department of Energy (DOE) researchers have found a way to make this conversion in *one hour*. Further, "[DOE] estimates that scaling up algae fuel production to meet the country's day-to-day oil consumption would take up about 15,000 square miles of land."[232]

The continental USA comprises 3,119,884 square miles. Therefore, the land needed to potentially replace US oil consumption with algae-grown oil represents about .005 (1/2 of 1%) of the land mass. Deserts in the USA comprise far more

---

[228] http://www.hemp.org/downloads/Biomass-Fuels-From-Hemp.pdf, Colorado School of Mines

[229] http://extension.oregonstate.edu/catalog/html/sb/sb681/

[230] http://www.agry.purdue.edu/ext/corn/pubs/agry9509.htm

[231] http://www.energytrendsinsider.com/2006/03/28/biodiesel-king-of-alternative-fuels/

[232] http://www.smithsonianmag.com/innovation/scientists-turn-algae-into-crude-oil-in-less-than-an-hour-180948282/

land than this, and elsewhere in the world even larger deserts are available.

While Exxon Mobil abandoned their major algae oil effort, other companies are moving ahead. Solazyme has, "produced from algae over 283,000 liters of military-spec diesel (HRF-76) for [a] United States Navy contract"[233] and Sapphire has a product fueling commercial jet liners and is able to produce "green crude", a replacement for crude oil that can be refined into gasoline, in open-farm desert locations.[234]

New Ways to Generate Hydrogen

Hydrogen is a fuel that burns without pollution. Other than the cost to produce hydrogen, the challenge has been storage. But massive decentralized production might make long-term storage irrelevant. Several promising approaches to generating hydrogen on demand have been prototyped.

Nanotrees, an artificial material which can be grown rapidly in massive quantities from commonly available materials, have been prototyped at the University of California, San Diego. Nanotrees use sunlight to separate water into hydrogen and oxygen.[235]

Another approach developed at Michigan Technological University uses full spectrum sunlight inside a special reactor chamber. Because it uses all of the available energy, efficiency of conversion is apparently 100 times greater than with conventional approaches. It uses water and methanol as inputs, and is reportedly, "convenient for scaling up commercially."[236]

Tidal Power

Tidal power, which captures energy from seawater movement, is starting to come into its own as part of the energy solution. A system soon to be deployed off the coast of

---

[233] http://investors.solazyme.com/releasedetail.cfm?releaseid=596912
[234] http://www.sapphireenergy.com/green-crude/faq
[235] http://www.gizmag.com/hydrogen-fuel-production-using-nanotrees/21769/
[236] http://www.kurzweilai.net/making-hydrogen-fuel-from-water-and-visible-light-at-100-times-higher-efficiency

Scotland is projected to produce 400 megawatts, and a South Korean system already deployed produces almost 250 megawatts. Such systems could power major cities such as New York and San Francisco, especially given that major cities tend to be coastal. Tidal power offers advantages over ground-based wind in aesthetics (being largely hidden from view), reliability and energy density given that water has far more energy potential per unit of volume than wind.[237]

High-altitude Wind Power (HAWP)

At high altitudes, wind speed is more consistent and generally stronger than ground-based wind. Further, there is much more room to build such systems than with ground-based windmills. HAWP works by tethering the wind-capturing device to the ground. The tether typically includes a power cable, though power may be delivered via laser or microwave as well. HAWP may use lighter-than-air lifting such as helium or hydrogen, or it may use an "aerostat" design that is designed to remain lifted by its aerodynamic qualities.

The most extreme potential source of HAWP would be the jet stream. Two significant scientific papers have been published about this, reaching different conclusions.[238] The first concluded that 1,700 terawatts of power are available, with climactic questions.[239] The second concluded that "only" 7.5 terawatts are actually accessible—but with major climactic impacts.[240] (This lower figure would still replace about 1/3 of Earth's present power consumption, provided further study can successfully address the climactic impacts.)

---

[237] http://www.theatlantic.com/technology/archive/2014/11/the-wind-farm-of-the-future-might-be-underwater/382225/

[238] In the early stages of scientific discovery, theoretical and even experimental dispute commonly happens. It is part of what makes science so exciting to scientists.

[239] http://www.awec2010.com/public/img/media/archer_caldeira.pdf

[240] http://www.earth-syst-dynam.net/2/201/2011/esd-2-201-2011.pdf

Less extreme approaches to HAWP are being developed now. Wind power densities can be three times higher at functioning altitude than with ground-based wind turbines.[241] There are multiple startups in this space. Google purchased one of them, Makani Power, saying that, "They've turned a technology that today involves hundreds of tons of steel and precious open space into a problem that can be solved with really intelligent software."[242]

While Google's implied endorsement helps to legitimize the viability of HAWP, others may surpass Makani in efficiency or reliability. Also, while wind power suffers from variability like solar, new storage technologies such as the Tesla battery packs will serve here as well.

New, Clear Power—a Road Not Taken

Nuclear fission has understandably frightened generations of people due to highly visible disasters. *Some entirely different designs physically eliminate the major risks.*

A Sound of Thunder

In the Norse religion, Thor is the God of Thunder. The element thorium is named in his honor—and apparently has the power to transform energy production for generations to come. It has been a road not taken.

Few are aware that when nuclear power was first being explored, reactor designers faced an historic fork in the road. At the time, plutonium was prized for its weapons potential. Therefore, the road taken was the one that generated toxic plutonium and other long-lived toxic byproducts. There was, however, a road not taken—a different road still available to us today. In today's world where nuclear war represents Mutual Assured Destruction, this different road could reduce the world's stockpiles of plutonium and other radioactive byproducts of uranium fission.

---

[241] http://www.altaerosenergies.com/wind.html
[242] http://techcrunch.com/2013/05/22/google-x-acquires-makani-power-and-its-airborne-wind-turbines/

Thorium-based fission was considered equally viable to uranium for energy production by the scientists of the time, and indeed demonstration reactors are now being built in India and China. (A thorium design does require a small amount of less-enriched uranium as feedstock.) In addition to being much safer than uranium, thorium is far more plentiful as well. Also, such a reactor is projected to produce few dangerous byproducts,[243] and a thorium reactor could use dangerous byproducts of present-day fission reactors as fuel, reducing those to less dangerous elements, thereby largely solving the problem of storing nuclear waste for vast expanses of time.[244]

Uranium Fission, Safe at Last?

In recent memory of Fukushima, it is difficult to become comfortable with uranium fission, especially with the awareness that the "Ring of Fire" volcanoes may have entered a period of activity that might, in turn, trigger massive earthquakes. Correlation has been established but not, to my knowledge, causation.[245] That said, other advanced fission designs that rely on uranium rather than thorium include physical safety features that are claimed to eliminate risk. (Admittedly, this has been claimed before of uranium fission, so critics' arguments should be carefully considered.)

Two substantial startups are developing "safe" approaches to fission. One of these is TransAtomic Power, which almost completely captures the remaining 97% of unused power in waste uranium. It does so in a manner that addresses the problem of storing nuclear waste. Rather than solid fuel pins, this design dissolves the nuclear waste into a molten salt.

---

[243] http://www.nei.org/News-Media/News/News-Archives/india-turns-to-thorium-as-future-reactor-fuel

[244] http://www.wired.com/2009/12/ff_new_nukes/all/, http://www.world-nuclear.org/info/Current-and-Future-Generation/Thorium/

[245] http://education.nationalgeographic.com/education/encyclopedia/ring-fire/

Crucially, this physically eliminates the risk of reactor melt-down, because the uranium is not aggregated into clusters capable of massive overheating.

An incident such as Fukushima would simply turn off the TransAtomic reactor.[246] Also, it works with uranium enriched to only 1.8%, vs. older designs of molten salt reactors that required 33% enrichment.[247] This fact has important non-proliferation implications. For example, the Iranians claim their uranium enrichment is for medicine, power, and energy; not weapons. Offering this design (or others discussed in this section) to them would put that claim to the test. The barriers to bringing forth such reactor designs are not technical but political.[248]

A second "new fission" startup claiming to offer similar benefits is TerraPower. It is backed by prestigious investors including Bill Gates. The company claims that, "Terra-Power's traveling wave reactor addresses [all of the] challenges associated with conventional nuclear reactors. The traveling wave reactor simplifies the necessary nuclear energy infra-structure, reducing overall costs and enabling a safe, secure form of nuclear energy." [249] According to the company, this design will use depleted uranium as fuel, create and burn its own fuel, minimize uranium enrichment and run for 40 years before replacement is necessary. There is no chemical separation and the entire fuel cycle is contained within the reactor core. It actually burns plutonium as fuel, converting it into less toxic elements. Commercial deployment is projected for the late 2020's.[250]

---

[246] http://transatomicpower.com/white_papers/TAP_White_Paper.pdf
[247] http://transatomicpower.com/products.php
[248] http://www.forbes.com/sites/hbsworkingknowledge/2014/09/24/we-need-a-climate-miracle-could-new-nuclear-provide-it/
[249] http://terrapower.com/pages/technology
[250] ibid.

Finally, the Integral Fast Reactor (IFR) discussed extensively by Tom Blees[251] is a design under development for a decade by the US Department of Energy from 1984 - 1994. This design could use either uranium or thorium as feedstock, capturing nearly all of the available energy. It apparently had physical design aspects that caused automatic shutdown in the event of a problem, regardless of human or automated fail-safes being present. The IFR project was canceled by the US Congress in 1994, three years before completion.[252] Critics assert that an IFR design is better in important respects than TerraPower's.[253]

Tower of Power

A unique design to harness the Sun for power generation builds a vast network of mirrors across an expanse of land. Sunlight hits the mirrors. The mirrors redirect this sunlight towards a central focal point on a tower. The intense heat thereby generated is used to produce power by turning a turbine, the same as traditional power plants.

The Ivanpah facility is an example of this, already producing electricity in the desert. Google, NRG Energy, and Brightsource have built a system with the capacity to generate 377 megawatts and power 140,000 homes.[254]

Many such facilities could be built in the decades ahead on desert land, across the globe. They can be built, as was this one, with respect for endangered species and still help to meet our future energy needs.

---

[251] *Prescription for the Planet*, Tom Blees
[252] http://www.ne.anl.gov/About/reactors/integral-fast-reactor.shtml
[253] http://bravenewclimate.com/2010/09/22/twr-vs-ifr/
[254] http://www.ivanpahsolar.com/

Solar Power Satellites (SPS)

Both the US Department of Defense (DOD)[255] and the government of Japan[256] have recently prepared analyses indicating the feasibility of using SPS as a power source. Says a US Army report, "there is general consensus among credible studies that SBSP (SPS) systems are technically feasible given a decade of development...." SPS is based on a simple premise: unlike solar energy captured on Earth, solar energy in near-Earth outer space is more intense per unit of area, far more widely available and on tap 24/7.

There are considerable technology development and maintenance issues. All can be addressed. It is a matter of engineering and of costs.[257] SPS power can be delivered to uninhabited areas via diffuse microwave (safe for birds, reportedly), converted to electricity via a rectifying antenna and then transmitted to wherever needed via cable and the electric grid.

Financial analyses have typically found SPS to be more expensive per unit of energy generated than power plants built on Earth. However, with financial analyses the assumptions are crucial. Analyses I have seen assume the launch of SPS components from Earth at present-day launch costs. (Currently, because of the inefficiencies of rocketry, a tiny fraction of a rocket's weight is the payload itself.)[258]

If we build SPS from lunar or asteroidal resources, for which the capability will exist in the decades ahead, or robotically assemble SPS in space from components inexpensively launched in quantity from Earth,[259] the financial picture will

---

[255] http://www.strategicstudiesinstitute.army.mil/pdffiles/PUB1254.pdf

[256] http://www.wsj.com/articles/japan-advances-in-space-based-solar-power-1426100482

[257] http://ssi.org/reading/papers/sun-powered-laser-beaming-from-space-for-electricity-on-earth/

[258] http://www.nasa.gov/mission_pages/station/expeditions/expedition30/tryanny.html

[259] http://news.co.cr/british-company-claims-biggest-engine-advance-since-the-jet/20059/, also: http://www.startram.com/home

become more favorable for SPS. (Should the space elevator become feasible, or the "high-altitude mass driver" proposed by Dr. O'Neill be built, it will be better still.)

Finances aside, SPS cause no environmental despoliation and can be built in effectively unlimited quantities in this century; especially if specialized robots are designed to perform two concurrent tasks: build SPS from resources derived from asteroid mining operations, and build more such robots.

Ocean Thermal Energy Conversion (OTEC)

OTEC takes advantage of the temperature differential between surface water and deep ocean water. "OTEC works best when the temperature difference between the warmer, top layer of the ocean and the colder, deep ocean water is about 36°F (20°C). These conditions exist in tropical coastal areas, roughly between the Tropic of Capricorn and the Tropic of Cancer."[260] Much of the world's near-coastal oceans around the equator have sufficient differentials. By mixing the two water sources in a special chamber, significant energy can be extracted.

Studies to date have not found OTEC to be cost-effective by itself. However, this may be changing with improved technology.[261] OTEC takes the form of a large oceanic platform. The platform can support synergistic activities such as fish or algae farming, as well as the tethering of high-altitude wind power devices—and potentially include living areas.

OTEC generates electricity by spinning a turbine through a closed loop evaporation/condensation cycle of a substance such as ammonia. (Other designs are possible, including one

---

[260] http://energy.gov/eere/energybasics/articles/ocean-thermal-energy-conversion-basics

[261] http://www.newscientist.com/article/mg22129580.900-20000-megawatts-under-the-sea-oceanic-steam-engines.html

based on thermoelectric materials.)[262] OTEC is functional technology, with extensive study and plans for deployment at Saga University in Japan.[263] India's National Institute of Ocean Technology at the Indian Institute of Technology, has calculated that OTEC plants placed in Indian coastal waters could produce 180 gigawatts of electricity, net of losses.[264]

A pilot plant has opened in Hawaii. It has a relatively small power output of 105 Kw.[265] However, this marks the first time an OTEC plant has been connected to the electrical grid. The company behind the project, Makai, has projects in conjunction with Lockheed, the US Department of Energy and the Office of Naval Research.[266]

To my knowledge, there are no serious concerns about environmental impacts from mixing shallow and deep waters.

Geothermal Energy

The deeper one drills into the Earth, the higher temperatures rise. Iceland has abundant geothermal energy that's easily accessible, thanks to volcanic activity. It has recently been found that by drilling deep holes in many other places, heat from deep in the ground can be similarly accessed. It also seems to cause small earthquakes, which makes the widespread viability of deep heat wells questionable.

In many places, the ground a few yards below the surface will maintain a constant temperature through the seasons. It is possible to place underground a tube made from heat-conductive material. A fan forces a steady stream of air through the tube, thereby raising indoor temperatures in winter and lowering them in summer.

---

[262] http://iopscience.iop.org/1367-2630/16/12/123019/
[263] http://www.ioes.saga-u.ac.jp/old_event/FDE2002/
  OTEC%20Power%20Generation%20Saves%20Mankind.pdf
[264] http://www.clubdesargonautes.org/otec/vol/vol11-2-1.htm
[265] http://www.makai.com/makai-news/
[266] http://www.makai.com/otec-ocean-thermal-energy-conversion/

Alternatively, such tubes could be designed to move a heat-conductive fluid through such a tube in a closed loop. The advantage of fluid over air is greater density of thermal mass. The disadvantage is that more energy is required to circulate the fluid. Such ground-coupled heat exchange systems have been successfully deployed, and once installed require almost no maintenance.[267]

Nuclear Fusion

Fusion has long been described as the fuel of the future. The opposite of fission, fusion is what powers the stars. Indirectly, thanks to the Sun, it is the energy that enables all life on Earth and all of our fossil fuel reserves. The question is how to safely and effectively generate it on Earth.

Fusion merges common elements. In some designs, containment of dangerous neutron particles poses challenges for widespread deployment of such a system, although arguably less so than many of the approaches to fission.

Little attention is being given to several highly promising alternatives that are free of the dangerous neutron emissions. Dr. Robert Bussard, former Assistant Director at the US Atomic Energy Commission (deceased), developed one such approach. Despite his intellectual preeminence in physics circles, his "Polywell" design struggled for funding.

Another aneutronic fusion startup, Lawrenceville Plasma Physics (LPP), is developing Focus Fusion. This aneutronic system was funded by NASA in an SBIR grant, and uses boron and hydrogen as fuel inputs. Both are plentiful and safe to handle.

Focus Fusion has achieved 1.8 billion degrees C, a record not matched elsewhere.[268] It has been featured in *The Economist* and highlighted by Google's *Solve for X* as the most promising current approach to achieving fusion.[269]

---

[267] https://en.wikipedia.org/wiki/Ground-coupled_heat_exchanger
[268] http://lawrencevilleplasmaphysics.com/risk-assessment/
[269] Disclaimer: I am on the Advisory Board of LPP

In 2014, Lockheed announced a new design for a fusion reactor that it promises will be rolled out into products by the mid-2020's, and able to replace all fossil fuel consumption by the 2030's. This design uses abundant tritium and deuterium as the inputs, and is expected to produce 100 megawatts, enough power for at least 50,000 homes. Such reactors would fit on a truck, produce no emissions and be safe.

While some have criticized Lockheed's "concept" announcement, the small size of the reactor (10' x 7') is claimed to make its testing and development much faster than larger designs. Lockheed expects to demonstrate a prototype in 2015.[270] However, no test results have yet been released or corroborated.

MIT has announced a much smaller and less expensive design for a "tokamak" fusion reactor that uses commercially available superconductors to create stronger magnetic fields. They expect their design to be functioning reliably by 2025 and provide 270 megawatts of power. Their ARC (Affordable Robust Compact) reactor design has been hailed by others in the field and was supported by the US Department of Energy and the National Science Foundation.[271]

With multiple credible parties pursuing designs that they expect to bear fruit in the next few years, fusion may soon no longer be called the fuel of the future.

Low Energy Nuclear Reactions (LENR)

In 1989, teams of scientists at two US universities announced within months of each other that they had achieved something deemed impossible: nuclear fusion at low temperatures. Experiments conducted soon thereafter at other institutions failed to replicate the results, and the professors were ridiculed.[272]

---

[270] http://www.lockheedmartin.com/us/products/compact-fusion.html
[271] http://www.kurzweilai.net/mit-designs-small-modular-efficient-fusion-power-plant
[272] http://undsci.berkeley.edu/article/cold_fusion_01

Since then, the general view in the scientific community has remained one of intense skepticism. However, a small cadre of credible scientists has continued the research. These have included researchers at MIT and SRI International, among others. The US Office of Naval Research continued to investigate LENR for many years following the fiasco in 1989, and has published its analysis which treats LENR as a real phenomenon.[273]

Various designs have been developed and tested since 1989. None has reached commercial viability. Currently, a LENR system called the E-Cat (Energy Catalyzer), which was developed by Prof. Andrea Rossi and Prof. Sergio Focardi of the University of Bologna, is the most widely watched.[274]

The most recent study of the E-Cat was conducted by a team from the Swedish Royal Institute of Technology, Uppsala University and Bologna University. It ran the E-Cat for 32 consecutive days, and the test results led to a remarkable conclusion for a scientific paper; all the more so considering the near-certainty of widespread professional ridicule:

> The quantity of heat emitted constantly by the reactor and the length of time during which the reactor was operating rule out, beyond any reasonable doubt, a chemical reaction as underlying its operation...In summary, the *performance of the E-Cat reactor is remarkable. We have a device giving heat energy compatible with nuclear transformations, but it operates at low energy and gives neither nuclear radioactive waste nor emits radiation.* From basic general knowledge in nuclear physics this should not be possible. Nevertheless we have to relate to the fact that the experimental results from our test show heat production beyond chemical

---

[273] http://lenr-canr.org/acrobat/MosierBossthermaland.pdf

[274] http://www.forbes.com/sites/markgibbs/2013/05/20/finally-independent-testing-of-rossis-e-cat-cold-fusion-device-maybe-the-world-will-change-after-all/

burning, and that the E-Cat fuel undergoes nuclear transformations. It is certainly most unsatisfying that these results so far have no convincing theoretical explanation, but the *experimental results cannot be dismissed or ignored just because of lack of theoretical understanding.*[275] (Emphasis added.)

Reportedly, Prof. Alexander Parkhomov of Lomonosov Moscow State University has claimed a successful replication of the E-Cat, with maximum power output of 2.58 times the power input.[276]

There is a saying that, "extraordinary claims require extraordinary proof." The claim that a potentially unlimited source of energy beckons from a source that violates current theory is surely such a case. Critics have pointed out that world-class energy research laboratories such as Lawrence Livermore have yet to test this design. At the same time, while many scientists call LENR impossible, we need to remember that the creation of the "impossible" has happened repeatedly in the history of scientific advances, each time overturning existing theory and ushering in a new paradigm. New theory is being proposed to explain what may be happening in LENR reactions[277] and further research will determine the truth about LENR.

A further caveat is Rossi's own track record. While his device stands alone on its merits or lack thereof, Rossi has a personal record that further emphasizes the need for rigorous skepticism and independent expert testing.[278]

---

[275] http://lenr-canr.org/acrobat/LeviGobservatio.pdf

[276] A paper reportedly submitted by Prof. Parkhomov, as yet unpublished, is here: http://www.e-catworld.com/wp-content/uploads/2014/12/Lugano-Confirmed.pdf

[277] http://www.journal-of-nuclear-physics.com/?p=501

[278] http://newenergytimes.com/v2/sr/RossiECat/Rossis-Italian-Financial-and-Environmental-Criminal-History.shtml

In addition to Rossi's project, there is a lower-profile startup pursuing a similar path and claiming transmutation of metals; a result that would evidently require fusion because it is incompatible with chemical processes. Brillouin Energy has conducted 50 internal tests under the leadership of two SRI International physicists, and has reportedly been able to reliably produce excess heat.[279]

Above, I have described energy technologies ranging from the mundane to the extraordinary. Though broad, this is not an exhaustive list. It shows that we have multiple promising approaches for achieving energy abundance. Some, such as vast hemp farms, we could start building now; others need further engineering work but will become feasible within a few years. A few show great promise and require further validation, research and development. The key understanding is that we may need only one of these approaches, built or grown in quantity, to provide for energy abundance—and there is every reason to believe that multiple of these will serve us in the decades ahead.

The Second Pillar: Abundant Matter

In the Scarcity Game, matter was for a long time viewed as a sometimes rare but ultimately available resource. The presumption was that more of something; even something rare such as gold, could always be discovered if enough resources were devoted to exploration and extraction. Recently, the more prevalent view has been that resources are not always going to be available and that the external effects of obtaining them, such as pollution, are increasingly high and unacceptable.

The basic issue with matter is collecting adequate quantities of necessary elements, then configuring the elements into structures that serve countless human wants and needs,

---

[279] http://brillouinenergy.com/science/experimental-results/

assuring an ample supply of everything without nasty side effects. It's easy to state yet also a great challenge.

Plastics and Graphene

An enormous portion of our present material needs have been addressed by plastics. There are arguably countless different plastic compounds, most currently made from natural gas and petroleum derivatives, although "green" biodegradable plastics made from plant materials such as corn and hemp have become increasingly commercially viable. Recently, some non-biodegradable plastics have been found to bring with them undesirable side effects including environmental damage, wildlife harm, and even hormone-like effects when ingested.

While plastics have also been criticized for creating enormous landfill and floating oceanic waste, this is a problem of technology deployment and not one inherent to plastics. Plasma converters, in particular, can reduce all plastics to energy and useful raw materials.

Plastics will continue to be used because they offer so many advantages. However, we increasingly have the capability to engineer naturally occurring molecules, which can be less problematic, for the same purposes. If plastics were the wonder material of the 20th century, it appears that engineered carbon will be the wonder material of the 21st century.

Carbon-based structures will in future substitute for many construction materials, being potentially lighter and stronger than steel and concrete. Graphene, in particular—a carbon lattice just one atom thick that's stronger and more flexible than steel—has a dazzling array of future uses. The range of possibilities is breathtaking, including perfected battery replacements, bodily augmentation, water and radiation purification, and instant wireless data transmission speeds (potentially enabling full immersion VR at a distance).[280]

---

[280] http://gizmodo.com/5988977/9-incredible-uses-for-graphene

While carbon-based materials such as graphene, bucky-balls and nanotubes may well be the ubiquitous "plastics" of the 21st century, we will still need sources of other elements and molecules. While recycling and nanotech-based mining and materials separation will greatly help, an additional source of raw materials of literally astronomical scope beckons.

Asteroids and the Limits to Growth

The Club of Rome's report, *The Limits to Growth*, which has attained the status of orthodoxy, delineated how growth is not limitless in a closed system such as a planetary environment. However, it has a serious flaw. It fails to take proper near-term account of the larger environment in which we live: the solar system.

At this moment, except for occasional impacts of meteors, the material resources of the solar system remain unavailable to us. In the decades ahead these resources—including the asteroids, the lunar surface, and possibly other planets and moons—will be mined. These resources will be used for all manner of manufacturing including a growing space infra-structure, finished products for use in space and for return to Earth, and eventually new human habitats.

The asteroid belt, a collection of natural resources ranging from particles to mountainous behemoths, occupies the region between Mars and Jupiter. Over 500,000 asteroids have been identified to date, with the rate of discovery accelerating.[281] So far, 871 asteroids with diameters of 1 km. or greater that are "near-Earth" (i.e., more easily mined) have been discovered.[282]

The US government is aware of the potential here. Indeed, "NASA is building drones to mine remote lunar and Martian

---

[281] http://www.universetoday.com/97571/how-many-asteroids-are-out-there/
[282] http://neo.jpl.nasa.gov/faq/#neo

regions".[283] Also, companies with well-credentialed staff and impressive backers are making plans to mine these resources. Putting the potential of asteroid mining into specifics, "a single 500-meter platinum-rich asteroid can contain more platinum group metals than have ever been mined in human history. Platinum group metals are so useful that 1 of 4 industrial goods on Earth require them in production."[284]

The lunar surface can be also mined for various materials necessary to build orbital infrastructure. Lunar surface soil contains oxygen, silicon, iron, titanium, calcium, aluminum, magnesium and many other elements and minerals. The Moon also contains crucial water ice.[285]

Europa is a moon of Jupiter that appears to host a planetary ocean with more water than is found in all of Earth's oceans.[286] Pluto, long imagined to be a dark wasteland, also harbors resources. Indeed, "It's very likely the mountains on the surface of Pluto, just as majestic as the rocky ones we have on Earth, are made from frozen water."[287]

Even Mercury, the hottest planet, has a far side that remains cold and rich in resources. It includes water ice which has been estimated at 19 trillion gallons, as well as recently discovered organic materials that resemble tar; materials that could enable the manufacture of all manner of plastic objects in space.[288]

If, in some future century, we should need more raw materials than those in the Main Asteroid Belt, we need not

---

[283] http://www.theatlantic.com/technology/archive/2015/08/robot-dark-side-moon-volcanoes/400430/

[284] http://www.planetaryresources.com/asteriods/#market-for-metals

[285] http://www.nasa.gov/mission_pages/Mini-RF/multimedia/feature_ice_like_deposits.html

[286] http://apod.nasa.gov/apod/ap120524.html

[287] https://www.newscientist.com/article/dn27906-pluto-wows-with-first-close-view-of-ice-mountains-on-its-surface/

[288] http://spacemath.gsfc.nasa.gov/weekly/4Page23.pdf

travel to other star systems. Resources that dwarf even the asteroids beckon in the region surrounding our solar system. To wit: "Astronomers theorize that there are approximately 10^{12} to 10^{13} comets in the Oort cloud totaling about 100 Earth masses."[289]

Population Growth and Matter Requirements

Critics are concerned that eventually population growth will exhaust any amount of resources; even the inconceivable amounts in and surrounding our solar system. However, the data shows no need for artificial limits.

While computer progress is now driving most technology and its social ramifications forward at exponentially expanding speeds, human requirements for raw materials should not increase exponentially. Population growth, which is commonly expected to drive such increases, tapers off drastically when children are not viewed as the source of social security.

Indeed, along with the recent rapid rise in incomes of Chinese and Indian people has come a sharp drop in average fertility rates worldwide. Specifically, "In the early 1970s, women had on average 4.5 children each; by 2014, total fertility for the world had fallen to around 2.5 children per woman."[290]

Some are viewing the reduction in birthrates with alarm. Some, such as Pope Francis, regard voluntarily avoiding having children as selfish.[291] Others are concerned on more pragmatic grounds: in a society with few young workers, who will provide for the needs of the elderly?

In my view, the rational concerns about this will disappear in a Celebration Society. Every child will be a person wanted not for his or her productive capacity but instead for the joy and wonder that are part and parcel of healthy childhood and family experiences. The human population may shrink over

---

[289] http://lcogt.net/spacebook/comets-kuiper-belt-and-oort-cloud
[290] http://www.unfpa.org/world-population-trends
[291] http://www.religionnews.com/2015/02/11/pope-francis-opting-not-children-selfish-choice/

time, but we will not go extinct from voluntary non-procreation.

Sophisticated proponents of limits to growth point out that, as all continuing growth is inherently accelerative by nature, given present levels of resource use our consumption of resources will outstrip even the solar system within a few centuries. However, this misses an essential point, as stated by Edward Abbey, "growth for the sake of growth is the ideology of the cancer cell."

Growth, to be meaningful and useful, must serve a purpose. Its purpose in a celebrationist society is the expansion of happiness. To that end, any person, equipped with a modest amount of matter, will in the future be able to create and endlessly recreate that matter into various forms that provide for necessities and amusement.

This presupposes effective, widespread nanotechnology assemblers and disassemblers, which leading nanotechnologists expect to arrive in the 21st century. Assuming that population levels off, as credible forecasts suggest, there will be no reason for an endless increase in demand for matter and we have sufficient matter to see us through the 21st century.

Nanotechnology—Ultimate Control Over Matter?

While the mining of asteroids and advanced recycling systems incorporating permaculture and plasma converters (to be discussed later) all offer us an enormous increase in the availability of useful elements and molecules, something even more powerful looms. Nanotechnology is real and its influence is rapidly rising.

In 2007, Batelle Memorial Institute brought together many leading lights from the field of nanotechnology to produce *Productive Nanosystems: a Technology Roadmap*. This almost 200 page document states, "Atomically precise technologies (APT) hold the potential to meet many of the greatest global challenges, bringing revolutions in science, medicine, energy, and industry. This technology roadmap points the way for strategic research initiatives to deliver on this promise."

In principle, nanotech ultimately promises to us a future decades hence in which matter can be assembled rapidly and automatically into various configurations as required, and subsequently disassembled into constituent molecules or even elements when that configuration is no longer required.

There are five types of nanotechnology, with different degrees of maturity and feasibility as of 2014:

1. Nanoelectronic systems, AKA semiconductor fabrication, are a $100 billion industry.
2. Atomically precise manufacturing, the "original concept" in nanotechnology, is a pending revolution.
3. Nanobots, the concept often mentioned in popular media, remain fictional.
4. Nanomaterials and devices have many niche applications.
5. Molecular design and synthesis is woven into chemistry, biopolymers and other materials sciences.[292]
6. Nanoscale manufacturing systems have been prototyped in the lab.[293] Nanoscale manufacturing of functioning electronic and medical nanodevices via nanorobots with nanomotors that are chemically powered, self-propelled and magnetically controlled has also been prototyped.[294]

Nanoelectronic systems advances will facilitate not only ever-faster and smaller computers, but also the interface between those computers and living systems.

Already a number of nanomaterials have entered the market. These include graphene, colloidal suspensions of metal particles, carbon nanotubes, and friction-reducing coatings.

Skeptics assert that what Eric Drexler, founder of the field, calls *mechanosynthesis*—the assembly of objects molecule by

---

[292] http://metamodern.com/2014/04/04/five-kinds-of-nanotechnology/

[293] http://www.rsc.org/chemistryworld/News/2010/May/12051003.asp

[294] http://www.kurzweilai.net/nanomotor-lithography-provides-simpler-affordable-nanofabrication

molecule—will not be a straightforward process at least in manufacturing applications. Some even believe that inter-actions amongst molecules will render this impossible.[295]

Ultimately, the feasibility of atomically precise manu-facturing will not be known until it can actually be tested in the decades ahead. Meanwhile, the field of nanotechnology has realized advanced electronics manufacturing techniques and has established new ways to make novel materials with revolutionary properties—materials that should greatly improve our control of matter.[296]

Nanotech should help make the creation and functioning of Celebration Societies easier. It is an enabling technology, but not a necessity. Nanotech aside, there is an important reason to expect that, in the decades ahead, demand for matter will be lessened from what a world of wealthy persons might otherwise consume.

True Recycling

When asked what he thought of Western civilization, Mahatma Gandhi replied, "I think it would be a good idea." I would say the same thing about recycling.

One concern about an abundant society is its generation of waste materials. After all, if our present world is generating mountains of garbage, a more abundant standard of living and consumption could generate even more.

There can be little doubt that using the world's oceans, rivers, air and other places as garbage dumps is a bad idea. Pollution is detrimental—to human health, to ecosystems upon which we depend, and even to productivity itself. Still, many corporations will continue to pollute as allowed because it is generally more profitable than recycling.

Corporations are not charged the full costs of the consequences of their actions, which requirement would dramatically change polluting practices in a matter of a few

---

[295] http://nanotechnologist.com/misc/index.html
[296] *Productive Nanosystems: A Technology Roadmap*, Battelle Memorial Institute.

short years. (It is worth noting that a complementary currency could be designed to potentially achieve the same result without the need for new laws, regulations or coercion.)

How, then, might we encourage more complete and effective recycling? We could make recycling efficient, convenient and economically attractive. Essentially, by reducing the cost differential between dumping waste into the environment and recycling it, more recycling will happen.

To pick one glaring deficiency, only about 6.8% of the total plastic used in the U.S. actually gets recycled, and much of the plastic cannot be efficiently recycled. The energy efficiency of conventional recycling varies from 96% (aluminum) to 21% (glass). [297] We can do much better.

A *plasma converter* transforms organic materials into a synthetic gas suitable for fuel, making the system self-powering, and converts non-organic materials into useful building materials such as bricks, concrete and insulation.[298]

According to *Biomass Magazine*:

> Japan has three plants in operation: a 166 ton-per-day pilot plant in Yoshi, co-developed by Hitachi Metals Ltd. and Westinghouse Plasma Corp., which was certified after a demonstration period from 1999-'00; a 165-ton-per-day plant in Utashinai City, completed in 2002; and a 28 ton-per-day plant commissioned by the twin cities of Mihama and Mikata in 2002. PlascoEnergy Group currently employs a plasma-arc waste demonstration plant in Ottawa, Canada, at the Trail Road Landfill while Advanced Plasma Power has built a

---

[297] http://discovermagazine.com/2009/jul-aug/06-when-recycling-is-bad-for-the-environment

[298] http://science.howstuffworks.com/environmental/energy/plasma-converter.htm

Gasplasma modular test facility in Faringdon, Oxfordshire, England.[299]

These are only the beginning of what is possible. In principle, the non-organic slag could be directed to a centrifuge, which would separate the elements by atomic weight, and then they would be harvested.[300] This may not presently be cost-effective, but in a celebrationist model of production costs will eventually become irrelevant.

I am not advocating plasma converters as the total solution to recycling. Some materials can easily and more effectively be handled independently. Sound production design can minimize the amount of waste generated at the outset.

There are ecological reasons to use principles of permaculture and also have gray water and brown water systems coupled to *biodigesters* that yield fertilizer, clean water, and methane gas for cooking and heating.

Elsewhere, it has been noted that ¼ of medicines find their origin in the amazon rainforest, whose steady destruction may be eliminating untold useful plant species. A recent discovery underscores this point. Polyurethane plastic has been considered non-recyclable; a material that will never degrade under normal conditions (although a plasma converter turns it into energy). Yale researchers recently discovered in the rainforest a fungus that eats polyurethane, and can even dissolve it within landfills.[301]

Likewise, a plasma converter will not generate complex compounds of minerals, helpful bacteria, and the other outputs of biodigesters or aquaponics that make such systems highly useful components of agricultural systems.

_____

[299] http://biomassmagazine.com/articles/2144/proving-out-plasma-gasification

[300] http://www.wisegeek.com/what-is-a-centrifugal-separator.htm

[301] http://www.fastcoexist.com/1679201/fungi-discovered-in-the-amazon-will-eat-your-plastic

Virtual Matter and Virtual Reality (VR)

When the experience of VR approximates the experience of "real" reality in the next few years, many and perhaps most of us will choose the simulation since it is the *experience* that we want, regardless of how it is delivered. Further, research is now establishing that the pursuit of experiences is far more satisfying than the pursuit of possessions.[302]

With the advent and widespread availability of VR, there will be a permanently reduced per capita demand for matter. It is a matter of costs and benefits: full immersion VR offers us advantages in time, expense, and maintenance.

As contrasted with VR, there are time delays associated with "real" matter. For example, if you'd like to drive a Lamborghini in the real world, you have to contact a dealer or rental company, pick it up or arrange delivery, and arrange payment. All of this takes time—and assumes that the particular color and model you want is available, and of course that you can afford the car.

Once possessions are no longer the required gateway to experiences, the craving for possessions should greatly diminish, probably approaching the minimum required so that an enjoyable physical existence may be sustained. Not only photos and videos but "physical" souvenirs will be digitized to be displayed and re-experienced whenever desired, but otherwise requiring no physical resources.

Other than enabling us to have experiences, possessions help us to achieve status; something which will be transformed in a Celebration Society. While owning an "original" artwork will carry a certain cachet, in my view this will be more a matter of the story behind one's possession than the object itself, since others will ordinarily be able to generate replications of the object.

---

[302] http://www.theatlantic.com/business/archive/2014/10/buy-experiences/381132/

VR is not some fanciful concept. It is already emerging into everyday life. For example, Marriott is already offering virtual travels.[303] VR tools such as the Oculus Rift and Google Glass are powering the conversion of spectator sports into participant sports, wherein fans can experience their favorite players' game conditions.[304] Qualcomm has created a VR/augmented reality, "global ecosystem of 175,000+ registered developers and ... 20,000+ apps with more than 200 million app installs worldwide."[305] IKEA's catalog app allows users to see how its products will look inside one's home via augmented reality. Theme parks offering VR environments are starting up,[306] and software that allows people using different VR platforms to share experiences is coming.[307]

The Third Pillar: Organizing Intelligence

Organizing Intelligence can be defined as any systematic expression of knowledge that interacts purposefully with matter and energy to generate a desired end result from them. It directs the interaction of the available matter and energy in order to produce whatever is required, and this direction takes the form of instruction or control of a system of production.

Organizing Intelligence requires some means of sensing the presence and attributes of available matter and energy (inputs, ambient conditions, etc.) and will adjust its directions according to both available resources and fulfillment of its purpose. Once sufficient outputs are produced, the system will stop until more are needed.

Therefore, it can be said that Organizing Intelligence is a combination of codified systems of knowledge and inputs to

---

[303] http://www.theverge.com/2014/9/30/6872047/marriott-virtual-vacation-demo.
[304] http://www.theatlantic.com/sponsored/ibm-how-technology-transforms/the-extinction-of-spectator-sports/168/
[305] https://www.qualcomm.com/products/vuforia
[306] http://www.cnet.com/news/zero-latency-vr-entertainment-revolution-begins-melbourne-australia/
[307] http://www.fastcompany.com/3051102/tech-forecast/altspace-comes-to-gearvr-making-shared-cross-platform-vr-experiences-possible

such systems of knowledge called perception or, more recently, sensors. Let's first consider systems of knowledge.

Historically, the codification of systems of knowledge took the form of human intelligence and the systemization of human knowledge. Books, mathematics, instruction manuals and other tools and disciplines might qualify, depending on their purpose and expression.

Sensors were historically limited to the human perception of conditions, either directly or through mechanized measurement and displays. Procedures were defined. However, for most practical purposes going forward, Organizing Intelligence will take the form of software and automated sensors.

The Essence of Software

Software is a set of instructions for doing something, often in a repetitive manner, with variations in performance based on differing conditions or requirements. It can be as simple as this:

1. Input X
2. Set X = X + 1
3. Output X
4. Go to Step 1

It can alternately be as complex as an AI, but for purposes of a Celebration Society our Organizing Intelligence need only be software with these characteristics:

1. Accepts as inputs specific forms of matter and energy, measuring each as appropriate and directing robotic control systems to manipulate them.
2. Uses pre-existing structures of matter along with precise quantities of input energy to modify precise quantities of input matter into a new and desired form of matter.
3. Monitor and collect all outputs, whether desired or not.
4. Repeat as useful.

To this I would add as a practical consideration that there must be extensive testing of any such system to establish reliability and determine possible risk factors and unintended side effects so they can be reduced to acceptable levels. For "mission-critical" systems, triple redundancy as used by NASA makes sense. Essentially, three identical systems operate in parallel. When one generates an output different from the others, that system is presumed to be defective and quickly replaced.

Note that this type of system accounts for matter, pollution, and waste, including forms of matter that are no longer desirable or used, by measuring pollution and waste as both outputs and potential inputs for future production.

The above may seem deceptively simple, and in principle it *is* simple. However, I submit that it offers us a way to transform matter into new and useful other forms of matter, which is both an answer to recycling and a basis for unlimited material wealth, given abundant matter and energy.

While our present-day Scarcity Game holds matter and energy to be limited resources, there is rising awareness that Organizing Intelligence is not a scarce resource. While the original of a program may take considerable resources to create, copies of that original are essentially free to produce.

Recently, we have seen an explosion of free software in the form of most apps as well as other programs such as browsers and practically everything from Google. This has educated the general public worldwide that the cost of delivering software far and wide is minimal if not actually free. (Of course, the business models that justify free software are designed to indirectly produce revenue. So long as profits are necessary, this will remain true.)

It is common to grouse about defects in software, particularly the Microsoft operating systems (although in that case much of the complaining is caused by peoples' reactions to being "forced" to use it). Indeed there is a saying in the software industry that version 1.0 of anything is the final test version, wherein the most eager users serve as real-world testers of the product. That said, software generally works quite well.

We rely on software to run practically everything of note in society. Examples include transportation systems, the power grid and sensitive medical procedures. Commercial flights are largely automated. LASIK eye surgery is done with such speed and precision that software guides the laser to ablate eye tissue. The only surgical role of the ophthalmologist—and it, too, is being replaced by a program that runs a second laser—is the cutting of the corneal flap.[308]

Some argue that complex systems require human supervision, and for a time this may be true especially with new systems. Eventually, however, most such complex systems will work with adequate reliability within operating parameters. Further, as we have seen elsewhere, the capability of AI's to independently assess and manage complex systems is growing. For example, there is now an AI program that predicts which genetic mutations will be associated with hundreds of complex diseases. It does so with 10 times more accuracy than comparable non-AI programs.[309]

Bugs and Dysfunctional Systems

Bugs are with us and will remain with us, perhaps indefinitely. However, criticisms of our increasing reliance on software as a society generally fail to consider (as do many criticisms, not merely of software) that it is not a choice between software and nothing. Software performs many tasks that we need, or much desire. If it were to cease providing this function, what would replace it?

While traditionally the answer was a return to human effort, increasingly that is no longer a viable alternative. There is literally no way that an individual human or a group of humans could effectively perform the tasks today provided by software, especially software working in conjunction with microprocessors in all manner of applications. Indeed, the much-discussed and rapidly emerging "internet of things" relies on the rapid migration of more and more intelligence and sensing apparatus to objects in our environment that were

---

[308] https://www.urmc.rochester.edu/encyclopedia/content.aspx?
ContentTypeID=85& ContentID=P00515

[309] http://www.kurzweilai.net/smart-program-predicts-key-disease-associated-
genetic-mutations-for-hundreds-of-complex-diseases

previously "dumb". When we can talk to our toaster, it may seem trivial and, to some, overkill. When we can talk to our vehicle with self-driving capabilities, it could be a lifesaver when we are tired, emotionally upset, or intoxicated.

Unlike "bugs" in human decision-makers, bugs in software eventually either get eliminated or are contained to specific limited conditions that are known and acceptable. Further, I would argue, the advent of open-source software systems (wherein user participation and expert response are customary) should help to assure a future in which bugs of all kinds are more rapidly identified and corrected. I believe that this will be the case when the entire operating system for the city-state is open-source.

Bugs can be introduced when a system is designed from scratch or when changes are made to an existing system. In the near-term, both types of bugs can be presumed in a Celebration Society. While it will not be possible to avoid or eliminate bugs with complete certainty, it will be possible to monitor all necessary systems both in software and the physical world for performance within acceptable tolerances.

Specifically, any output that has significant real-world consequences will be monitored continuously by triple-redundant systems. If any of the three monitoring systems detects a condition that varies outside of tolerance, it will sound an alarm. If neither of its sister systems immediately corroborates the reading, that system will be presumed defective and flagged for diagnosis and repair. However, if all three of the triple-redundant monitoring systems identify a problem simultaneously then the broader systems will presume that there is a problem.

For example, suppose the temperature within a public room is to stay within the range of 75 – 78 degrees F. If the sensors that monitor temperature detect a reading of 79 degrees, they will activate a cooling system. If the reading does not drop to 78 degrees, they will signal a problem. The problem will immediately come to the attention of AI's, robots and/or people who are charged with maintaining a comfortable environment. They will check other sensors to determine the nature of the problem.

If the problem is determined to be something non-urgent, perhaps an air conditioner compressor failure, it will be scheduled for repair. If the problem is determined to be urgent, such as a fire or perhaps a temperature rise that goes beyond comfort and risks health, remediating the situation will be of higher priority, and other measures such as evacuation may be taken.

In the decades ahead, we can presume that the systems of the initial Celebration Society will be designed and built with bugs included. Even with simulations prior to physically building the initial society, bugs will remain.

In all likelihood, bugs will remain with us forever in complex systems. Bugs are only recognized as such when a problem is detected. Such detection in an automated system depends on using a sensor(s) to monitor a relevant variable(s) to ensure that the value(s) remain(s) within an acceptable range.

The advantage a Celebration Society will have in bug detection, diagnosis and correction is unlimited deployment of sensors along with AI modeling of important systems that can rapidly identify, analyze and isolate the causes of bugs. So, although there may be a larger number of bug-related problems initially, at least as compared to traditional societies, continuous process improvement will assure that this rapidly diminishes towards an acceptable level.

If this seems optimistic, consider the work of W. Edwards Deming, an American systems thinker who pioneered to concept of continuous process improvement. Japan embraced his thinking, raising it almost to a cult status. (There is a Deming Prize, awarded annually.) It has been argued that this is the main reason for Japan's rise from an exporter of balsa wood trinkets in the 1950's to the world's leading exporter of high-end consumer electronics circa 2000. (Critics mention the immense paperwork associated with the Prize and some of the methods. However, with advanced sensors and real-time computer interaction and recording of data, it should be possible to drastically reduce the labor requirement.)

Dysfunctionality is Tolerated Today

Important legacy systems worldwide are riddled with defects, with inadequate diagnosis and poor management. Therefore, a Celebration Society doesn't need perfection; it instead needs a process that quickly and objectively identifies dysfunctions within systems and remedies them immediately when possible, or flags them for adjustment and further study.

Legacy systems often make life unnecessarily hard. For example, in Venice my wife and I watched as two workers struggled to move an appliance down a narrow street that was wide enough for all known uses when it was built centuries ago. Likewise, modern building codes, written long ago for safety, now can prevent more advanced building solutions from being implemented.[310] By creating important new systems from scratch, with self-monitoring and testing built in to the process, it should be possible to have complex systems which, while imperfect, are continuously monitored and improved via feedback.

Apparently, legacy software systems exist that are mission-critical yet no one understands them fully. In at least one case, it is reported that a "company runs a piece of national infrastructure which affects more or less every business and home in the country. They screw up, the whole country gets clobbered.... That company is still to this day running that same application [begun in the 1980's and evolved], and three-quarters of what it does is completely unknown."[311] (My wife assures me from her 22 years of experience at IBM that this is not uncommon for legacy systems.)

In the future, when fully immersive VR is available, systems will be modeled in VR and changes can be introduced there before happening in the real world. (This is what vendors of electronic casino games already do, albeit in far simpler form. Flaws in payouts cannot be tolerated either from a

---

[310] http://www.dovetailinc.org/report_pdfs/2011/dovetailbuildingcode1011.pdf
[311] Tim Elliot, posting on *Quora*.

regulatory or practical perspective, and so enormous numbers of simulated runs are performed at high speed by software before a game is released.) While the VR software may itself have bugs or fail to incorporate a bug from the real-world system, it will nevertheless help to reduce real-world problems.

Eventually, with AI's that are capable of thinking a million times faster than humans, testing can be done far faster than in the past. Many bugs will be identified and eliminated before they have any effect at all on humans. Further, systems will continue to be monitored real-time in all critical parameters, forever.

Dealing with Malware

In considering bugs, I am not thinking of malware but of unintentional errors. Malware is any software designed by a hostile or abusive actor for a purpose antithetical to that of the end-user. Historically, most malware has been designed and used by young people seeking to entertain themselves, by petty criminals seeking to steal financial resources and the like.

Increasingly, however, more sophisticated malware has been designed and used by governments seeking advantage over other governments or for theft of corporate secrets. Stuxnet is the most advanced example to be deployed in recent times. Apparently created by Israeli and/or US-based operatives working on behalf of their government(s), it was designed to attack a particular kind of Siemens controller used in nuclear separation, causing the centrifuges to self-destruct. It is widely credited with being far more advanced than typical malware "viruses", "worms" and the like. It was specifically designed and used to disrupt the Iranian nuclear program.

North Korea reportedly waged a cyberattack on Sony as revenge for a Sony movie that ridiculed the North Korean leader. Likewise, it has been claimed that the Chinese Army has a specific Unit 61398 that is expressly responsible for cyberattacks on US businesses and others. Also, when Russian hackers took down Estonian institutions via cyberattack in 2007,[312] it was generally considered a state-orchestrated attack. It is quite likely that other governments are doing the same now, and they will do so increasingly in the future.

In the decades ahead, malware will remain a problem and probably an increasing one. For this reason, it seems to me that mission-critical systems in a Celebration Society need to be run on a closed intranet with very strong proof of ID for entry. (Because all locations in a Celebration Society city-state will be physically reachable in a matter of minutes, biometric security requiring physical presence would seem feasible.)

Looking ahead a century or more, should we achieve a planetary Abundance Game, it is difficult to see the value of malware. This is not to say that it could never happen, since it might constitute an interesting game for some people. However, if the purpose of malware is to play a game, the purpose could be served within a fully immersive VR environment without the risk of adverse consequences to the target or the perpetrator.

There are now entire factories operating essentially automatically, with the inputs of matter and energy controlled by software Organizing Intelligence. Handfuls of humans "supervise" the process; a prudent measure until a future time when today's software bugs and viruses may be eradicated through superior AI design and supervision of software. Admittedly, there is the possibility of AI's being dedicated to mischief, but the only defense is other AI's—not unaugmented people, who will be far too slow in their responses.

Organizing Intelligence to Generate Necessities

Software based Organizing Intelligence can direct the production of all human necessities in the decades ahead, including food, shelter, water, energy, clothing, medical care, companionship and novelty. (Babies actually learn via novelty.)[313] Fabrics are woven, cut, and stitched into clothing

---

[312] http://www.theguardian.com/world/2007/may/17/topstories3.russia
[313] http://www.theatlantic.com/health/archive/2015/04/babies-learn-through-being-surprised/389420/

by robots. Robots are starting to have the delicate touch and accurate sensors needed to plant and harvest crops. Homes and other buildings can be 3D printed, or modularly constructed by machines from components manufactured by other machines.

As discussed elsewhere, medical care is increasingly automated. Companionship can be provided in a non-technological way by other people and animals, and increasingly, by human-like and animal-like robots.[314] Novelty can be provided by software on a video screen with some means of interaction, or by physical objects with embedded intelligence and sensors.

In the future, the gap between automated production of *necessities* and the automated production of *everything* will narrow. As to whether it will ever fully close, only time will tell. But the gap is irrelevant to creating a viable, sustainable Celebration Society. For that, we just need that the basic necessities of everyone be met and that people have a life-enhancing environment in which to thrive.

---

[314] http://www.parorobots.com/

Part V: Other Supportive Technologies and Resources

> Technology is a gift of God. After the gift of life it is perhaps the greatest of God's gifts. It is the mother of civilizations, of arts and of sciences.

> *~Freeman Dyson*

Many technologies and other resources stand ready to support a Celebration Society. More are emerging all the time. As the technological tidal wave continues to gather force, whole fields of knowledge and research are coming into existence now in an historical blink of an eye.

Given that technological advances have accounted for almost all of the progress in human history,[315] we should be very wary of discounting the transformational impact of technological change—especially as the rate of change is exponential and accelerating.

Broadly speaking, technology can be defined as anything expressed as a codified body of knowledge and then used to leverage or augment human capabilities. From this understanding, products are technologies when they enable more or better production, or enhance the quality of life. A hammer is technology at its most physical and simple; software is technology at its most abstract and complex. Further, every expression of technology can be modified to make it more suitable for a specialized purpose(s), as for example the ball peen hammer used in metalworking.

A generation ago, we had programmers. Today, there are myriad programming specialties including fields where programming blends with other fields in what is called *convergent technology*. One example is bioinformatics, which combines

---

[315] Research suggests that all other forces have been trivial by comparison. (See: *World Population and Social development Index, 2000 BC – 2000 AD.*)

computer science, statistics, mathematics, and engineering to analyze and interpret biological data. As software pervades more and more aspects of life and society, organizing intelligence becomes ever more potent.

Though technologies are frequently improved, unless they work adequately well at the start they are not useful; they are either researched further or discarded.

New technologies can elevate discarded or ignored resources so that they become important and useful. These newly useful resources are then able to augment or enhance human capabilities.

I have compiled what I consider to be the most important supportive technologies and resources into categories:

- New approaches to education
- New forms of money
- Healthcare sustaining long vigorous life in the direction of immortality
- Advanced agricultural technologies
- Production of abundant clean water
- Achieving universal communications
- Fast, cheap, onsite manufacturing
- The *Mother Plant*, a resource that can empower many other things

All of these technologies and resources are available now or poised to blossom in the next decade or so. Together, these and various other enabling technologies will allow us to create a new paradigm for the dwelling of humans in balance with natural ecosystems.

Education for Tomorrow

In my view, education has historically served three primary purposes:

1. Preparing children for adult citizenship
2. Cultivating skills that can be used to earn money
3. Instilling values commonly held

In a Celebration Society, all of these will be different from the norms of today. It will also include a fourth purpose, the pursuit of knowledge for delight in learning.

We need to assure that tomorrow's adults embody the qualities and competencies that will be essential to tomorrow's Celebration Societies. What are those qualities? In my view, among them must be: creativity, curiosity, respectfulness, honesty, self-control, intelligence, inclusiveness, playfulness, generosity, devotion, kindness, integrity and wisdom. What will it take to cultivate today's children into adults who embody such qualities and transmit them to society?

The winner of the $1 million 2013 TED Prize, Sugata Mitra, identified the origins of the present-day educational system in the needs of the British bureaucracy and its successful engineering of schools to meet those needs. As with so much else, we are living with legacy systems developed many years ago to meet needs that no longer exist; needs we have forgotten and yet unconsciously serve.

College was envisioned as something for the aristocracy. The present pre-college educational system was designed to transform farm kids into good industrial workers; cogs in a vast production machine. Such workers needed to accept authority as well as rigid schedules, and to perform work without necessarily understanding how it fit into any larger picture. Today, the crying need is for something radically different. Said James P. Hogan, "There was something wrong with a society that spent millions trying to make computers and robots imitate humans while at the same time training humans to behave like robots."[316]

Even a passing familiarity with technology trends makes it clear that the work of tomorrow will bear little resemblance to factory work or, for that matter, office work of today. Here are some attributes of tomorrow's work environment:

- Collaborative projects will increasingly supplant individualistic ones.

---

[316] *Cradle of Saturn*, James P. Hogan

- All of the non-secret/non-proprietary knowledge of humanity will be almost instantly available in vast online, networked databases thanks to the internet.
- AI agents will comb those databases, looking for the answers to specific questions and also seeking patterns in the data that may be relevant to the user's needs.
- With AI's analyzing all manner of data and sensory inputs tirelessly and at superhuman speeds, the need for human analysts will plummet.
- The combination of AI's, robotics and sensors will make much if not most labor by people uneconomical and therefore obsolete. ("We need only extrapolate ... a little way into the future to reach an important tipping point, the point at which human technology renders the ordinary human technologically obsolete.")[317]

What will remain for people is creativity, at least to some extent. Present-day mainstream education does little to cultivate this most precious ability, soon to become perhaps the last bastion of economic value-added by people. (While China recently had a national five-year plan to focus educational initiatives on development of creative thinking, it's not clear what success this achieved.)[318]

Do We Need Behavior Modification?

In the Scarcity Game, the presumption within all types of societies is that children must be forced to learn behaviors that are suitable for the society. There is little room for the concept that suitable behaviors can arise naturally from eagerness to fit in and be a valued member of society. Schools have often functioned as factories in which all of the children are forced to dress the same, sit or stand in precise groupings, participate in the same lessons at the same times and, in general, function as cogs in an educational machine.

---

[317] The Technological Singularity, Murray Shanahan
[318] China Education Resources, Inc.

This prepared them for life as cogs in an industrial machine. However, with that industrial machine now morphing into something else entirely, this is a less and less helpful type of experience. Even so, when children rebel or otherwise do not fit in, they are often coerced to do so.

Consider the beating of children. This is an easy way to change unwanted or destructive behaviors; far easier than seeking to understand behavior from a child's point of view and encourage change more gently, at least from the busy parent's point of view. And, when life is harsh and brutish, it is understandable that parents would seek such shortcuts. After all, their remaining time might be spent on survival.

But now consider what the child learns. Might makes right. The large and powerful have the right to impose their will on the small and weak. And so bullying, a chronic social problem in many cultures, is sustained across the generations. Women, who are generally smaller, are physically abused by men. Further, there is no bright line separating "physical discipline" from brutalization.

People who have been brutalized have an increased tendency to brutalize others. Indeed, among the most violent of criminals, it has been found that a particular set of harsh circumstances needs to have befallen that person in order for their pathology to manifest. For example, evidence is now coming to light that even a psychopath who is raised in an extremely nurturing, violence-free environment can become a healthy and productive member of society.[319]

It turns out that we humans have a lot of checks and balances built into our physiology that tend to prevent violence to one another. According to social psychologist Albert Bandura, "it requires conducive social conditions rather than monstrous people to produce atrocious deeds. Given appro-

---

[319] http://www.theatlantic.com/health/archive/2014/01/life-as-a-nonviolent-psychopath/282271/

171

priate social conditions, decent, ordinary people can be led to do extraordinarily cruel things."[320]

Anyone who doubts this has at least two challenges. First, there are the famous experiments of Stanley Milgram in which ordinary people decided to administer dangerous shocks to others because an authority figure told them to do so. Second, does anyone believe that average Germans of the Nazi period were more inherently evil than the Germans of the earlier Bismarck period or the Germans of the early 21st century?

What are the actual tendencies of small children? Are they innately selfish and cruel, as some have alleged? Various studies have now shown that children appear to have an innate sense of good and of bad, often acting in an altruistic fashion. Toddlers are empathic natural helpers, willing to help others even at some cost to themselves.[321]

Researchers have identified factors that appear in nursery school and correlate to future criminal behavior. Fortunately, these factors can also be changed.[322]

This is not to say that people are incapable of indifference, taking from others, or even active hostility to the less fortunate. Obviously those are entirely possible, and equally obviously children who grow up in socially diseased environments that foster an "us vs. them" mentality may turn to gangs or even terrorism.

Enforcing Outdated Societal Values

It has been said that one can judge the degree of civilization of a society by how it treats its children and its elders. In advanced nations of the West, the elderly are generally

---

[320] http://web.stanford.edu/~kcarmel/CC_BehavChange_Course/readings/ Additional%20Resources/Bandura/bandura_moraldisengagement.pdf

[321] http://www.smithsonianmag.com/science-nature/are-babies-born-good-165443013/

[322] http://www.telegraph.co.uk/news/science/science-news/11774861/Future-criminals-can-be-spotted-at-nursery-school-study-suggests.html

warehoused; shut away and left to die.[323] (Said Pope Francis, "in this empire of the god money, things are thrown away and people are thrown away."[324]) While the majority of Western children are generally given a safe environment, decent health care, clothing, shelter, and enough to eat, a significant percentage of children lack these basic necessities.

But even amongst those given the necessities, many are still raised in families where intense competition is favored over cooperation, where they are subjected to the pathologies of their parents, and for much of their lives are locked away in industrial era school-factories, in which the qualities of good drones are inculcated.

There is also the recent yet historically aberrant concept of the "nuclear family" wherein two adults or even just one are somehow expected to meet all of the needs of children. In rural Thailand, for example—a place where each child has many "uncles" and "aunts"—the notion of a nuclear family is regarded as an unnatural, sadly isolated lifestyle.[325]

Children so treated will naturally rebel. It is not natural for children, especially boys, to sit still and pay attention to repetitive drills whose purpose may not be understood for years, if ever. Since so many children are failing to "behave", there is a solution with an entire industry supporting it: medicate them!

According to a US Centers for Disease Control study, "An astounding 19 percent of high school-age boys – ages 14 to 17 – in the U.S. have been diagnosed with ADHD and about 10 percent are taking medication for it... (in addition) 11 percent

---

[323] http://www.motherjones.com/media/2014/10/atul-gawande-being-mortal-interview-assisted-living

[324] http://www.theatlantic.com/international/archive/2015/09/pope-francis-advice-to-millennials-cuba/406435/

[325] I lived in Thailand on two occasions, during which I visited rural communities. I was struck by the prevailing warmth, generosity and feeling of extended family into which I was included.

of Americans age 12 and older are taking antidepressant medication."[326] In Britain, Ritalin prescriptions have *quadrupled* in a single decade.[327]

What kind of dysfunction must a society have to so aggressively medicate children with amphetamines (Adderall), other stimulants (Ritalin, Concerta),[328] and antidepressants? Either these medical conditions are being over-diagnosed or behaviors natural to children are incompatible with the way children are being raised and taught.

Consider a child being raised today in a system that favors memorization of facts and skills to meet test-taking requirements. Imagine that child drugged on Ritalin for years to force a vibrant imagination into compliant attention. Now imagine him or her as an adult 20 years hence, desperately needing creative thinking skills, self-confidence and initiative—yet perhaps incapable of these.

Scientists have determined that two of the skills possessed by Thomas Edison that allowed him to become such a successful inventor were an ability to reason from analogy and to learn from failure—skills that the current educational model fails to inculcate.[329]

Certain forms of suffering leave generational changes in genetics.[330] Lysenko was a Russian geneticist whose work was discredited because he believed that environmental changes could be inherited. He was almost universally dismissed for generations. The reality, as we now understand, is that while

---

[326] http://www.wnd.com/2013/04/radical-increase-in-kids-prescribed-ritalin/

[327] http://www.theguardian.com/society/2012/may/06/ritalin-adhd-shocks-child-psychologists

[328] http://www.drugabuse.gov/publications/drugfacts/stimulant-adhd-medications-methylphenidate-amphetamines

[329] http://www.theatlantic.com/magazine/archive/1995/12/the-undiscovered-world-of-thomas-edison/305880/

[330] http://www.newscientist.com/article/mg20827852.500-epigenetics-can-take-us-towards-a-saner-future.html

his concept was crude and easily disproven in that crude form, it had some merit. Epigenetics is the study of how genes express themselves and are read by cells. Expression of genes varies significantly according to the circumstances in which the organism lives, and may even vary according to the experiences of one's recent ancestors.[331]

Quite apart from the cultural transmission of values and behaviors, if a person is brutalized, what epigenetics are triggered that may have influence upon that person's offspring? Consider the possibility that we are living in an epidemic of brutalization. In America, and almost certainly elsewhere, "...Half of all kids are traumatized... And nearly a quarter experience two or more stressful childhood events, setting them up for worse physical and mental health later in life."[332]

In the present day, most people either grow up in societies where life is short and harsh, where people scrape and strive from dawn to dusk just to survive, or they are "fortunate" and grow up in societies where the necessities are met, but where they are taught a set of beliefs and given experiences founded upon harsh, unending scarcity and vicious competition.

Changing Work Requirements

In pre-industrial societies, children learned a trade through apprenticeship. It was a sensible way to transmit culture and skills, but it no longer served production once industrialization entered the picture.

Industrialization and industrial-era models are crumbling around us. In Silicon Valley, there are fast-growing companies with officers in charge of play! They understand that, to attract and keep the kinds of workers they require—workers who think creatively and refuse to function as drones—they need to engage playful tendencies in a way that supports the corporate purpose. However, the prevailing educational system is woefully inadequate to produce these kinds of workers;

---

[331] http://news.yahoo.com/inherit-experiences-inside-weird-world-142103088.html
[332] http://www.theatlantic.com/health/archive/2014/12/half-of-all-kids-experience-traumatic-events/383630/

the kind who truly think outside the proverbial "box" rather than merely talk about it.

Paul Graham is founder of the world's most successful high tech startup incubator system, Y Combinator. Y Combinator has produced more than 500 companies with an average value of $45.2 million since its inception in 2005. Presumably, as founder of the affiliated Startup School, Mr. Graham knows what kind of education "produces" the kind of people who can start and successfully develop such companies—the kind of companies coveted by policy makers.[333]

Graham refers to the average school as a part-time prison, where the quality of teaching is so low that kids don't take it seriously and this builds rebelliousness into the culture.

> The real problem is the emptiness of school life.... School is a strange, artificial thing, half sterile and half feral. It's all-encompassing, like life, but it isn't the real thing.... If life seems awful to kids, it's neither because hormones are turning you all into monsters (as your parents believe), nor because life actually is awful (as you believe). It's because the adults, who no longer have any economic use for you, have abandoned you to spend years cooped up together with nothing real to do. *Any* society of that type is awful to live in. You don't have to look any further to explain why teenage kids are unhappy.[334]

---

[333] These companies do not tend to create a lot of jobs. It has been estimated that the *total* number of jobs created by Y Combinator companies to date is about 9 – 10,000. (A complication is that most will use contract providers for much of their work, indirectly creating more jobs.) Policymakers who say they expect high-tech startups to meet the need posed by the coming jobs crisis are either ignorant or being disingenuous.

[334] http://www.paulgraham.com/nerds.html

What kinds of qualities does Graham think are important in founders of high tech startups? He lists five key ones: determination, flexibility, imagination, naughtiness ("they care about getting the big questions right, but not about observing proprieties") and friendship.[335] How many of these do you think a typical school inculcates?

Graham is not alone in this view. Wrote a long-term educator:

> Our children have sacrificed [their] natural curiosity and love of learning at the altar of achievement, and it's our fault.... parents, teachers, society at large—we are all implicated in this crime against learning... [we taught kids] that it's better to quit when things get challenging rather than risk marring that perfect record.
>
> Above all else, we taught [kids] to fear failure. That fear is what has destroyed [their] love of learning.... Is that what we want? Kids who get straight A's but hate learning? Kids who achieve academically, but are too afraid to take leaps into the unknown?[336]

College was originally developed to cultivate leadership qualities in the upper classes. It therefore offers a very different educational experience than do the lower grades. However, by the time students reach college age, some view it as a much-needed escape from prison while others view it as an extension of the professional preparation that was high school. In very few cases is college viewed as the natural place to explore and master one's life purpose.

Further, college apparently does a poor job of cultivating skills necessary to thrive in the 21st century. Sociologists Richard Arum and Josipa Roksa studied 2,300 college students using the Collegiate Learning Assessment (CLA), which

---

[335] http://www.paulgraham.com/founders.html
[336] The Gift of Failure, Jessica Lahey

assesses critical thinking, written communication, problem solving, and analytic reasoning. They found that quite a few students did nothing to develop these skills during their time in college. Specifically, 45 percent showed no significant improvement in two years of college and 36 percent showed none after four years.[337]

Thoughtful parents look at the vast range of knowledge necessary to thrive in a modern society, and they want to stuff as much of that knowledge as possible into their kids' heads. It's understandable, but short-sighted. When people live in a world offering continuous access to all manner of information, coupled with AI's offering assistance in everything of note, what will matter is one's ability to learn, to appreciate, to put things into context with good judgment, to grow, and to create.

Having a large repository of facts in one's biological memory will soon matter no more than does penmanship today. Given all that computers can do and will soon be doing, what is to be the role of humans in our productive system and how can we best prepare children to thrive in such a world?

New Approaches to Education

In my view, in a Celebration Society children should be offered many forms of safe stimuli and encouraged to pursue those that interest them. Often, these will be the interests and activities of their parents or other close adults, a process known in ancient societies as apprenticeship or family dharma. (When children had different interests, efforts were often made to find a suitable mentor.)

They should be offered all manner of learning opportunities to flourish in exploring and developing their natural interests, passions, and gifts. There will be no incentive to discourage a child from pursuing a field of interest because it is impractical, since the potential earning of an income will

---

[337] Academically Adrift: Limited Learning on College Campuses, Arum and Roksa

be irrelevant or, at most, secondary to the pursuit of happiness.

Such an approach to education will be viable once we have achieved fully functioning celebrationist systems of production. Meanwhile, some human work will be required in society and education may need to accommodate this.

McAfee and Brynjolfsson argue that self-organizing learning environments (SOLE's) may offer part of the answer. Programs such as Montessori, a particular type of SOLE, have given us leaders such as the founders of Google, Amazon, and Wikipedia.

In such environments, kids form teams, use search technology, have back and forth discussions, and eventually develop ideas that are often correct. They perform ideation, broad-frame pattern recognition, and complex communication—skills people still perform better than computers.[338]

To their credit, after arguing that a specific set of skills can set humans apart from computers, McAfee and Brynjolfsson do acknowledge that, "After spending time working with leading technologists and watching one bastion of human uniqueness after another fall before the inexorable onslaught of innovation, it's becoming harder and harder to have confidence that any given task will be indefinitely resistant to automation."[339]

The widespread interest in STEM (science, technology, engineering and math) education is an attempt to prepare people for the jobs of tomorrow. Right now, it's having mixed results. It's not the content of education that's problematic so much as the context; making what is learned meaningful to students. In this regard, various promising initiatives to shift the educational experience are arising.

---

[338] *The Second Machine Age*, McAfee and Brynjolfsson
[339] ibid.

For example, *Discovering the Art of Mathematics: Mathematical Inquiry in the Liberal Arts*, is a curriculum developed at Westfield State University by Julian Fleron and funded by the National Science Foundation. It is designed to cultivate an attitude towards math in which it is, "...taught as both an intellectual discipline and a creative endeavor—where math is *made*, not just discussed."[340] Likewise, an educator has figured out how to teach elements of calculus to five year olds.[341]

The books of mathematician and actress Danica McKellar have won enthusiastic reviews from math teachers because they make math relevant and accessible to one of its hardest audiences: teenage girls.

A still more radical approach is being practiced in an increasing number of schools. Writing in *Right-Brained Children in a Left-Brained World*, authors Jeffrey Freed and Laurie Parsons essentially advocate for this approach, known as unschooling. Unschooling is a movement that began in 1968 with the emergence of Sudbury Valley and other such schools. Such a school exists as a place where kids are given stimulating challenges to evoke curiosity and exploration, but do not have a set curriculum or testing.

In unschooling, kids are not forced into rote memorization, nor into anything else. Indeed, some of these kids do not choose to learn to read until they are much older than when reading is usually taught. However, when eventually self-motivated to learn these skills, they can learn them far more rapidly than do youngsters forced to learn the same material.[342]

---

[340] http://www.theatlantic.com/education/archive/2014/10/teaching-math-to-people-who-think-they-hate-it/381125/
[341] http://www.theatlantic.com/education/archive/2014/03/5-year-olds-can-learn-calculus/284124/
[342] https://www.psychologytoday.com/blog/freedom-learn/201002/children-teach-themselves-read

How do unschooled kids fare in adulthood? A study of such adults found that 83% went on to some sort of higher education (compared to the US average of 62.5%).[343] 78% were financially self-sufficient, 48% were in fields that could be described as creative arts and among those who were always unschooled the percentage rose to 79%. 53% were entrepreneurs. A remarkable 77% had a clear relationship between their adult employment and their childhood interests and activities. 77% stated that unschooling, "enabled them to develop as highly self-motivated, self-directed individuals." Finally, "For 72 of the 75 respondents, the advantages of unschooling clearly, in their own minds, outweighed the disadvantages."[344]

It seems to me that these results closely mirror the kind of education that Paul Graham holds to be ideal for tomorrow's entrepreneurs. Not everyone has access to unschooling at the present time. However, access to online education is rapidly proliferating across the globe, which opens a new possibility.

Khan Academy offers a free online education to anyone with access to the internet. Originally designed for young children, it now has a vision of free education through college. This seems to be an excellent supplement to self-organizing learning environments.

One great challenge of such online education is the high dropout rate. Since students started the program without coercion and in hopes of success, their dropping out may be due to either a lack of adequate support or a loss of interest in the material.

If Khan Academy were married to a particular educational complementary currency design, known as the SABER, which rewards and systematizes tutorial support, I believe the whole

---

[343] www.Higheredinfo.org/dbrowser/index.php?measure=32
[344] https://www.psychologytoday.com/blog/freedom-learn/201406/survey-grown-unschoolers-i-overview-findings

system would show massive synergy. If this were also combined with unschooling, wherein Academy courses were organized to serve specific interests rather than merely as a curriculum, the results could be spectacular.

Another possible approach that attracted much fanfare but, to date, arguably little success[345] is the MOOC, or massive open online courses. These are essentially courses taught via webcast and so are theoretically accessible to anyone, anywhere, and even possibly any time. It now appears that, rather than viewing these courses as stand-alone tools, they should be structured as powerful components of broader educational experiments.

One of the most promising developments in education is the One Laptop per Child movement which, coupled with the push for a bare-bones $100 laptop, promises a future in which education is personalized to the child's speed and style of learning as well as the child's interests. This will be especially enhanced by the advent in the near future of infinitely patient and flexible AI tutors. Already, AI is starting to replace textbooks.[346]

Many children learn best by doing and not by lecture. Personal computers are, perhaps, the ultimate tool for this purpose—especially when they are eventually coupled to VR. (If you question whether a $100 laptop can support advanced AI and VR capabilities, consider that today's laptop is the supercomputer of 20 years ago.)

The skills we call reading and writing are about to be transformed. Already, there is no need for an average person to learn penmanship beyond the ability to fill out a form or leave a note. Typing will also soon become an unnecessary skill, since one can communicate just fine by dictating to a computer, which converts spoken words into text. Writing

---

[345] http://www.newyorker.com/science/maria-konnikova/moocs-failure-solutions, also http://www.nytimes.com/2013/12/11/us/after-setbacks-online-courses-are-rethought.html
[346] http://www.theatlantic.com/education/archive/2015/03/the-death-of-textbooks/387055/

then becomes about using language to understand, create, and convey ideas far more than it is about the physical means of expression.

Reading, too, is changing. It seems that people are increasingly oriented towards learning in short bursts of information. As near-instantaneous access to the world's repositories of information becomes ubiquitous, with AI assistants to quickly find what is wanted, few will see any point to reading large amounts of information for the sake of learning it.

Games as Educational Tools

Games, long derided as being distractions from education, are being discovered instead to serve as powerful tools that can enhance the outcomes of learning or even as teaching methodologies.[347] The decision by families to play games together at home is being seen as beneficial to education.[348] Further, studies are finding that playing video games improves learning capabilities more generally, not just the skills taught in the game.[349]

The emerging field of *serious games* redesigns training and educational experiences into games in order to enhance retention, feedback, enthusiasm, access to limited resources, willingness to take risks and...increase happiness. It is increasingly driving education and training in major organizations. For example, serious game developer Totem Learning, offers an immersive experience of how serious gaming can substitute for traditional employee orientation. Its clients include Coca-Cola, HP, 3M, Raytheon and other substantial companies.[350]

---

[347] http://www.theatlantic.com/education/archive/2014/07/are-multiplayer-games-the-future-of-education/374235/

[348] http://www.theatlantic.com/education/archive/2014/07/how-family-game-night-makes-kids-into-better-students/374525/

[349] http://www.kurzweilai.net/playing-action-video-games-can-boost-learning, http://www.pnas.org/content/early/2014/11/05/1417056111.abstract, http://www.theatlantic.com/education/archive/2015/02/teaching-in-the-age-of-minecraft/385231/

[350] http://www.totemlearning.com/technology/

The breadth of activity in this field is evident from the following list of topics covered in the Serious Games People group on LinkedIn:

> ...we talk about games to teach sexual education, a Disney incubator for educational games startups, grants that you can apply for from the U.S government if you are creating educational games, a UN app competition to build a peace-promoting app, how virtual reality can revolutionize learning and last but not least, games to analyze history plus our game of the month, which is an interactive story about the Yellow Fever epidemic in 18th century Philadelphia.[351]

Augmented and Virtual Reality

Probably the most disruptive developments in the field of education will arise from transforming the space in which education is delivered. As discussed above, different ways of delivering content and of structuring the relationship between educator and student will have profound effects. However, these may pale in comparison to the effects of VR and augmented reality platforms.

Said Peter Diamandis:

> How do we fix education? We make it fun, taught by the world's best, on a personalized basis. And we make it *free*.

> With the help of virtual reality, a young student learning about dinosaurs in the Jurassic period won't have to just read about it in a textbook – they'll be able to put on a VR headset and literally explore the VR-equivalent of Jurassic Park.

---

[351] www.gameplaylearn.com, Anuar Andres Lequerica

Students studying physics will be able to 'step inside' a virtual environment where they build (and destroy) huge structures, fly through the planets, and stand next to a virtual Isaac Newton as he discovers his laws of motion.

Remember the Holodeck from Star Trek? There are a handful of startups that are trying to re-create this exact experience.

Add to this the ability for Artificial Intelligence and VR to work collaboratively, where a virtual version of world's best history professor delivers a personalized lesson for your child at a pace and in a language best suited just for them.

We will see these technologies dematerialize, demonetize, and democratize access to educational resources that the best and the brightest don't even have today.

In other words, the software will become freely available to the world, and a child in rural Tanzania will have access to the same resources as a student at Harvard or MIT.[352]

A world in which such learning environments are universally available will inevitably transform its approach to education. Likewise, the lines between education as something one must do, education as something one loves to do, and immersive entertainment will blur until it becomes hard to tell one from the other. At that point, we will have achieved a world in which people learn because they find the knowledge useful or fun—and the learning is tailored to their personal learning style and interests. That will be celebrationist learning.

Meanwhile, we still have widespread educational practices that are actually counterproductive. The coercion of focus is a prime example.

---

[352] E-mail sent 9/13/15

Coercing Focus at the Expense of Daydreaming

While the ability to focus is obviously important to completion of tasks and long-range planning, current educational models often presume that focus must be drilled in; coerced. The experiences of children in unschooling environments such as Sudbury indicate that focus naturally arises when the child finds something fascinating.[353]

But there is an even more damning problem with coercing focus. Mind-altering drugs such as Ritalin, used to force this focus, may cause permanent changes in brain chemistry similar to those caused by cocaine use.[354]

Research has now established that daydreaming—the bane of many educators because it is superficially in opposition to focus—is in fact vital to human development and functioning. The strictures against daydreaming or wandering attention appear to arise because the types of daydreaming that spur motivation and help people to rehearse important skills and performances are conflated with wishful thinking, which saps energy.[355]

Dr. Scott Barry Kaufmann has described these findings (emphasis added):[356]

> *Daydreaming helps students achieve the very things educators assume it hinders...* half a century ago, Yale psychologist Jerome Singer (found) daydreaming to be a commonplace part of human experience. He identified something he called 'positive-constructive daydreaming'.

---

[353] http://www.psychologytoday.com/articles/200604/education-class-dismissed
[354] http://newswire.rockefeller.edu/2009/02/04/ritalin-may-cause-changes-in-the-brains-reward-areas/
[355] http://www.bakadesuyo.com/2011/10/does-fantasizing-give-you-the-motivation-to-a/, "Positive fantasies about idealized futures sap energy", *Journal of Experimental Social Psychology*, July 2011
[356] *Psychology Today*, March/April 2014

This is the use of daydreaming for future planning. Since Singer, researchers have faced a gnawing question: given that many of us spend about half of our waking hours on this, what's the evolutionary reason?

One study[357] found that people who daydream have the best-developed ability to control their own attention. Another study found that students who were encouraged and provided with time to imagine their academic future lives and practice the necessary skills had important gains. These included more connection with the school, more motivation to do well, more strategic options for doing well, better attendance and fewer behavioral issues.

Another study tracked a group of children over 30 years. It followed them for many indicators of creative and scholastic promise. *The strongest factor in predicting personal achievement including significant creativity, more than grades and intelligence tests, was having a clearly defined future vision of their lives.*

Research at York University discovered that people who can resist a small immediate reward to pursue a later but larger reward use daydreaming.

Santa Barbara psychologists asked study participants to generate unusual uses for a common object, and those given the opportunity to practice daydreaming were 40% percent more creative.

---

[357] Led by Jonathan Schooler, University of California, Santa Barbara. The findings appear to be universal, including the US, Europe, China and Japan. The findings corroborate those of Eric Klinger, that daydreams and night dreams both reflect current concerns.

Daydreaming represents a different kind of intelligence than that measured on standardized tests. It's no less valuable. It also appears to inculcate mindfulness; a trait that's highly associated with mental health and high functioning in life.

Studies also suggest that leading scientists use daydreaming in their work.[358]

Finally, "Many highly creative writers, artists and scientists were major daydreamers as children. The long list of highly accomplished daydreamers includes Einstein, Newton, the Bronte family, W.H. Auden, and C.S. Lewis."[359]

Does this behavior sound like something that should be medicated away?

I close this section with one of the most shocking recent discoveries in the field of education. It concerns autism. Autism has long been regarded as a dysfunctional state; one offering little hope of a normal life. However, it is now clear that, at least in some cases (and possibly many if not all) the autistic brain is not deficient but rather unsuited to our present educational system.

As mentioned earlier, the autistic brain has been found to be hyper-functional. The autistic child is not vegetating but rather lost in a world of his or her own observation and daydreaming. This can translate into a level of genius that suggests we may be in need of a new term. A "black swan" example is the prodigy Jacob Barnett. Diagnosed with autism at an early age, he was shunted to "special education" and expected to essentially live as a vegetable.

Instead, Jacob's mother home schooled him and focused her whole educational effort on understanding and encour-

---

[358] http://www.theatlantic.com/education/archive/2014/11/the-creative-scientist/382633/

[359] *Psychology Today*, March/April 2014,

aging his passions. The result: a young man who may become one of the greatest physicists of all time. Admitted to college classes at age 8, he has developed a new theory that may solve some of the great unanswered questions in physics.

His TEDx talk explains far better than I could hope to do who he is, what he has accomplished, and what may become possible by rethinking autism.[360] The Perimeter Institute, where he is completing his Ph.D. while still a teenager, also shows the potential of an educational institution based on cultivating passion rather than meeting arbitrary standards.[361]

If we have vital aspects of something as fundamental as education turned upside down, might other aspects of society that are equally fundamental also be misunderstood? Let's now turn to a subject that most of us believe we understand—money.

Artificial Scarcity or Monetary Abundance

Neither finance experts nor economists commonly understand money at a deep level, though they usually think that they do. What they understand is the design, expression, and operation of one particular monetary architecture that prevails across the globe. It never occurs to most of them that different architectures are possible and might lead people to behave differently than does the one with which they are familiar.

Currently, the common understanding is that capitalism is the only viable system of production, and capitalism is assumed to rest on the bedrock of central bank issued money (except in the minds of hard money advocates; more on this below). While humanity's reliance on capitalism will likely remain while we transition to celebrationism, so long as our primary financial system is based on scarcity, we can never have universal abundance. In the following section, I will

---

[360] https://www.youtube.com/watch?v=Uq-FOOQ1TpE
[361] http://www.macleans.ca/news/canada/jacob-barnett-boy-genius/

discuss national money and the opportunity to improve its functioning with complementary currencies.

Scarcity and Money

Today, our world is driven towards hyper-competitiveness by artificial scarcity. It is hard-wired into our money. In every nation, a central bank that is generally privately owned charges interest for the use of their money. Paying that interest requires endless growth just to pay the interest to the owners of the central banks; growth that could otherwise benefit the rest of the economy.

The effects of this money are leveraged by a *fractional reserve* requirement. Essentially, banks can now lend 9 units of money for each unit that they hold as a deposit. When banks are collectively optimistic about the economy, they use this power to make loans to businesses and the effects multiply throughout the economy. When they become collectively pessimistic, the reverse happens.

Today's money mostly exists as pieces of paper and electronic journal entries. It may be structured by the government as bonds, notes or other financial instruments, but all of these have equivalents in the private sector. There is nothing inherently special about this type of money other than the fact that it alone can be used to pay taxes, and it alone is recognized as *legal tender* that must be accepted in payment of debts. It is issued by central banks.

Central banks perform certain functions in modern economies. Specifically, they are:

> responsible for overseeing the monetary system for a nation (or group of nations). Central banks have a wide range of responsibilities, from overseeing monetary policy to implementing specific goals such as currency stability, low inflation and full employment. Central banks also generally issue currency, function as the bank of the government, regulate the credit system, oversee commercial banks, manage

exchange reserves and act as a lender of last resort.[362]

There will always be a place for central bank-issued money, so long as it is required for paying taxes. However, some of its policy functions and goals may be more effectively accomplished through the addition to the monetary portfolio of complementary currencies (see following).

Limitations of Today's Money

Many fans of Adam Smith believe that our problem with money is the substitution of worthless *fiat* (government issued paper) money for "hard" money such as gold and silver. They somehow missed Smith's caution that gold and silver have no intrinsic worth; he stated in *The Wealth of Nations* that supplies of these can drastically change over time and so, therefore, can prices.

Along with other elements of production, gold and silver supplies will soon greatly increase, driving down their prices and thereby reducing their value as backing for money. (Asteroid mining assures this result in the 21st century.)[363]

But if hard money is not truly "hard," and fiat money is essentially inflatable paper, what is the solution? Right now, all of the world's central bank-issued currencies are of different appearances but share the same *architecture*. Their interest, fractional reserve, and other design characteristics are optional.

Because national currencies are issued separately by different central banks, those banks usually keep the worst inflationary tendencies of their respective governments in check to preserve the benefits of foreign trade and investment.

---

[362] http://www.investopedia.com/terms/c/centralbank.asp

[363] http://www.forbes.com/sites/kitconews/2013/01/25/asteroid-mining-becoming-more-of-a-reality/

Penalties for wayward governments include collapsing exchange rates, higher interest rates and capital flight.

It has been estimated that the US needs more than $3.6 trillion of infrastructure repairs by 2020.[364] Some local governments raise needed funds through privatization—sale of assets such as bridges, office buildings and roads for cash to private owners who then charge rent to users. This is a short-term expedient that only postpones and increases the debt burden upon the next generation.

The problem is that there is simply not enough *national money* available for infrastructure repairs. That $3.6 trillion must come from somewhere—either decreasing the money spent elsewhere or increasing revenues from taxes and fees. The alternative, that government spends $3.6 trillion it doesn't have, either creates a massive debt burden whose interest payments will drag down the economy in the future or, if not borrowed, causes inflation. Yet, without the needed money, engineers flip burgers and the publicly owned roads crumble.

This is an absurd mismatch of needs and resources. Complementary currencies are ways to match underutilized assets with unmet needs. They do so on a voluntary basis; no coercion is required. Any municipal or state government could begin a complementary currency for infrastructure repairs, and quickly put many of its unemployed to work doing something useful. So, too, could a committed private group— or a public/private partnership.

Governments are risk-averse. They are rarely to be found among the ranks of first-adopters or innovators (though they can play a central role in funding basic research), unless there are no other possible solutions to a problem. Once one present-day national government has demonstrated success in a major way with complementary currencies others will consider their use. Once many governments have enjoyed

---

[364] http://www.infrastructurereportcard.org/executive-summary/

success by strengthening their monetary portfolio, many others will likely join because of clear, established benefits.

Alternately, if a private group develops a complementary currency design that offers major benefits on a local basis[365] and duplicates that success to multiple such locales, consistently producing the expected benefits, it is likely that such a currency design will be adopted across that nation and, soon, by other nations.

Currencies of Abundance

Today's financial and economic systems, all of which use the same architecture of money worldwide, prize *efficiency* but not *resiliency*. Ecological systems science has found that sustainable systems balance resiliency and efficiency, and in fact tend to have more resiliency than efficiency.

Essentially, a greater number of elements in the ecosystem equates to more resiliency. An ecosystem comprised of one type of prey for each type of predator is most efficient. However, a shock to one such species can decimate the whole system. On the other hand, a system comprised of multiple types of predators and prey—as typically happens in nature—means that the ecosystem can take shocks, make adjustments, and come back.[366]

In the absence of resiliency, growth happens faster. Since capitalism prizes growth, it has emphasized efficiency. However, these "booms" of economic growth are always followed by "busts" because the *monetary monoculture* has little ability to handle shocks to the system.

Complementary currencies are a powerful tool to enable economic resiliency because they have different architectures

---

[365] The average income in Curitiba, Brazil is estimated at 30% higher than its neighbor cities. http://www.lietaer.com/2010/09/the-story-of-curitiba-in-brazil/

[366] http://capitalinstitute.org/wp-content/uploads/2015/01/Quantifying-Economic-Sustainability-Goerner-Eco-Econ-2009.pdf

than national money. Characteristics such as interest, fractional reserve, government issuance, and others commonly associated with national money may or may not be included in their design. Other characteristics, particularly those designed to foster certain kinds of behavior deemed desirable, may be engineered into them, thereby stimulating such behaviors without need of regulation or law.[367]

Complementary currencies are often wrongly called "alternative currencies". Properly understood, however, they do not replace but rather *complement* the existing national money, with each type of money doing well what the other does poorly. The result is a *portfolio effect*; a concept crucial to modern finance and not previously understood as applying to monetary architectures.[368]

Complementary currencies are issued on an as-needed basis within a community. The volume and usage of money are determined by a network of voluntary agreements based on trust. (Trust is also essential to other types of money.)

Complementary currencies can greatly leverage the productive power of an economy rapidly and without major disruption, allowing people to do necessary work such as infrastructure repair that would otherwise require new taxes.

They can be created by government agencies or by private groups, at different levels from the local to the transnational. They are amenable to implementation based on either "conservative" (purely private), "moderate" (public/private), or "progressive" (purely public) principles. (Partisans seeing common ground may well join forces for mutual benefit.)

From a political standpoint, complementary currencies are that rarest of ideas: a dream come true for all viewpoints. Properly understood, they threaten no one and offer benefits to all, either directly or indirectly.

Complementary currencies require no new taxes or regulations, and can be created and run through private

---

[367] *The Future of Money*, Bernard Lietaer
[368] https://medium.com/@jonathan_kolber/a-theory-for-global-economic-stability-d1c1a22d61de

initiative. No government involvement is required, though governments could encourage the process of adoption. They bring competition to that last and greatest bastion of monopolies; money.

Complementary currencies also offer an effective, viable tool to help us meet major social needs of the time: better education, environmental restoration, dignified work that pays well (for now), and provision for the needs of children and the elderly.

Here are some highlights of complementary currencies:

- Money is not value neutral, as has generally been assumed by economists. Its design architecture either encourages or discourages specific behaviors. Our present national money design fosters competition, nationalism, production without regard for sustainability, and profit at the expense of other values.

- The unexamined monetary monopoly is far more pervasive and influential than decried monopolies such as cable television, telephone, electric utilities, and so forth. It is indeed economists' great blind spot.

- Complementary currencies are not a new idea; they are a very old idea now being resurrected. One of the greatest societies of antiquity, whose accomplishments in some important ways surpassed our own, apparently relied on complementary currencies working alongside national money.

- A simple complementary currency—bus tokens—transformed Curitiba, Brazil, in one generation, from a place of slums literally knee deep in garbage into the "ecological capital of Brazil" with a standard of living 30% higher than its neighbors. In 2010, it won the Global Sustainable City Award. No government funding, regulation or borrowing was used.

- Switzerland, long heralded as a bastion of capitalism, has a secret. During recessions, many Swiss businesses use the WIR, a complementary currency, alongside the Swiss Franc. The WIR's architecture causes velocity of money—literally, how many transactions happen—

without need for government stimulus via deficit spending, thereby addressing the core practical problem of Keynesian economics.[369] The WIR bolsters Swiss stability. To wit, "from 1948 to 2003, WIR bank transactions were highly countercyclical. This stabilizing effect should be of interest for monetary policy. After all, if a secondary currency can be an effective financial stabilizer, then standard monetary policy is not optimal... More recent data does not change that conclusion."[370]

- Before World War II, Europe was in its own great depression. Germany in particular was suffering from the Versailles reparations. Unemployment stood at 30% in many places. Two communities, one in Germany and one in Austria, implemented local complementary currencies. Within weeks, their unemployment rates had been slashed to 5% and use of these currencies spread—until the central banks wrongly perceived a threat and shut them down. Shortly thereafter, Hitler came to power on a pledge of restoring the economy and national greatness. (According to Dr. Hjalmar Schacht, President of the Reichsbank during the first half of Hitler's reign over Nazi Germany, the Nazi's surge in popularity was primarily fueled by "poverty and unemployment.")[371]

- In Brazil and Switzerland, complementary (AKA social) currencies have been endorsed by the central banks.

- Complementary currencies can be designed to foster specific behaviors. We could, for example, design a currency that promotes "green" behavior. It would function as a voluntary tool alongside national money.

---

[369] Keynes was aware of demurrage but thought inflation to be preferable because, in his view, people would instead choose to use competing types of money without that feature. He advocated that governments inflate during boom times and reverse it during leaner times, but governments generally find the advantages of deficit spending too attractive to reverse.

[370] http://www.ewp.rpi.edu/hartford/~stoddj/BE/WIR_Panel.pdf

[371] *Hitler's Banker: Hjalmar Horace Greely Schacht*, John Weitz

Complementary currencies are discussed much more fully in the book *New Money for a New World*. In order to pass gracefully through the transition period from scarcity to abundance, we can use a tool such as this.

Complementary currencies are certainly not *the* solution to creating a Celebration Society. However, they are an important tool and our job of conversion would be much harder without them. Eventually, since money is a way of allocating scarce resources, we should reach a state of societal evolution where it is no longer needed. But that will take decades if not generations.

The Mortality Option

Accelerating scientific breakthroughs in brain and
longevity research make healthy life extension
increasingly likely.

2015 – 16 State of the Future Report, the Millennium Project

Like other fields where transformation may be imminent, longevity research (AKA life extension) sharply divides doctors and scientists. The goal of life extension is extended healthy life span; not merely more years but more healthy years, with the eventual goal of allowing healthy immortality.

On one side, we find those who dismiss the very possibility as remote. One prominent advocate of this view is Ezekiel Emanuel, a medical ethicist who wrote about why he wishes to die at age 75.[372] Another is Jay Olshansky, professor of public health at the University of Illinois at Chicago. To such scientists, medical practice should be based on a high level of certainty. They favor so-called gold standard therapies that have proven effective and safe in clinical trials with thousands of patients, and they see no such results here.

---

[372] http://www.theatlantic.com/features/archive/2014/09/why-i-hope-to-die-at-75/379329/

This is an understandable position. However, those of us who are experiencing the effects of aging and would prefer to avoid further decay do not have the luxury of such certainty. Given that human trials of anti-aging therapies will take years if not decades, we are making a bet. We can either place a bet to wait, as these doctors recommend, experiencing the generally slow but sometimes catastrophic ravages of aging, or we can try therapies that many scientists and doctors would call experimental.

To the skeptics, such therapies are most likely a waste of money and may carry dangerous side effects that may not show up until significant time has passed.

There is another group of scientists who regard the limited yet promising human anti-aging indications as worthy of action now,[373] especially when added to studies of other animals where healthy lifespan has been increased by 20% or more.[374] The benefits seen in animal studies are reasonably expected to transfer to humans using the same therapies, given that the genes and cellular structures are comparable. Perhaps even more significantly, the anti-aging scientists are being joined by a growing number of self-made billionaires who are backing such research.

There are institutes being founded and funded to understand aging and how to slow, halt or even reverse its ravages. Examples—and the list is growing—include Buck Institute, The University of Michigan, the University of Texas, University of California San Francisco, and the Mayo Clinic.

Google has founded the California Life Company (AKA Calico), whose stated mission is, "We're tackling aging, one of life's greatest mysteries. Calico is a research and development

---

[373] http://www.dailymail.co.uk/sciencetech/article-2011425/The-person-reach-150-alive--soon-live-THOUSAND-claims-scientist.html

[374] http://www.kurzweilai.net/fullerene-c60-administration-doubles-rat-lifespan-with-no-toxicity

company whose mission is to harness advanced technologies to increase our understanding of the biology that controls lifespan. We will use that knowledge to devise interventions that enable people to lead longer and healthier lives. Executing on this mission will require an unprecedented level of interdisciplinary effort and a long-term focus for which funding is already in place."[375]

Noted biotechnology pioneer Craig Venter also has a startup for this purpose. Interestingly, even without new discoveries in longevity and life extension, the human lifespan worldwide has been rising steadily at a rate of 3 months per year for over a century. Though they do not have formal institutes focused upon longevity research, the medical schools at Harvard and Stanford are also actively researching in this area.[376]

Determining that an intervention will significantly increase human lifespan will require either studies going on for decades or a way of measuring human aging on a much shorter time scale. For now, we can explore treatments that have low risk and the potential for efficacy.

There are already some commercially available supplements, practices, and exercise tools that appear to offer some of these benefits. These supplements include resveratrol, glutathione, SOD, and green tea. Practicing a Mediterranean Diet is a helpful practice.[377] A newer example is the dietary supplement TA-65™.[378] Likewise, the PowerPlate™ device (based on technology originally developed to counteract the decaying effects of weightlessness on astronauts) has been

----

[375] http://www.calicolabs.com/

[376] http://www.theatlantic.com/features/archive/2014/09/what-happens-when-we-all-live-to-100/379338/

[377] http://www.resveratrolnews.com/telomeres-governor-of-longevity-or-just-a-marker-of-ageing/1034/

[378] http://www.tasciences.com/clinical-research/

documented to counteract certain conditions associated with aging.[379]

A recently released product from Life Extension Foundation following 15 years of Harvard and other research, NAD+ Cell Regenerator, shows promise of multiple anti-aging benefits.[380] (It is also the basis for an impressively credentialed startup, Elysium, which has multiple Nobel laureates on its team. Like Life Extension, Elysium offers the product as a dietary supplement because of FDA barriers to approval.)[381]

The antiaging supplement TA65 was originally offered at a price of $4,000/month, seeming to validate concerns that this technology would be restricted to the wealthy. However, like almost all technologies, improved manufacturing and economies of scale have caused the price to plunge. It is now $200/month, and a synthetic version (expected in a few years) will in 20 years or so be available in generic form, potentially for much less.

What all of these supplements and exercise technologies have in common is that they increase the length of *telomeres*, the "caps" on the end of our DNA strings that limit how many times the strand can duplicate itself without error.

Indeed, preventing the shortening of telomeres or even lengthening them may prove to be the "holy grail" of longevity research—at least until nanotechnology can repair damage in real time. In addition to substances such as TA-65 that increase telomerase, researchers are finding other methods for potentially doing this. Cancer cells have a mechanism called "alternative lengthening of telomeres (ALT)", which might in future be harnessed for healthy cells.[382]

---

[379] http://powerplate.com/education-training/published-studies

[380] http://www.lef.org//Magazine/2015/1/Next-Generation-Vitamin-Provides-Hope-To-Aging-Societies-Worldwide/Page-01

[381] http://www.technologyreview.com/news/534636/the-anti-aging-pill/

[382] http://www.kurzweilai.net/how-cancer-cells-assure-immortality-by-lengthening-the-ends-of-chromosomes

Further, scientists have now figured out how to use DNA to guide 3D printing and expect to be able to use it to precisely print tissues or even complete organs in future. Should this prove true, when accidents or illness damage or destroy tissue it will become possible to print and insert replacement tissue or whole organs with no risk of rejection.[383]

Thoughtful people will argue that, even if we can repair or replace bodily functions, our brains will remain the "final frontier" of anti-aging research. Here, too, there is good news: researchers at Penn State are so confident of their ability to develop functional medicine to regenerate lost or damaged neurons—even scar tissue in the brain—that they have launched a crowdfunding campaign to take it to readiness for clinical trials.[384]

In the decades ahead, nanotechnology is expected to enable the generation of tiny machines that can traverse our bloodstreams, either strengthening metabolic processes or correcting damage. For example, *respirocytes* are a proposed substitute or enhancement for red blood cells, and expected to be far more efficient. They could potentially enable a person to hold their breath under water for hours, or perform other feats of physical endurance far beyond present limits.[385]

Ray Kurzweil is perhaps the leading advocate of immortality as an option in this century. His argument centers on the fact that the technology to enable cyborgs (a human/machine fusion wherein human capabilities are restored or even enhanced) is already with us and rapidly advancing.

Few people consider a hearing aid to be a "cyborg" enhancement. However, when the hearing aid is permanently implanted, such as a cochlear implant, it becomes such.

---

[383] http://www.kurzweilai.net/dna-guided-3-d-printing-of-human-tissue

[384] http://www.kurzweilai.net/crowd-funding-campaign-hopes-to-accelerate-clinical-trials-of-new-brain-repair-discovery

[385] http://www.kurzweilai.net/respirocytes

Vision is starting to be restored to the blind with implantable eyes. Artificial limbs are becoming more lifelike in their appearance and functionality.[386] Scientists have been able to create workable interfaces between computer chips and brains.

While limited direct neuron-to-chip interfaces have been developed at Max Planck Institute,[387] a different approach appears to be coming. Stanford researchers have prototyped implantable chips that will be smaller than a pen point capable of being remotely powered, executing medical commands and reporting results via radio. The chips are expected to be able to directly interface with the brain, mapping its function in real time.[388]

Even more radically, it may become possible for computers and brains to directly communicate without wires or implants. "When 'magnetoelectric' nanoparticles (MENs) are stimulated by an external magnetic field, they produce an electric field. If such nanoparticles are placed next to neurons, this electric field should allow them to communicate."[389] Already, tests have found that mouse brains respond to this stimulus.

It is unclear how the potential of artificial body parts will match up against increased ability to re-grow damaged or missing parts. It may become an individual decision, based on different trade-offs.

Like the proverbial camel's nose under the tent, the replication of organs' capabilities in machines that can be implanted within living persons is expected to increase, organ by organ, function by function. Each such step will have

---

[386] http://news.co.cr/mind-controlled-robotic-arm-has-skill-and-speed-of-human-limb/21403/

[387] http://www.biochem.mpg.de/478344/01jenmuefro

[388] http://www.kurzweilai.net/a-tiny-ultrasound-powered-chip-to-serve-as-medical-device

[389] http://www.newscientist.com/article/dn27676-20-billion-nanoparticles-talk-to-the-brain-using-electricity.html#

compelling reasons, offering a far better quality of life to certain people who benefit from it. For example, if brain tissue damaged by Alzheimer's or another degenerative condition can be replaced by a chip implant and this is determined to be safe, who will say that this is a bad idea? Yet the net effect, over time, is that we are facing the prospect of full replication—and even enhancement—of human capabilities.

As stated previously, IBM expects to achieve replication of the functions of the human brain in a computer by 2019.[390] (There is no need for cell-by-cell replication; there is great redundancy in brain subsystems.) All of this points to a near-future in which the functionality of the brain is understood, and it is possible to conceive of a time circa mid-century when one's individual brain can be "mapped" and the information content captured and stored in a computer.

Much as an airplane performs the same function of flight as a bird, I expect that AI research will soon lead us to a time when AI's replicate all manner of human intellectual functions, but differently and more efficiently.

At some point soon, Kurzweil and others of similar viewpoint argue, we will have the option of downloading ourselves into computers. This view presumes us to be information patterns rather than immortal souls. (If souls are real, the downloaded creation will be a replica rather than a person—though from an outsider's perspective there may be no discernible difference.) Also, by gradually evolving ourselves from biological organisms to cyborgs, there is every reason to expect that we shall retain our present sense of self.

Barring catastrophe, this would constitute a bona fide immortality option. Another option would be that once decay processes in the body are understood and can be corrected or prevented, people will be able to establish themselves in a body that remains healthy and youthful. This, however, has the disadvantage that an accident could still end one's life. In artificial housing, one could be backed up like files are today.

---

[390] http://www.scientificamerican.com/article/graphic-science-ibm-simulates-4-percent-human-brain-all-of-cat-brain

I expect that both options will be attained and used by many persons in this century, probably with real-time mapping of biological brains via nanobots.

Assuming that biological processes will soon be well-enough understood that aging can be halted or reversed, the remaining causes of death will be war and accidents. The unrelenting focus of news media on frightening information notwithstanding, overall deaths from combat as a percentage of population was *sixty-fold* higher in 1950 than in 2010. Specifically, in 1950 it was one person in 5,000 and in 2010 it was one person in 300,000—worldwide.[391]

Recently, traffic accidents have been killing more people than armed battles.[392] The advent of self-driving vehicles (most commercial flights are essentially automatic already) will reduce deaths from traffic accidents as well. Google's self-driving cars, accompanied by a person only for legal reasons, have logged over 700,000 miles of safe driving on US roads.[393]

Meanwhile, immortality as an option would be far less attractive if one had to experience it with crippling disabilities. Fortunately, there are multiple pathways now being explored towards restoration of function:

- Regeneration of damaged tissues and even limbs. For example, regeneration of severed spinal cord function is starting to be achieved.[394]
- Artificial organs that replace or even surpass natural ones.
- Soon, nanobots capable of traversing the body via the bloodstream and lymphatic system should be able to

---

[391] *Better Angels of Our Nature*, Steven Pinker,
http://www.theatlantic.com/features/archive/2014/09/what-happens-when-we-all-live-to-100/379338/
[392] ibid.
[393] http://www.bbc.com/news/technology-28851996
[394] http://www.iflscience.com/health-and-medicine/nasal-leads-paralyzed-man-walk

monitor for abnormalities in bodily tissues and organs. (Each such nanobot need only monitor for a single cell type). When an abnormality is detected, the cell could be killed or possibly restored to normal function.[395]

The pursuit of youth and beauty are big business today:

- Plastic surgery is a $12 billion industry in America alone.[396] Most of these treatments are purely for beautification.
- Even larger is the US cosmetics industry, at $56 billion.[397] Cosmetics have a powerful influence on how women appear, with men often oblivious to how extreme is the effect.[398]

There will not suddenly be a vast increase in the percentage of bodies that are youthful and beautiful in a Celebration Society. However, over time, we can expect the following to happen:

- Advanced technologies for slowing or even reversal of aging will become widely used.
- Advanced food growing and delivery methods will lead to a general increase in health.
- Advanced techniques, many using stem cells, will allow for rejuvenation of skin and other tissues far beyond plastic surgery.
- Organs, including skin, will be grown in vats or even printed, and then swapped for the aged or otherwise damaged organs in a body.

---

[395] http://www.iflscience.com/health-and-medicine/dna-nanobots-will-seek-and-destroy-cancer-cells

[396] http://abcnews.go.com/Health/Healthday/story?id=4506248

[397] http://www.statista.com/topics/1008/cosmetics-industry/

[398] The video "from ugly to pretty" shows what a 19 year old girl, arguably at the height of her comeliness, does to create such a look.
https://www.youtube.com/watch?v=Y9O5bi9UoFo

- Nanotech and engineered viruses will be used to repair and augment brains, which may eventually be further augmented by nanotech networks that will suffuse cranial tissue and circulate through blood and lymph, communicating in real time with larger computer networks and the Internet.[399]
- Use of bona fide age reversal technologies such as telomerase enhancers, in vivo genetic engineering, nanotechnology scavengers and viruses engineered to adjust one's DNA may emerge.
- Eventually, lifespan may be extended a day for every day lived, with bodies maintained in youthful vigor and beauty. This will constitute immortality for all practical purposes.

Even if physical immortality proves elusive, a Celebration Society is fully possible. Immortality is only an enhancement. Still, assuming it to be forthcoming, all of this will take decades to fully achieve on a widespread basis, and nearly everyone desires the company of beautiful bodies, at least part of the time. Partly this is the correlation between beauty, youth and health which, while imperfect and subject to social variation, explains sexual attraction.

Another part of this is certainly the desire for the life-affirming company of youth, which is a healthy and bonding quality when held in a context of service. Young animals have an infectious exuberance. On the other hand, when someone loves an old person, as many of us do, I submit that what we love is the wisdom, kindness and character this person exudes. We would prefer that their body be healthier and more youthful, if for no other reason than the person's liberation from ailments and physical restrictions.

We are moving from a world in which people have "disabilities" to one in which various augmentations are increasingly common. Soon, artificial eyes will offer better

---

[399] Though a highly intriguing prospect, some leading researchers in nanotechnology do not regard it as feasible.

vision than 20/20 (as LASIK can already do), with ability to see in light frequencies ordinarily invisible to people. Artificial ears, or implants to existing ears, will offer people the acuity of cats. Bones and muscles will be enhanced with capabilities in the direction of the "bionic man".[400]

Sometime later in the 21st century, bodies could apparently become like clothing: we may be able to "put on" a body that we like for a time, or modify an existing body in various ways, either temporarily or permanently. The effects of this on personal identity, social structures and human relationships can hardly be overstated.

Agriculture for Tomorrow

> The new Age of Wonder might bring together wealthy
> entrepreneurs... and a worldwide community of
> gardeners and farmers and breeders, working together
> to make the planet beautiful as well as fertile,
> hospitable to hummingbirds as well as to humans.
>
> ~*Freeman Dyson*

Not all powerful technologies are high-tech. Technology may be viewed as any agency by which knowledge and tools systematically augment human capabilities. Various organisms can become such tools, offering astonishing benefits. For example, fungi can help us address huge problems including cleaning polluted soil, serving as insecticides, treating viruses, protecting homes and generating fuel.[401]

---

[400] http://www.ted.com/talks/aimee_mullins_prosthetic_aesthetics
[401] http://www.ted.com/talks/paul_stamets_on_6_ways_mushrooms_can_save_
the_world

Permaculture

One such technology, permaculture ("permanent agriculture"), combines many ancient understandings of agriculture with recent research findings into a synergistic whole.[402] While not essential to the creation of a Celebration Society, it may prove quite helpful.

Few people have any idea of the power of permaculture. It is a system that takes more time to establish than traditional monoculture agriculture but, once established, continues to produce abundant food with limited maintenance. It can produce, "better food security and higher crop and diet diversity" than conventional alternatives.[403]

In permaculture, certain animals are respected as parts of the system. They are viewed as beneficial throughout their lifecycle. People have a symbiotic rather than parasitic relationship with these animals. In particular, rotational grazing is used to feed herbivores while strengthening the land and plant life. It can prevent or even reverse desertification, a growing crisis worldwide.[404]

Unfortunately, as yet academia has rarely studied permaculture which makes this section of the book speculative. Academics who have studied permaculture report that, "permaculture deserves a closer look."[405] I therefore regard it as too interesting to ignore.

Critics note its lack of efficiency, in that farms are not structured as vast rows of monoculture plantings conducive to factory farming. It is true that yield of a given food product *as measured solely by volume*, is highest with factory farming—until that system depletes the soils and extraordinary measures must be taken.

But what of flavor, freshness and nutritional value? In these aspects, which are what make food desirable (given

---

[402] *Introduction to Permaculture*, Mollison and Holmgren
[403] http://www.theguardian.com/global-development-professionals-network/2013/apr/23/farming-methods-agroecology-permaculture
[404] https://www.youtube.com/watch?v=vpTHi7O66pl
[405] https://pcnpg.files.wordpress.com/2010/03/enviro-anthro.pdf

adequate volume), permaculture wins. It brings the production of food as close to the consumption as possible. Tied into robotic and AI systems, it will provide for timely delivery of the freshest produce. It is a system that integrates human activities into a network of biological (and, in future, robotic) activity. Properly designed and monitored, this network optimizes its own sustainability.

Such networks in proximity to each other create virtuous feedback loops that strengthen each other, exchanging resources and maintaining a broader balance. Mycelium networks, an essential if hidden component of healthy permaculture systems, are discussed in detail below.

Also, as factory farming advances from today's rigid machines that require farming to be adjusted to suit the capabilities of the machinery, with tomorrow's intelligent and flexible machines it will be possible to transfer the advantages automation offers us from factory farming to permaculture. This will offer us the best of both worlds.

Some key benefits of permaculture, whether automated or human-cultivated, include:

- Biodiversity is enhanced. Ecological systems science shows us that sustainable ecosystems combine resiliency with efficiency, emphasizing resiliency more heavily. The key factor promoting resiliency is diversity of species. Without such diversity, anything that kills off a single species can destroy the whole system.
- Reversal of desertification. While acknowledging that desert ecologies have their value, vast deserts have arisen where land was formerly lush and fertile. During its Dynastic period, Egypt was known as the breadbasket of the world. It was a massive grain exporter, and today that is reversed thanks to desertification.[406]

  Such lands could better serve humanity and support rich ecosystems if they were once again green and productive. A vast and growing swath of Africa,

---

[406] http://www.canadiangeographic.ca/blog/posting.asp?ID=425

Asia, Brazil and Australia's interior is desert and I expect that there will be overwhelming support for drastically reducing this desert if it allows for better living conditions, diverse ecosystems and production of abundant water. The simple measure of restoring migratory herds of animals has huge potential.

Further, a project called *Greening the Desert* reports the rapid conversion of desert land that receives almost no rainfall to highly productive land. Mushrooms— never before seen in this area of Jordan—spontaneously appeared. If it can be corroborated by major institutions, this important experiment provides a template for the transformation of deserts.[407]

- Otherwise extending the range of agriculture. Permaculture systems in Austria and elsewhere are growing fruit trees at elevations not normally considered possible. (This is clearly deserving of academic study.)[408]

- Capture and distribution of needed water. Permaculture uses techniques that implant special material into soil, creating an underground sponge. It also directs rainfall into patterns of flow and storage that optimize capture and use.

- Restoration of depleted soils. The capability to self-fertilize on an ongoing basis and even to restore depleted soils to high nutrient and moisture holding levels.

- Defense against erosion. A permaculture system mixes plants with shallow, medium and deep roots in close proximity. Some of these help to secure soil against erosion, while other root systems offer other benefits to the whole.

- Networks facilitate cooperation among plant species. As will be discussed below, underground mycelium networks greatly enhance resource allocation.

---

[407] https://www.youtube.com/watch?v=sohI6vnWZmk (5 minute introduction), http://www.nakedcapitalism.com/2012/05/greening-the-desert.html (textual summation)

[408] *Sepp Holzer's Permaculture,* Sepp Holzer

- Creation of ecovillages. "Ecovillages are human-scale, full featured settlements in which human activities are harmlessly integrated into the natural world in a way that is supportive of healthy human development, and which can be successfully continued into the indefinite future."[409] As I envision it, a Celebration Society city-state may be comprised of such ecovillages, sharing a central city infrastructure that offers economy of scale benefits with the sharing of resources as mutually agreeable.

Though permaculture may sound like a romantic notion looking backward, there are important differences from pre-industrial agriculture as it was often practiced. Unlike much of pre-industrial agriculture, permaculture relies on a deep understanding of biological systems and of ecological systems theory.

Permaculture includes these new understandings:

- It is not so much the amount of rain or irrigation that an area receives that matters as the amount captured.
- A particular kind of charcoal, called *terra prieta* or *biochar*, can be infused into land (e.g. desert, prairie, etc.) early in the process of converting it to perma-culture. Properly placed, it acts as an underground sponge for moisture, and serves as the springboard for a micro-ecology to emerge which then spreads out into the vicinity, gathering and holding more moisture.[410]
- An extinction event millions of years ago wiped out 90% of Earth's plant life. Many plants that survived largely did so through a symbiosis with mycelium, fungal networks that can spread underground in tendrils with far more surface area than plants' own root systems.

---

[409] *Ecovillages: New Frontiers for Sustainability*, Jonathan Dawson
[410] *The Biochar Solution*, Albert Bates

Research shows that plants coexisting with these fungi can enjoy much better water and mineral transportation, and grow faster. The monoculture "plants-as-factories" view of agriculture has deprived plants of these symbiotic allies for generations by killing mycelia with fungicides.[411]

- The correct preparation of land early in the conversion process, including use of deep furrows and strategic placement of rocks, pools and other surface features to control heat and humidity will guide the kind of permaculture ecology that evolves over the next few years. This will generate a new microclimate.

Issues in Agriculture

Advocates for biotechnology, and GMO's in particular, argue that they are doing essentially the same things as previous selective breeding except more efficiently. That said, some of their transplants cross the species barrier in a way that would otherwise be impossible, with unknown wider consequences.[412]

Biotechnologists might take pause from our experience with antibiotics, whose inventor Alexander Fleming warned us that improper use of antibiotics could lead to exactly what we have today: resistant strains of bacteria.[413] Just as bacteria have evolved in response to antibiotics, so too will organisms that share environments with GMO organisms evolve. Already, *superweeds* are becoming a problem.[414]

---

[411] *Mycelium Running*, Paul Stamets
[412] http://news.bbc.co.uk/2/hi/science/nature/8070252.stm,
http://abcnews.go.com/blogs/technology/2012/09/neon-genetically-modified-glofish-could-threaten-natural-species/
[413] http://www.nobelprize.org/nobel_prizes/medicine/laureates/1945/fleming-lecture.pdf
[414] http://www.ucsusa.org/sites/default/files/legacy/assets/documents/food_and_agriculture/rise-of-superweeds.pdf

We simply cannot know the full consequences at this time. As we learn again and again with pharmaceuticals, there are unexpected side effects from new substances. When those substances live, breed, and spread, the consequences can be still greater. The lack of penalties for suppressing publication of adverse studies means that we cannot know if we have a complete picture of documented risks.

GMO's are a complex subject, and some supporters have become opponents and vice versa.[415] GMOs do have the potential to address serious food issues. There is a wider gap between the scientific community, 88% of whom regard GMO's as safe, and the public (only 37% of whom agree) than with any other issue including climate change.[416]

There are forthcoming technological alternatives to GMO's. For example, "controlled environment agriculture" systems can keep pathogens away by maintaining a positive air pressure environment with ionization and limited use of ozone to kill airborne microorganisms, alongside beneficial predators such as dragonflies, ladybugs and if necessary flying microdrones to kill destructive insects. (Currently, such drone systems are prohibitively expensive, but they need not be in a Celebration Society—and once successfully deployed their costs will plunge, like other advancing technologies.)

Robotic farming is already starting to be commercially viable, as evidenced by an indoor Japanese lettuce farm[417] and facilities now being planned and built in the US and Canada. The expected advantages are significant:

> Compared to conventional farms (and depend-
> ing on the exact configuration and technologies

---

[415] http://www.nytimes.com/2015/04/25/opinion/sunday/how-i-got-converted-to-gmo-food.html

[416] http://www.pewinternet.org/2015/01/29/public-and-scientists-views-on-science-and-society/

[417] http://www.digitaltrends.com/cool-tech/japan-automated-factory-lettuce

used), they're around 100 times more efficient in terms of their usage of space, 70-90% less reliant on water, with a lower CO_2 footprint. Foods are grown without the use of pesticides, they're nutrient-rich, and free from chemical contaminants. And because they can be built virtually anywhere, (these) can serve communities where certain foods aren't normally grown.[418]

If certain microorganisms remain a threat to crops, advanced systems of sensors, AI, and robotics can apply pesticides and fungicides in a narrowly targeted manner with close monitoring instead of widespread application.

In such environments, it should be possible to grow all manner of heirloom and other non-GMO plants that do not store or ship well but are otherwise prized for flavor and nutrition, with only limited concern for pests and pathogens.

What we do know about the future of GMO's is that their use (or lack thereof) will be driven more by politics than by science. The same is true of synthetic biology (discussed elsewhere), which is coming fast with the potential to effect even more profound changes. Selective bans on such technologies are already happening in many countries. This will then leave it to countries without such bans to deploy the technology and serve as test environments for the rest of us.

It appears that little of Earth's land area has remained untouched by human activities dating back to ancient times. Such so-called pristine wildernesses as the Amazon rainforest, Serengeti of Africa and Yellowstone in the United States were greatly shaped by human activity.[419] This demonstrates that the notion of some idyllic pre-human condition to which much

---

[418] http://io9.com/how-vertical-farming-is-revolutionizing-the-way-we-grow-1730550597
[419] http://www.bbc.co.uk/programmes/b011wd41

of Earth's land could be returned is essentially a romantic fantasy.[420] The land *has* been transformed (and not just by human activities) since ancient times. The right question is not how to cease modifying the physical environment. It is instead: how can we cultivate ecosystems that respect and preserve the diversity vital to sustainability, consistent with a flourishing human civilization?

This is not only a matter of ethics but one of practicality. Research has found that, "Nearly half of the medicines in use today have their origins in natural products, mostly derived from terrestrial plants, animals, and microorganisms"[421] yet only a small fraction of the organisms on Earth have been studied for medicinal potential.

What treasures, such as potential cures for cancer, diabetes, and other medical crises await us in nature? The cure for the next Ebola, SARS, or even the pandemic long-awaited by epidemiologists such as Dr. Michael Osterholm[422] may lie in wait patiently awaiting discovery—if we do not obliterate it first. In particular it is little known that corals and the organisms that call coral reefs home offer us significant medical benefits.[423] It is likely that further medical uses await discovery.

In the movie *Avatar*, the whole of planet Pandora was networked through an underground system of tendrils connecting the plants and animals. Like other great science fiction, *Avatar* touched on some deep truths. Mycelia are tiny

---

[420] https://www.newscientist.com/article/dn27945-myth-of-pristine-amazon-rainforest-busted-as-old-cities-reappear/

[421] http://www.nature.org/ourinitiatives/habitats/oceanscoasts/explore/coral-reefs-and-medicine.xml

[422] http://www.nejm.org/doi/full/10.1056/NEJMp058068

[423] http://coralreef.noaa.gov/aboutcorals/values/medicine/,
http://www.nature.org/ourinitiatives/habitats/oceanscoasts/explore/coral-reefs-and-medicine.xml,
http://www.smithsonianmag.com/smart-news/sea-coral-makes-excellent-human-bone-grafts-180953121/

hair-like fungus tendrils that can extend for great distances underground, connecting the root systems of various plants in the vicinity. Indeed, the largest living organism ever recorded is a fungal mass spanning 2,200 acres in Oregon. It is over 2,000 years old.[424]

We do not yet know how far mycelium networks can extend in connecting groups of plants within acreage, but it is already clear that they enable exchange of information and, on that basis, water and minerals. This in turn makes the ecosystem of plant life healthier, more resilient and better able to support the animals that coexist as part of that system.

In 2011, as an experiment, I watered a tree on our property with a mycelium mixture. It was, at the time, essentially identical to a tree that had been planted 15 feet away. As of 2015, the mycelium-enhanced tree is 6 feet taller, with significantly more foliage, a wider trunk and more branches. This is admittedly only an anecdote, but it is consistent with what some others who use mycelium soil additives are reporting.

It appears that there are several reasons why we do not presently have a world in which permaculture is the normal way of producing food:

- Government subsidies and regulations that favor factory farming.[425]
- The perception that permaculture cannot produce large quantities of food to meet human and animal requirements. This is fallacious based on several considerations:
  - The same land that produces the food can also serve as dwelling space for humans and animals, including both rural and urban aspects—the use of rooftop gardens and indoor multistory farms with artificial lighting allows for urban farming.

---

[424] *Mycellium Running*, Paul Stamets
[425] Food, Inc.

o There is far more land available than we presently use. For example, roughly 2/3 of the world's land is desert or desertifying[426] and much of it could be reclaimed into lush environments through permaculture. (If the world's population were to have the density of New York City, it would all fit into the State of Texas.)[427]

- The belief that permaculture cannot be mechanized enough to be efficient. This is understandable, when viewed through the lens of factory farming, in which vast tracts of monoculture food (e.g. wheat) are grown and harvested largely by stupid machines run by fewer and fewer people. When viewed through a different lens, the situation is wholly different. Imagine living in a permaculture community where food production is viewed basically as a large cooperative gardening effort. At certain times, neighbors come together to help with particular challenges. Other times, people tend their own gardens and there is a common area.

The common area is tended by human workers—for now. In the future, people who enjoy this activity will be free to continue it. However, the majority of the human workers will be replaced by intelligent robots that can discern one type of food from another, how ripe something is, and whether it is to be picked for harvest or to be thrown away into a biodigester, which recycles all organic wastes of the community into fertilizer, biogas, and usable water.

Some people who favor permaculture think that robot servants should not be part of a permaculture system. This makes no more sense than saying that a machine should not be used to dig the initial furrows, or that other machines should not be used to cut or move trees and large rocks. That said, those who wish to create Celebration Society permaculture systems devoid of advanced technology will be free to do so with like-minded people.

---

[426] https://www.youtube.com/watch?v=vpTHi7O66pI
[427] http://persquaremile.com/2012/08/08/if-the-worlds-population-lived-like/

Within decades, the costs of these intelligent robots—including human-level tactile capabilities, senses and judgment—will fall enough that people will even use robots to tend their home gardens. Then and forever more, the growing of food will become primarily a hobby for people and a requirement for machines.

This is not fanciful talk. All of the elements of this scenario already exist or are on the drawing boards.

Permaculture is also essentially a *local* system of production: local production of food, building materials, and even water and energy. Local production can be locally recycled, through the use of composting and *biodigesters*.

By organizing communities on the basis of permaculture principles, with plastics and fuel derived from carbon neutral sources such as hemp, the pressure for resources to be harvested wholesale and unsustainably is diminished. (Such plastics can be fabricated to be biodegradable, as desired.) The pressure to strip mine mountain tops, clear cut forests, and similarly ravage the environment will diminish as more and more communities are organized in this manner.

We will still need metals, rare earth elements and other minerals that are not necessarily local in origin. However, advanced technologies will increasingly make these available from recycling, seawater, asteroids and—ultimately—harvesting and recycling via nanotechnology. Also, transportation of materials and products from one locale to another can be a carbon neutral activity thanks to future energy sources.

Friends, family and I can all attest to the distinction between permaculture organic produce and regular organic produce. The permaculture flavors are more complex and interesting. Presumably—and here I am speculating—the mycelium network and other permaculture techniques enable these plants to either generate unique phytonutrients or gather more and different trace minerals into their fruits and vegetables.

I will further speculate that these flavor differences may correlate to some as yet undiscovered health benefits. (This is but one of many examples of research that I expect a Celebration Society to undertake.) Regardless of that, permaculture produce will command higher prices than conventional organic produce—thereby creating another revenue source for a Celebration Society using these principles.

Permaculture-based communities tend to embrace values of sustainability and respect for nature. While these are a good start, more is needed for a comprehensive and stable Celebration Society.

High-tech Food Production

One out of seven people doesn't get enough to eat, and the worst harm is to children. Over 5 million children die annually due to malnutrition-related issues. Coastal fishing has been ruined in the USA and other places by fertilizer runoff, and bottom trawling is destroying an area of the ocean floor the size of Russia each year.[428]

Currently, 70% of the fresh water on Earth is used for growing food. Even apart from abundant sources of clean water (as described below), precision agriculture techniques (including monitoring of all ambient conditions for crops) will lower this by 35 – 40% with a 25% increase in production—and this is without such radical advances as closed multi-story farming systems. Precision agriculture will be possible for the same reason that universal surveillance is coming: sensors will be very cheap and small, easily produced in huge quantities.

One major problem with food production is insufficient arable land. One-third of the world's land area is deserts,[429] which do not produce food. As discussed elsewhere, it appears that permaculture techniques can convert deserts to highly productive food systems by capturing the water that falls and then gradually creating their own microclimates that recycle much of the water.

---

[428] *Abundance: the Future is Better than You Think,* Diamandis and Kotler
[429] http://www.universetoday.com/65639/what-percentage-of-the-earths-land-surface-is-desert/

Apart from permaculture, multistory food factories can use artificial sunlight to grow food as required. One promising design, not yet to my knowledge prototyped on a multistory basis, are closed *aquaponics* systems that use fish such as tilapia to produce fertilizer and protein, while growing plants both for human consumption and to feed the fish.[430] In the next decade or two, it will be possible to make these factories run robotically under AI supervision.

Beyond this, lab grown meat has been prototyped, including the world's first $200,000 hamburger. Like all new technologies, the prototype is far more expensive than later production, and research shows that in future lab-grown meat will be far less expensive in water, feed, physical footprint, waste products and eventually even cost per pound than so-called *factory farming*,[431] a system that has the following detriments:

- Antibiotics must be used to keep these animals, packed in crates like sardines, from dying of epidemics, and the result has been an upsurge in antibiotic resistant bacteria, contributing to a human health crisis.
- The excrement from these animals ruins local eco-systems and waterways.
- The meat often contains residues that are unhealthy to eat.
- The conditions in which these animals live would be called torture if applied to people. They do experience physical pain, and some recent research suggests that non-human mammals may have emotions similar to what we do.[432]
- Enormous quantities of water are required.

Lab-grown meat has none of these problems, being simply cells fed a nutrient bath and grown on scaffolding into desired

---

[430] http://ag.arizona.edu/azaqua/ista/ISTA9/FullPapers/Rakocy1.doc

[431] https://www.youtube.com/watch?v=waro4LJDZvU

[432] http://www.theatlantic.com/health/archive/2014/04/does-your-dog-or-cat-actually-love-you/360784/

shapes. Further, vegan meat substitutes now offer the look and texture of real meat, with some offering similar flavors as well.

Cutting Edge Solutions to Other Problems

There are, of course, a multitude of problems besetting humanity. Not all are easily solved. However, some of the great problems are far closer to a permanent solution than most people now believe possible. Here, I will touch upon these— with the understanding that most of these technological solutions did not exist even a decade ago.

Abundant Fresh Water

There is no shortage of water on Earth. The shortage—and it is increasing—is one of clean, fresh water (AKA potable) rather than dirty or salty water.

Water crises are widely foretold in this century. Elsewhere, I discuss in general terms how abundant clean energy allows for purification of water through reverse osmosis (RO). Already, this is producing 20% of the water consumed by Israeli households. By 2016, 50% of Israeli water will be produced this way, at a cost of 58 US cents/cubic meter, or 1,000 liters, which represents the average Israeli per capita weekly water consumption.[433]

This same technology can be deployed elsewhere as needed. Reverse osmosis is being enhanced with nanotech filters. Further, radical and complete localized solutions to water production that do not need much energy are at hand.

Legendary inventor Dean Kamen has invented the Slingshot, a water purification system the size of a dormitory refrigerator. Input any kind of water and out comes pharmaceutical grade water. It can purify 250 gallons a day using the

---

[433] MIT Technology Review c/o *Future Energy eNews*, March 2015.

energy of a hair dryer. Further, the power source is an extremely rugged Stirling cycle engine that can burn any organic material—for example, cow dung, which is commonly used as fuel in India. In addition, the device will clearly have important medical uses in remote places.[434]

A portable technology—at least for drinking water—comes to us thanks again to nanotechnology. Engineer Michael Pritchard devised the Lifesaver bottle in response to Hurricane Katrina, when even the US government was unable to provide adequate drinking water.

With a hand pump and a filter, this device looks like many others. The magic is in the filter. Using nanotechnology, its pores are only 15 nanometers, small enough to block even viruses, along with all other pathogens. A single handheld unit's filter is good to produce 6,000 liters of clean water from any available water source, and it automatically shuts itself down when the filter fails. A pallet full of jerry can units can produce 1 million liters of water.[435] The cost, the company informed me, is 57 cents a day for four people—less than 15 cents a day per person. According to Pritchard's calculations, everyone on Earth can now be provided with ample clean water for drinking and cooking for $20 billion.[436]

All types of commonly available water can be input to the system. $20 billion may sound like a lot, but when the case is made that this is cheap compared to the benefits in social stability, longevity and slashing human diseases by about 50%, it seems likely that the funds will be found—if not all at once then in stages. With an optional carbon disc, the unit can also remove heavy metals and endocrine disrupting hormones.[437]

---

[434] http://www.slingshotdoc.com/about-slingshot-dean-kamen/
[435] http://www.lifesaversystems.com/lifesaver-products/lifesaver-jerrycan
[436] http://blog.ted.com/michael_pritcha/
[437] http://www.lifesaversystems.com/

In addition to providing new sources of clean water, technology can prevent water wastage. For example, old and damaged plumbing and transportation pipes waste 20% of the clean water in the US alone. New nanomaterials will allow the replacement of these pipes and all new pipes with self-repairing models, eliminating this waste.[438]

Sensor arrays will enable smart water management systems, wherein as soon as a leak is sprung its location and severity will be known and it can be flagged for repair based on urgency. IBM is developing these systems right now.[439]

A nanotech-based new type of sand captures water in desert soil, decreasing use by 75%, reducing desertification and potentially helping alongside permaculture techniques to reverse deserts into productive areas.[440] Terra prieta, a special type of carbon, performs a similar function.

Dead zones exist in coastal areas around the world where major rivers deposit into oceans. Research by mycologist Paul Stamets and Battelle Memorial Institute has found that mycelium fungus can assist in the reclamation of waters contaminated by hydrocarbons such as oil spills and factory farming effluent.[441]

Ubiquitous Access to Information

The lack of access to the world's knowledge has made it harder for poor and third-world people to advance, whether in education or knowledge of how to price and sell their products. Universal internet access will address this.

---

[438] http://www.digitaltrends.com/cool-tech/self-healing-plastic-inspired-by-squid-teeth

[439] http://www.ibm.com/smarterplanet/us/en/water_management/nextsteps/solution/J103636F12674V34.html

[440] http://phys.org/news/2009-02-hydrophobic-sand-combat-shortages.html

[441] http://www.ted.com/talks/paul_stamets_on_6_ways_mushrooms_can_save_the_world

In 2011, Huawei began sales of an $80 Android smartphone, distributing 210,000 units in the first 6 months.[442] Likewise, the Indian government has partnered with Datawind to introduce a $35 Android smartphone with a 7" screen.[443] Datawind is now exporting these as cheap tablet devices.[444]

With such units offering increasingly ubiquitous broadband connections and powered by inexpensive solar systems, people all over the world will have access to the internet, online virtual banking enabling savings and investment, as well as the means to locate and communicate with like-minded individuals elsewhere. Seen in this light, the so-called Arab Spring may be only the first wave of internet-enabled social changes to come.

For this to happen, we will need widespread deployment of wireless broadband internet. Google and Facebook are teaming up to bring broadband to the world via balloons and drones.[445]

Rapid, Automated Production On-demand

3D printers are now enabling businesses to accelerate or reduce the costs of product development and business processes. They are also allowing the production of superior consumer products, especially in vital medical devices. These benefits are expected to rapidly proliferate across the world. Here are some of the key benefits already realized:[446]

- Reducing inventory costs. Holding inventory is costly. 3D printing production increasingly enables manufacturers to make what is needed, when and where it is needed.

---

[442] http://techrice.com/wp-content/uploads/2012/08/Chinas-Smartphones-Have-the-Whole-World-Talking-FD.docx
[443] http://www.forbes.com/sites/peterhigh/2014/11/19/the-35-tablet-that-is-changing-the-education-landscape-in-india/
[444] http://venturebeat.com/2011/10/26/aakash-android-tablet-exclusive/
[445] http://www.technologyreview.com/news/542161/facebooks-internet-drone-team-is-collaborating-with-googles-stratospheric-balloons/
[446] http://www.forbes.com/sites/ricksmith/2015/06/29/7-ways-3d-printing-is-already-disrupting-global-manufacturing/

- <u>Rapid and inexpensive prototyping</u>. Historically, Ford Motors needed to invest 6 months and 6 figures in developing each mold for a prototype engine. Now, using 3D printing they need only 4 days and cost $4,000.

- <u>Customization of products on demand.</u> Now, if you need a knee replacement your surgeon can scan it and 3D print a perfect replica. Likewise, Invisalign is enabling ultra-precise tooth alignment using 3D printing.

- <u>Extending product life.</u> Historically, spare parts for a product disappeared from production a decade or so after it was made. Now, with digital design files, those parts can be printed on demand as required.

- <u>Enabling innovation.</u> Because 3D printing enables geometries that are not possible via any other manufacturing method, many new types of product designs are becoming possible.

- <u>More efficient designs.</u> Instead of machining multiple parts which must then be assembled, a 3D printer can print the assembled parts as a single part. This results in stronger and more efficient parts. For example, GE replaced a fuel injection system requiring 21 parts with one 3D printed part that was five times stronger, had 15% greater fuel efficiency and saved over $1 million per plane.

According to TechCast Global:

> [3D printing] allows three-dimensional printing of prototypes, products, and even living tissues by building them up from thin layers of material. Sophisticated software ... controls the printer's moveable platform and nozzle. The nozzle deposits powdered metal, plastic, or living cells, mixed with a liquid binder or sintered with a laser, and the process repeats layer after layer.[447]

---

[447] *3D Printing*, TechCast Report, 11/20/14.

The range of applications and precision of 3D manufacturing are both rapidly increasing. Although printing small parts has been a common use, much larger objects can now be constructed. Further, given that these printers are far cheaper than massive industrial manufacturing operations, the potential exists for much more decentralized, fast and cheap creation of products.

Prices continue to plunge. They are now about $1,000 for a personal unit suitable for small applications. Larger ones suitable for 3D printing of, for example, homes or vehicles, are considerably more expensive but still much cheaper than entire factory setups. One Chinese company is using a large 3D printer to build up to 10 homes a day on-site, much faster than conventional home construction.[448]

Further, items are created on-demand, one at a time, and therefore this offers the potential for far greater customization of products.

In what may become the ultimate refinement of 3D printing, nano-scale printing is being achieved using laser lithography. The technique is suitable for nano-scale objects such as tiny machines.[449] While not needed for most macro-scale products, nano-scale will enable complete precision when required.

Multiple colors, metals and carbon fibers are being added to the materials suitable for 3D printing. MIT recently announced a 3D printer that can mix up to 10 materials in a single printing process.[450] Should 3D printing become feasible for a wide variety of materials together being fabricated into individual products, this could actually become the basis for printing on-demand a huge variety of physical products.

The range of products that can be made onsite, on-demand and customized to user specifications is rapidly expanding. To the extent that 3D printing can do all of this,

---

[448] https://www.youtube.com/watch?v=u5W7WSYKtXo
[449] http://www.kurzweilai.net/microscopic-3d-printing
[450] http://www.engadget.com/2015/08/24/mits-newest-3d-printer-spouts-10-materials-at-a-time/

and at a price competitive with conventional manufacturing, it will empower people to meet their needs for physical objects with less need for supportive infrastructure, faster and in a more sustainable manner. This will enable people who presently cannot afford infrastructure such as factories and specialized production equipment to leapfrog into 21st century manufacturing.

3D printing should also enable local manufacture of all manner of finished products, without much need for transportation of components or assemblies. That will enhance local self-sufficiency.

Not all production will or should be solely local. For quite a while, I expect that extremely capital-intensive, IP-rich manufacturing such as computer chips and many other high-tech items will not be part of the Celebration Society production system but will be purchased in exchange for national money. When there are enough Celebration Societies to justify such shared infrastructure, that may change.

Abundant Lighting and Off-grid Electricity

Currently, much of the world uses dirty, dangerous, expensive, and inefficient kerosene for lighting. They do so because they lack access to an electric grid. Much as cellular communications have been enabling third world nations to leapfrog old telecommunications infrastructure, new systems combining solar panels, lithium batteries, and LED's are poised to enable the same with lighting (and other) household energy needs.

Such systems are now commercially viable at an installation cost of about $140 per household, and are 100 times more efficient at generating light than kerosene lamps. Further, innovative financing mechanisms are being combined with the technology to make this happen. It would be possible to electrify the entire off-grid world by 2025.[451]

---

[451] http://www.huffingtonpost.com/skoll-foundation/how-to-light-the-off-grid_b_7564126.html

CO2 Emissions

While other greenhouse gases, especially methane, pose separate risks of climate change, carbon dioxide (CO2) remains the focus of most concern. A recent invention from Lawrence Livermore Laboratories may offer an inexpensive, retrofittable and reusable solution for power plant emissions— which represent much of the CO2 emissions on the planet. Indeed, "Power plants are the largest source of carbon pollution in the U.S., accounting for roughly one-third of all domestic greenhouse gas emissions."[452]

The Livermore invention uses nanotechnology in combination with sodium bicarbonate (baking soda). Tiny beads are exposed to smokestack emissions, for example from coal power plants, and capture the CO2. The beads can then be heated to extract the CO2 and reused.

Says Livermore:

> Drawbacks of current carbon dioxide capture methods include corrosivity, evaporative losses and fouling. [This method offers] rapid and controlled carbon dioxide uptake and release over repeated cycles... an order-of-magnitude increase in carbon dioxide absorption rates for a given sorbent mass. The microcapsules are stable under typical industrial operating conditions and may be used in supported packing and fluidized beds for large-scale carbon capture.[453]

Even more radically, chemists at George Washington University have developed a process to convert atmospheric CO2 into carbon nanofibers. "Such nanofibers are used to make strong carbon composites, such as those used in

---

[452] http://www2.epa.gov/carbon-pollution-standards

[453] http://cleanleap.com/could-these-tiny-beads-be-solution-stopping-co2-emissions,
http://www.nature.com/ncomms/2015/150205/ncomms7124/full/ncomms7124.html #compounds

the Boeing Dreamliner, as well as in high-end sports equipment, wind turbine blades and a host of other products," said Stuart Licht, Ph.D., team leader.

The process reportedly is quite efficient, "using only a few volts of electricity, sunlight, and a whole lot of carbon dioxide." Fibers build up on a metal plate, from which they can be periodically scraped and then sold.

Licht estimates electrical energy costs of this "solar thermal electrochemical process" to be around $1,000 per ton of carbon nanofiber product. That means the cost of running the system is hundreds of times less than the value of product output. At this time, the system is experimental. Licht's biggest challenge will be to ramp up the process and gain experience to make consistently sized nanofibers.

Most importantly, Licht calculates "with a physical area less than 10 percent the size of the Sahara Desert, our process could remove enough CO2 to decrease atmospheric levels to those of the pre-industrial revolution within 10 years." Such an extraordinary claim must be replicated by others to be fully credible. It is another potentially game-changing technology for the planet.[454]

The Mother Plant

> If cannabis were discovered in an Amazon rainforest today, people would be clambering to make as much use as they could out of the potential benefits of the plant.
>
> ~ *Donald L. Abrams, MD*

---

[454] http://www.kurzweilai.net/diamonds-from-the-sky-approach-to-turn-co2-into-valuable-carbon-nanofibers

The plant's Latin name means the 'useful hemp'.
Species designated sativa (useful) are usually among
the most important of all crops.

~*Andrew Weil, MD*

This section may upset people who hold
particular views about the *cannabis sativa*
plant. I don't wish to be unnecessarily
upsetting, but I would be doing a disservice
were I not to offer explanation of the many non-
psychoactive benefits this plant is poised to
offer in helping us to create a Celebration
Society. That said, it is a useful but not a
necessary resource.

The Scarcity Game has not been kind to mothers. Misogyny is rampant throughout the world, often justified on selectively interpreted religious grounds or even biology. This is despite the evidence that two of the most successful civilizations in human history, Dynastic Egypt and the Central Middle Ages, had equality of the sexes—and that present-day societies that embrace females as leaders tend to be more successful as well.[455] In this section, I will explore why I believe that cannabis should help to enable a Celebration Society and be re-branded as, "the Mother Plant".

Cannabis serves as a cautionary tale, but not in the way many people think. Demonized in the 1930's by a campaign of willful disinformation, it became a poster child for how spheres of monetary influence, unchecked by an informed citizenry, can wipe out huge potential benefits to humankind.

---

[455] http://www.wsj.com/articles/a-better-world-run-by-women-1425657910

In his epic book *1984*, George Orwell depicted a society in which falsehood becomes truth whenever the government so decrees. America came close to an Orwellian reality with its campaign against cannabis—subsequently adopted in most of the world due to America's influence and, frankly, its bribes.

Cannabis offers a superior way to do many useful things. Henry Ford once built a car of plastic made largely from cannabis hemp, and it was so durable that there is a famous photo of the car withstanding an axe blow by Mr. Ford himself. During World War II, the United States government was so desperate for certain materials that it created a short film advocating the aggressive, widespread growth of cannabis. It was called, *Hemp for Victory*.

Characteristics of the Mother Plant

What characteristics would qualify something to be called the Mother Plant? Such a plant would need to, essentially by itself, meet all the basic needs of humanity. Such a plant would provide:

- Food in its seeds and oil—nutritionally balanced such that one could eat it alone for long periods and survive in good health.
- Energy that is clean and abundant.
- Clothing that can be either sturdy and strong or silk-like.
- Housing by being readily made into solid building materials, with the added benefits of thermal mass, as well as insect, mold and fungus repellent qualities.
- Environmental sustainability by replacing petro-chemical products as sources of various plastics—with controllable biodegradation.
- Environmental remediation, improving soil where planted.
- Health benefits ranging from preventative to curative, including management of many types of pain, treatment of degenerative diseases and conditions including some of the most difficult neurological conditions, helping with the treatment of many cancers without

231

harmful side effects, prevention of stroke damage,[456] a powerful combination of antioxidants and an effective treatment for depression, without significant harmful side effects when used responsibly.

- Protection against the use of dangerous drugs, such as alcohol. To wit, "A survey of evidence showed a correlation between increased marijuana use and less alcohol use for people ages 18 to 29 … (causing) a reduction in the social harms resulting from alcohol use. Reducing traffic injuries and fatalities is potentially one of the most important."[457]

Cannabis offers all of these benefits. Over 10,000 years ago cannabis was apparently the first cultivated crop[458] and it is believed by certain scholars to have been used in early Christian (and possibly Vedic or Hindu) anointing ceremonies. In modern Hinduism, cannabis use is fundamental for millions of Shiva worshippers. Cannabis has been found buried in ancient Chinese tombs, as well as ancient sites excavated in Greece and Egypt.[459]

Cannabis hemp was cultivated very widely in the early USA. Presidents Washington and Jefferson cultivated it. Benjamin Franklin made paper from it, some of which was used for US founding documents. The original "Stars and Stripes" was reportedly sewn from hemp cloth.

While some seek to differentiate hemp from "psychoactive" forms of cannabis, they are both *cannabis sativa*. (Or, less commonly, *cannabis indica*.) THC is always present; cannabis

---

[456] Per the US Government's own patent on medical uses of cannabis, US 6630507.

[457] http://www.nytimes.com/2013/10/27/us/few-problems-with-cannabis-for-california.html, http://alcalc.oxfordjournals.org/content/49/3/292.abstract

[458] What if Cannabis Cured Cancer?

[459] http://www.thestar.com/business/tech_news/2008/11/27/2700yearold_marijuana_found_in_chinese_tomb.html

with a very low (typically less than 3/10 of 1%) THC content is generally legal and called hemp. Further, raw cannabis is not psychoactive; the THCa form is naturally present in raw cannabis and only when heated does it become the psychoactive THC.[460]

Hemp can also be crushed to produce a variety of useful oils. It offers a light green food oil with a superb nutrient profile. Hemp seed oil was at one time a primary ingredient in exterior and interior oil-based paints. The use as fuel oil is noted for the lack of refinement required, making it an ideal diesel fuel replacement. So-called *hash oil* is much darker and richer in medicinal properties, depending on its cannabinoid profile.

Cannabis contains approximately 400 different compounds, only a few of which have been studied. These few offer an astounding array of medical benefits, according to journal literature. For example, high CBD oil—low in THC, and therefore legal for shipment almost everywhere—is useful all by itself in treating multiple conditions.[461]

Cannabis hemp is a rapidly growing, vigorous shrub that can flourish in most types of soils—a wider range than many other food crops. It actually enhances the soil in which it grows. It is four times more productive of woody pulp and fiber than trees, which makes it an ideal replacement for paper, woven products and certain construction materials, thereby saving forests and their ecosystems. As discussed elsewhere, it is also an excellent source of biomass.

Those who saw the movie *The Graduate* will recall when the wise elder whispered his career advice to the young graduate in the form of a word. His word was, *plastics*.

Today, he would almost certainly whisper a different word, *graphene*. This recently discovered, miraculous form of carbon offers a staggering array of benefits, with more being discovered. (Some of these benefits are covered elsewhere in this book.)

---

[460] http://www.ncbi.nlm.nih.gov/pubmed/19728318
[461] http://www.projectcbd.org/

A part of the Mother Plant that often goes to waste—the inner hairlike fiber—has recently been discovered to offer a simpler equivalent of graphene for at least one vital application. An American Chemical Society paper describes hemp fibers as "graphene like",[462] and it is apparently far cheaper to manufacture in quantity.[463]

The Mother Plant is not required for a Celebration Society. Nevertheless, it will make the achievement of such a society easier in multiple ways.

Many cannabis users report that its use enhances their ability to dissolve unwanted social barriers and, especially, to enhance intimacy. However, some report paranoia as well—but it is hard to distinguish plant-induced paranoia from paranoia induced by the authentic possibility that the government will use all manner of entrapment and may lock the user away for years with rapists merely for enjoying this plant.

Why is such an amazing plant not widely cultivated throughout the world?

The Past and Future of Cannabis Prohibition

While cannabis has a long and storied history of cultivation and use throughout much of the world, our current Prohibition originated in America.

In the early years of North American colonization and of the American Republic, cannabis cultivation was highly encouraged and, at times, legally required. Until made illegal, cannabis was widely used as medicine.[464]

During WWII, the US Government needed massive new sources of fiber for rope and other uses. The US government

---

[462] http://cen.acs.org/articles/91/web/2013/05/Energy-Storing-Nanomaterial-Made-Hemp.html.

[463] http://www.bbc.com/news/science-environment-28770876, http://www.techtimes.com/articles/12963/20140814/weed-not-graphene-may-be-a-better-supercapacitor-what.htm.

[464] https://www.fas.org/sgp/crs/misc/RL32725.pdf

created and promoted the film *Hemp for Victory*, and as a result 400,000 acres of hemp were planted to meet its needs for war resources.[465]

Following the war, the US government flipped its hemp advocacy upside down; from *Hemp for Victory* to a film named *Reefer Madness*. (Indeed, an attempt was evidently made to collect and destroy all copies of *Hemp for Victory*. One copy survived in the Library of Congress.) Subsequently, *Reefer Madness* was included in high school curricula across the country. What happened?

According to both the *Vaults of Erowid* (a federally approved 501(c)(3) non-profit educational organization that provides information about psychoactive plants and chemicals) and an article in a 1938 issue of *Popular Mechanics,* a new invention called a *decorticator*, would have allowed far more efficient use of hemp to produce paper and other fibrous products, thereby eliminating paper mills and trees grown for this purpose. It would have threatened significant business interests.[466]

(The article, entitled "New Billion-dollar Crop", mentioned that "[hemp] is used to produce more than 5,000 textile products, ranging from rope to fine laces, and the woody 'hurds' remaining after the fiber has been removed contain more than seventy-seven per cent cellulose, and can be used to produce more than 25,000 products, ranging from dynamite to Cellophane.")

This was the final salvo in the battle for control of America's paper production. Randolph Hearst, the newspaper and lumber baron, reportedly feared a major loss of revenues and aligned with his son-in-law Harry Anslinger, an opportunistic minor government official. Anslinger hated Mexicans and blacks, and demonized cannabis as "marijuana"—a denigrating reference to its Hispanic name.

---

[465] http://www.naihc.org/hemp_information/content/hemp.mj.html

[466] www.erowid.org/plants/cannabis/cannabis_culture11.shtml, also *The Emperor Wears No Clothes: Hemp and the Marijuana Conspiracy* by Jack Herer, and Reprint of *Popular Mechanics* article from www.globalhemp.com/1938/02/new-billion-dollar-crop.html

He rallied support against this "marijuana" drug being imported from Mexico and the Caribbean, so that many of the legislators who voted for his bill did not realize that they were criminalizing the hemp plant grown in their own gardens and communities. To strengthen support, Anslinger and his cronies lied to the US Congress about the American Medical Association (AMA) position. In 1937, the AMA actually opposed Prohibition, regarding cannabis as a safe drug.[467]

In 1972, the National Commission on Marijuana and Drug Abuse recommended that small-scale distribution and possession of cannabis for personal use be made legal once again. Since then:

- Over 12 million Americans have been arrested for marijuana possession.
- US taxpayers have spent over $20 billion dollars enforcing criminal marijuana laws.
- One in eight inmates incarcerated for drug crimes is serving time for cannabis, costing over $1 billion per year.[468]

Almost half a century later, America seems poised to finally adopt the Commission's simple recommendations. The medical science is clear—cannabis prohibition has no scientific basis. Even if use of the plant may have some deleterious effects, those pale in comparison to the effects of alcohol and tobacco, neither of which offers the manifold benefits of cannabis.

Does Cannabis Prohibition keep us safer? Not according to L.E.A.P. (Law Enforcement Against Prohibition). Its membership consists of retired judges, sheriffs, police officers, DEA agents, and prosecutors. Each of these persons became disenchanted with what they call the "Failed War on Drugs." They share a conviction that the right solution is not endless money spent on paramilitary operations to fight drug gangs—

---

[467] http://www.marijuanalibrary.org/AMA_opposes_1937.html
[468] http://norml.org/component/zoo/category/celebrating-35-years-of-failed-pot-policies

gangs which literally could not finance their existence without Prohibition.

Neither, in LEAP's view, should America have a law enforcement/prison system that gives huge bounties to law enforcement officials for drug busts and that has created a multi-billion dollar private prison system, with a higher per capita rate of incarceration than any other Western nation. Rather, LEAP stands for regulated use and treatment for drug users who have problems—essentially, the program recently adopted in Colorado and Washington State, though to date only for cannabis.

Perhaps the harshest indictment of the War on Drugs came in an interview with a former Mexican drug cartel member, a senior Mexican intelligence official, and a veteran American counter-narcotics agent—together with 75 years of drug trade experience. Among the comments made was this, "The U.S. government, like the Mexican government, finds itself fighting against a certain bad guy one day and alongside him the next.... There's no real fight against drugs. It's all a perverse game of interests."[469]

Recent research underscores previous findings that cannabis is a remarkably safe herb to consume, at least for adults.[470] Nevertheless, the US government's Drug Enforcement Administration (DEA) continues to list cannabis as Schedule I, meaning that it has no recognized medical use and is equally dangerous to heroin. Who seriously believes this? Even the former head of the DEA, Michelle Leonhardt, was unable to assert this under oath, ducking the question repeatedly in testimony before Congress.[471]

---

[469] http://www.theatlantic.com/international/archive/2015/07/chapo-mexico-drug-war/398927/

[470] http://www.salon.com/2015/02/23/study_marijuana_is_even_less_dangerous_than_we_thought/

[471] http://www.huffingtonpost.com/2012/06/21/michele-leonhart-dea-crack-heroin-marijuana_n_1615270.html

Anyone who still favors Prohibition might wish to consider this question: where is the crime wave in Colorado? Where is the surge in hospitalizations or in driving accidents? Murders and burglaries dropped sharply in Denver County following Colorado legalization.[472] Opponents have scrounged for "evidence" supporting their prejudices.

For example, in 2014 a foster parent locked a child in a car in order to be free to smoke pot. The incident was widely discussed; far beyond an ordinary murder. While despicable and tragic, the crime happened before the criminal got high. Opponents have even cited a satirical *Onion* story about deaths on Day 1 of legal pot in Colorado as if it were factual, and they made much of a tourist who consumed more than 6 times the recommended dosage and then fell off a balcony with unsafely low railings. Much as the Women's Christian Temperance Union is today remembered as a historical oddity, I expect future generations will likewise remember supporters of Cannabis Prohibition.

The approach of regulated access has been tried and proven successful in Portugal in recent years.[473] It has now arrived in the US and, so far, there have been no overdose deaths or other egregious societal effects. Since the US has been leading the world's antidrug efforts, the end of US prohibition will presage a new day for cannabis on planet Earth. Ironically, it is the uses of cannabis as a medicinal drug that may well most powerfully drive this change.

Medical Uses

For decades, the USA banned research into the medical uses of cannabis, which has recently been eased for selected research projects. The United States Department of Health and Human Services filed and obtained a patent on medical uses of cannabinoids, US 6630507. At the same time,

---

[472] http://www.denverpost.com/news/ci_25495907/sharp-drop-homicides-denver-so-far-this-year

[473] http://www.tdpf.org.uk/blog/drug-decriminalisation-portugal-setting-record-straight

cannabis remains a Schedule I drug on the Drug Enforcement Administration's list, meaning a drug with no medical benefits, like heroin. This contradiction remains unexplained.

Nevertheless, during the US research embargo (only partially lifted) the medical uses of cannabis continued to be studied in freer countries. Leading medical scientists were interviewed in the documentary *What if Cannabis Cured Cancer?* Many hundreds of peer reviewed journal studies imply that it may do so, at least in certain cases, along with multiple anecdotes including heartbreaking stories of small children left to die by the limitations of conventional medicine and—apparently—saved by cannabis.

In his documentary *Cannabis Madness* (no doubt a dig at *Reefer Madness*), CNN's Chief Medical Correspondent Sanjay Gupta explores this further. Dr. Gupta attributes the health benefits of cannabis to its CBD compound. There are actually hundreds of cannabinoid molecules in cannabis, and to my knowledge all of those tested to date have shown medical benefits.

There is a 1 in 4 chance that you or someone in your family has or will have cancer.[474] While it is too soon to say that cannabis—not smoked but taken in a more concentrated manner, and not necessarily a psychoactive form—cures cancers, it clearly offers potential for mitigating the side effects of chemotherapy and perhaps even for treating the cancer diseases[475] themselves, with more modest side effects and lower cost than conventional approaches.

While medical science doesn't yet have definitive answers to the efficacy of cannabis against diverse forms of cancer, there is significant evidence suggesting this possibility. My own father suffered from three types of cancer before his

---

[474] http://www.greenmedinfo.com/blog/cancer-ancient-survival-program-unmasked

[475] According to oncologists, "cancer" should not be thought of as a single disease but as an umbrella term for a number of related cellular disorders.

death, and I wonder how many more years we might have shared had the truth been known.[476] How about you and people in your life? Whom have you lost?

Another illness that has recently reached epidemic proportions is diabetes. A recent large study[477] indicates that cannabis is important medicine for treating and managing this pernicious disease. Specifically, in the US over 29 million people are currently diagnosed with diabetes. This is nearly 10 percent of the US population. Further, "Diabetes remains the 7th leading cause of death in the United States (with) a total of 234,051 death certificates listing diabetes as an underlying or contributing cause of death."[478]

Medical marijuana has been the focus of several studies examining potential diabetes treatment. One such study, published in the *American Journal of Medicine,* found that active users of marijuana had a more productive carbohydrate metabolism than people who didn't use marijuana. Murray Mittleman, Associate Professor of Medicine at Harvard and author of the study, said, "(Marijuana users') fasting insulin levels were lower, and they appeared to be less resistant to the insulin produced by their body to maintain a normal blood-sugar level."[479]

The study comprised over 4,657 men and women participating in the National Health and Nutrition Examination Survey between 2005 and 2010. 48 percent had smoked marijuana at least once and 12 percent were current cannabis smokers. The researchers controlled for other factors that might impact diabetes risk, such as gender, income, alcohol use, cigarette smoking and physical activity. Even after these adjustments, the current marijuana users showed fasting insulin levels that were 16 percent lower than those of former users or those who had never used the drug.

---

[476] His last words were, "The book. We've got to finish the book!" (Referring to this book, for which he served as a sounding board.)

[477] http://healthland.time.com/2013/05/21/marijuana-the-next-diabetes-drug/

[478] http://www.diabetes.org/diabetes-basics/statistics/

[479] http://healthland.time.com/2013/05/21/marijuana-the-next-diabetes-drug/

These findings are applicable to both types of diabetes. In Type 1 diabetes, said the authors, a lower fasting level might eliminate the need for an insulin injection at that time. While injections wouldn't be completely eliminated, it could decrease the number needed per day.

It is worth noting that the study did not discriminate between strains of cannabis, and that certain strains have much higher concentrations of certain cannabinoids than do others. Also, smoking delivers much lower doses of cannabinoids than, for example, juicing the raw plant—which also removes the psychoactive effects. Such approaches may yield even better diabetes control.

While many other medical benefits of cannabis have been documented, the potential for alleviation of the cancer and diabetes epidemics alone should warrant major research and the immediate cessation of Cannabis Prohibition.

Likewise, cannabis use results in lower body fat, better BMI readings and similar indicators of superior weight control. All of these appear to be side benefits of the cannabis user's body being better able to process insulin. Published in The American Journal of Medicine, these findings were based on, "...a nationally representative sample of over 4,600 adults."[480]

Some people argue that cannabis renders users dysfunctional. Of course, any drug can do this when used improperly or to excess. But admitted frequent users have included leading public figures such as Carl Sagan, David Letterman, and a host of others who can hardly be called dysfunctional people. (All vertebrate animals have receptors for cannabinoids. In healthy animals, these are produced within the body and known as *endocannabinoids*.)[481]

---

[480] http://www.theatlantic.com/health/archive/2013/05/study-why-pot-smokers-are-skinnier/275846/
[481] What if Cannabis Cured Cancer?

Others argue that it poses a danger to youth or that it is a "gateway" drug. Analysis of drug-related crimes and youth drug use in Colorado, which has legalized recreational marijuana use by adults, indicate that both drop when marijuana is legalized. A Brookings Institution report concluded, "It's too early to judge the success of Colorado's policy, but it is not too early to say that the rollout, or initial implementation, of legal retail marijuana has been largely successful."[482]

Additionally, since alcohol use generally precedes use of cannabis among youth who go on to use "hard" drugs, to make this argument on a logical basis one would have to say that alcohol is a gateway drug.

Medical research cited by the Drug Enforcement Administration's own Administrative Law Judge, Francis Young, in his formal opinion recommending its removal from Schedule I, found cannabis to be remarkably safe. Said Judge Young:

> Nearly all medicines have toxic, potentially lethal effects, but marijuana is not such a substance. Marijuana, in its natural form, is one of the safest therapeutically active substances known to man. By any measure of rational analysis marijuana can be safely used within a supervised routine of medical care.[483]

For all of its benefits, cannabis is like any other useful substance. It can be abused. There is research that indicates heavy, long-term use—in particular, by teenagers—can have lasting detrimental effects on the brain.[484] Similar research indicates that heavy, long-term use of alcohol can have lasting, detrimental effects to not only the brain but many other organs as well.

---

[482] http://www.theatlantic.com/features/archive/2014/08/life-with-legal-weed/375966/

[483] DEA Docket # 86-22, 57.

[484] http://www.northwestern.edu/newscenter/stories/2013/12/marijuana-users-have-abnormal-brain-structure--poor-memory.html

There will always be people who abuse experiences and substances, whether these be gambling, sex, tobacco, alcohol, cannabis, or other things. Those who claim that cannabis is a gateway drug are missing the fact that people who want to escape intolerable circumstances will keep trying things until they find something that enables them to escape. Indeed, the very fact that addictive people move on from cannabis to harder drugs indicates that cannabis isn't offering them the escape that they seek.

Excluding cannabis cultivated to be free of THC, today's cannabis reportedly tends to have a much higher concentration of THC than the plant traditionally had. Maximizing THC has inevitably come at the expense of reducing many of the other 400+ cannabinoids naturally found in the plant—some of which may modulate and regulate the effects of THC.[485] This is yet another consequence of Prohibition. Had the plant remained legal and widely available, there would have been no incentive to aggressively concentrate its high-inducing properties.

Drugs of all sorts can be abused and can have harmful effects. Even excessive aspirin can be harmful. Research published in prestigious journals such as *The Lancet* are raising important questions about the safety of chronic heavy use of cannabis.[486] Such heavy use, which many would characterize as abuse, arises because the user is seeking escape from intolerable circumstances. (See the Rat Park experiments, discussed elsewhere.)

There is an international treaty on controlled substances that prohibits cannabis. However, treaties can be changed—and this one includes a vital exemption for medical uses. For example, during all of the current worldwide regime of cannabis Prohibition Sri Lanka has enjoyed national distribution of cannabis-infused ayurvedic pharmaceutical products on the grounds that they are traditional medicine. I am aware of nothing inherently geographic about such a right; it would

---

[485] http://www.ncbi.nlm.nih.gov/books/NBK230721/
[486] http://www.thelancet.com/pdfs/journals/lanpsy/PIIS2215-0366(15)00167-4.pdf

seem that other nations could offer those same medicines. Further, cannabis was a widely prescribed medicine in America until the 20th century. That, too, is tradition.

Cannabis may be efficacious against some of the most pernicious diseases for which there is presently no treatment. Currently, ALS (Lou Gehrig's disease) has an average survival time of 3 years, with no cure or effective treatment in mainstream medicine. Given that medical researchers have been prohibited from studying the plant, it is noteworthy that some said this:

> Based on the currently available scientific data, it is reasonable to think that cannabis might significantly slow the progression of ALS, potentially extending life expectancy and substantially reducing the overall burden of the disease...There is an overwhelming amount of preclinical and clinical evidence to warrant initiating a multicenter randomized, double-blind, placebo-controlled trial of cannabis as a disease-modifying compound in ALS.[487]

Since the medical uses of cannabis are increasingly recognized by the medical and scientific communities as extending to a large percentage of the citizenry in all nations, the vast array of scientific medical studies afford us a basis for widespread cultivation of cannabis, and the other benefits will be a byproduct. (Perhaps the best use of cannabis for its preventive health benefits is juicing the whole raw plant, a use which is devoid of psychoactive effects because non-psychoactive THCa only becomes psychoactive THC when heated.)[488]

---

[487] "Cannabis and amyotrophic lateral sclerosis: hypothetical and practical applications, and a call for clinical trials", *American Journal of Hospice & Palliative Medicine* 27: 347-356

[488] Jung J, Meyer MR, Maurer HH, Neusüss C, Weinmann W, Auwärter V. (Oct 2009), *Journal of Mass Spectrometry*

In his recent CNN documentary, *The Marijuana Revolution,* Dr. Sanjay Gupta cites research that cannabis may forestall or even reverse Alzheimer's disease and potentially other types of dementia as well. There is a dementia risk of "one in six (for persons) over the age of 80".[489]   Given that this prospect frightens most of us, and assuming that further research substantiates these cannabis results, who would still support Prohibition?

Food Uses

Research can quickly establish how thoroughly cannabis could make good use of fallow lands, or even replace other crops. While total replacement of other crops would be absurd, it could remove much of the world's pressure regarding food production as well as distribution, since cannabis can grow in widely different soils and environments. It is nutritionally superior to most grains. The protein content of hemp seed is comparable to soybeans and egg whites.[490]

Given the gross inefficiency of meat production at producing nutrition,[491] redeploying some of that grazing land to cannabis would be more productive, as hemp seed is one of the most complete and balanced vegetable sources of protein, offering all of the essential amino acids as well as essential oils (alpha linoleic acid and linoleic acid, which are converted in the body into the other essential oils) similarly to chia seed; another incredible source of nutrition.

Cannabis sativa seed has a mild nutty taste. No doubt, when entrepreneurial creativity is applied to making this into a diverse variety of foods we will see a wide diversity of product offerings, as has happened in Colorado with the medical uses.

------

[489] http://www.alzheimers.org.uk/site/scripts/documents_info.php?documentID=102

[490] http://www.fao.org/fsnforum/sites/default/files/resources/Hempseed%20as%20a%20nutritional%20resource-%20An%20overview.pdf

[491] http://www.news.cornell.edu/stories/1997/08/us-could-feed-800-million-people-grain-livestock-eat

Part VI: Living in a Celebration Society

The more you praise and celebrate your life, the more
there is in life to celebrate.

~Oprah Winfrey

Celebration brings a community's attention and appreciation to that which it cherishes. In so doing, it brings forth more of whatever is cherished. Every time we celebrate yesterday's achievements, we inspire future achievements that lead to tomorrow's celebrations. Further, celebration brings forth in us the qualities that we most admire. It is a way of elevating ourselves and, at its best, a source of sanctity and awe.

A society focused on celebration will thereby naturally encourage its youth to great deeds and remind everyone of the value of service. Nobility will again refer to a quality of spirit rather than an accident of birth. Vision will be of central importance, and systems will be informed by values.

In a Celebration Society, a new vision and system will provide for the basic needs of everyone regardless of their personal productive capacity. It will give residents and Citizens the chance to feel valuable and valued, according to their interests and passions as appreciated by others. This will be neither communism nor socialism, though some persons who are seeking a simplistic understanding or are prejudiced against the message of this book will use those labels. All new ideas draw such ire.

Communism is a system that proposes common ownership of the means of production. In practice, this has always meant that some central authority determines what everyone must do and what they may possess, usually to the benefit of that authority's membership. (While small communal societies might be able to function on the basis of consensus, there is no certainty of this.) Celebrationism will require neither forced redistribution of assets nor forced labor. Private ownership will remain for so long as people find it meaningful.

Instead, by making assets far easier to create and to duplicate, their value will greatly diminish. While, for example, prime real estate with an ocean view will remain valuable, anyone without such physical real estate will be able to enjoy much of its benefit through virtual or augmented reality or travel.

While some will compare celebrationism to *luxury communism*,[492] there is an absence in celebrationism of any need for confrontation between capital owners and others. Also, luxury communism remains rooted in the Scarcity Game: its proponents advocate taking the means of production away from capitalists rather than recognizing that these means can become universally available.

As a practical matter, we will not suddenly transition from capitalism to celebrationism. It will likely take decades. Most systems of production are not yet fully automated, and we will need to incentivize those who understand the non-automated aspects.

Celebrationism will provide for all not by "redistributing" away from those who are prosperous today but rather by using automation in a new and far more powerfully productive manner. Such a shift will require a fundamental re-thinking of the nature of production and of society; a re-thinking at least as great as the shift from agricultural society to the industrial era. (It is similar to though not identical with what Jacques Fresco called a resource-based economy.)[493]

It will require that we be willing to replace certain beliefs that never were or are no longer substantiated by evidence. This transformation will require a re-thinking of much about how we exist as a species. This does not come easily to most people. Said multibillionaire Ray Dalio, founder of the world's most successful hedge fund, "I believe that the biggest problem that humanity faces is an ego sensitivity to finding out whether one is right or wrong and identifying what one's strengths and weaknesses are."

---

[492] http://www.theguardian.com/sustainable-business/2015/mar/18/fully-automated-luxury-communism-robots-employment

[493] https://www.thevenusproject.com/en/about/resource-based-economy

Some of that re-thinking will harken back to time-honored perspectives. For example, I believe that Benjamin Franklin—a man renowned for the energy he invested in self-examination and self-improvement—would have been happy living in a Celebration Society. A successful businessman, he was able to retire at age 42 to what he called a "life of leisure". However, what he meant by this was a life spent enjoying the company of others, pursuing scientific discoveries, sharing his wisdom, serving as a statesman, and contributing to civic projects.

The most benevolent and philanthropic of the American Founders, Franklin hoped that the tribute paid him after his death would be, "He lived usefully" and not, "He died rich".[494] To Franklin, a life of service was a life well lived.

Never in recorded history has a society existed like a Celebration Society. The closest known parallel is the civilization of the Central Middle Ages (CMA), and those records are fragmentary. We find some indications of what life might be like in a Celebration Society in an unlikely place: rat experiments on addiction.

A Rat Park for People

> It's not the drugs that make a drug addict, it's the need
> to escape reality.
>
> ~ *"Riley", Sense8, Episode: Demons*

Most present-day societies criminalize addicts, with devastating consequences for those persons, their families, and often their communities. Already, we have evidence that dysfunctional behavior such as addiction will become much less of a problem in a Celebration Society.

---

[494] http://www.theatlantic.com/business/archive/2015/09/how-america-lost-track-of-benjamin-franklins-definition-of-success/400808/

Rodents are often used in the testing of medical drugs just prior to human trials because these results are believed by most medical researchers to predict human results significantly better than chance. Human trials of new drugs are performed to assure their safety and efficacy. That said, if something fails to work for rodents, human trials do not occur. Further, recent brain research strongly suggests that non-human mammals can have emotional responses.[495]

Enter *Rat Park*. It's one of those outlier experiments that defies the conventional wisdom to such an extent that the common reaction is to throw up one's hands and ignore it. Rat Park was an ongoing experiment for about 20 years at Simon Fraser University in Canada, led by psychologist Dr. Bruce K. Alexander and his team of colleagues.

Rather than accept the conventional wisdom that some property of opiate drugs made them inherently addictive, Alexander wondered if the methodology used for testing addiction was impacting the results. The lab rats used for these tests—Norwegian white rats—are intelligent, curious, highly social, and physically active; much like humans. To test for addiction, these rats were isolated in cages that offered no mental or physical stimulation; essentially, placed in solitary confinement for life. Alexander hypothesized that such conventional tests showed only that, "Severely distressed animals, like severely distressed people, will relieve their distress pharmacologically if they can."[496]

The finding of Alexander's experiments, confirmed in multiple tests, was that it is impossible to induce addiction in rats living in a Rat Park environment. They refused the drugs, even when mixed with their favored sugar water.

What does this say about people? It suggests that much human addictive behavior is not a function of the substances themselves but the desire to escape desperately unsatisfying living conditions.

---

[495] http://www.theatlantic.com/health/archive/2014/04/does-your-dog-or-cat-actually-love-you/360784/

[496] http://www.brucekalexander.com/articles-speeches/demon-drug-myths/164-myth-drug-induced

Researchers have identified what is called the "addictive personality"—a person who becomes addicted more easily than normal; whether it be to alcohol, other drugs, nicotine, gambling, sex, internet porn, etc. The Rat Park results suggest that perhaps such persons are simply more emotionally sensitive than most to not having their needs met by the environment in which they live.

A partly corroborating experiment involving rats was conducted at the University of Illinois. Instead of addiction, it studied whether rats placed in socially rich environments with other rats and toys would become more intelligent than rats who lived in solitary confinement. They did.[497]

We probably won't call an environment that's designed to optimize well-being for people Human Park. Regardless of its name, such an environment will balance rural and city elements in a manner that affords residents the advantages of both types of living: ample access to nature coupled with the cultural, intellectual and physical diversity of a city. It will include elements of cities, towns, and rural locales in synergistic mutual support—similarly to how Adam Smith described the way that the leading cities related to their countrysides in his time.

Most food production will be local, meaning it will be fresh, nutritious and delicious, while minimizing waste due to spoilage and costs of transportation. Further, fruits and vegetables can be grown that offer extraordinary health benefits.[498] Given that this will be a place where addictive compulsions toward excessive behaviors—be they drug-related, sexual, gambling, or otherwise—will presumably not find much traction, it becomes difficult to imagine what life in such a culture will be like.

This is surely an experiment worth performing—and it can be argued that a kind of Rat Park experiment was accidentally

---

[497] http://www.sciencedirect.com/science/article/pii/0014488673900903

[498] For example, a particular variety of guanabana found in Central America serves as a gentle, potent sedative. It does not, however, transport well so greenhouses would be required.

performed during the Vietnam War. The results were generally consistent for people with what the Rat park experiments would have predicted:

> *Time Magazine* reported (that) using heroin was 'as common as chewing gum' among U.S. soldiers, and there is solid evidence to back this up: some 20 percent of U.S. soldiers had become addicted to heroin there, according to a study published in the *Archives of General Psychiatry*. Many people were understandably terrified; they believed a huge number of addicts were about to head home when the war ended.

> But in fact some 95 percent of the addicted soldiers — according to the same study — simply stopped. Very few had rehabilitation. They shifted from a terrifying 'cage' back to a tolerable one, and so they no longer used drugs to escape. (While addiction in returned Vietnam Vets has remained higher than the general population, this may be attributed to PTSD, the feeling of being unwelcome and disrespected by their countrymen, and other such factors rendering their environment unsatisfactory.)

> Professor Alexander argues that this discovery is a profound challenge both to the view that addiction is a moral failing and the view that addiction is a disease taking place in a chemically hijacked brain. As he argues, '...addiction is an adaptation. It's not you. It's your cage.'[499]

Critics will argue that certain substances cause permanent changes in brains via a single dose, and cite this

---

[499] http://www.huffingtonpost.com/johann-hari/the-real-cause-of-addicti_b_6506936.html

as proof that those chemicals are inherently addictive. The Rat Park experiments suggest a more nuanced interpretation. It seems likely that such neurological changes will, at most, merely increase the predisposition—a predisposition that may be averted from manifesting by a nourishing environment.

This view is supported from a different angle. According to neuroscientist Marc Lewis, a psychologist and former addict:

> The disease theory, and the science sometimes used to support it, fail to take into account the plasticity of the human brain. Of course, 'the brain changes with addiction. But the way it changes has to do with learning and development — not disease.'
>
> All significant and repeated experiences change the brain; adaptability and habit are the brain's secret weapons. The changes wrought by addiction are not, however, permanent, and while they are dangerous, they're not abnormal. Through a combination of a difficult emotional history, bad luck and the ordinary operations of the brain itself, an addict is someone whose brain has been transformed, but also someone who can be pushed further along the road toward healthy development. (Lewis doesn't like the term 'recovery' because it implies a return to the addict's state before the addiction took hold.)
>
> [Addiction is a response to] a particular emotional wound the substance helped them handle, but once they started using it, the habit itself eventually became self-perpetuating and in most cases ultimately served to deepen the wound... addiction really is habit; we just don't

appreciate how deeply habit can be engraved on the brain itself.[500]

In Rat Park, all rodent needs and many desires were met. While we cannot know what the human equivalent will look like, we can envision possibilities.

Dreams of Enchantment and Royalty

Many little girls grow up dreaming of being princesses, taken away into an enchanted life by a Prince Charming figure. For centuries, such wishes have been indulged by older and wiser people as mere fantasies; never attainable but harmless. Still, I expect that for millions of adult women—and millions of adult men as well—such dreams of a royal life remain, though suppressed.

The "princess vacation" is popular in Japan. Women will save thousands of dollars to have a special one-time vacation in Europe where they live the life of a princess, attend a royal ball, and briefly live the fantasy. In addition, they will spend months learning the etiquette, fashion, dance, and other skills necessary to playing such a role, if only briefly.[501]

In a Celebration Society, there may well be a new system of government starting with administrative, legislative and judicial branches—along with a fourth. It has been said that one problem in America is that the presidency is burdened with some of the functions ordinarily performed in other nations by royalty, including ceremonial leadership and being elevated above the ordinary as a symbol. On the other hand, royalty in most places is hereditary and therefore some members are beloved while others are merely tolerated or even despised.

---

[500] http://www.salon.com/2015/06/27/addiction_is_not_a_disease_a_ neuroscientist_argues_that_its_time_to_change_our_minds_on_the_roots_of_ substance_abuse/,
The Biology of Desire: Why Addiction is Not a Disease, Marc Lewis
[501] http://www.washingtonpost.com/wp-dyn/articles/A2128-2005Jan11.html

The fourth branch of government in a Celebration Society could be a *meritocratic royalty*. Such royal status would be attained not through birth, good fortune, or bribes but rather through extraordinary acts of service, given freely in a spirit of bettering humanity and one's society. This would be a new kind of royalty.

Since there is no limit to the amount of service that can be rendered to our fellow people and the other beings who inhabit and share this world with us, there is therefore no limit to how many may ascend to the status of royalty. That said, it should neither be trivialized nor easy. It should be something achieved through service at an extraordinary level; service that itself serves as a hallmark and inspiration to society. These royals will thereby be beacons for the best values of a Celebration Society and of humanity, and naturally entrusted with leading celebrations and in other roles of great importance.

Viewed in this manner, every girl may dream to someday become a princess and every boy a prince. I would say that, to attain such an exalted status, one would have to not only devote one's life to one's fellow beings but also be willing to go through all manner of challenges to one's *shadows*; what those schooled in archetypal psychology call the dark side which must be fully experienced, transmuted and then integrated into one's being. This might take the form of a second rite of passage beyond that of Citizenship.

The choice to pursue a life of service in order to become a member of the Royalty is only one option that will become available to Citizens of a Celebration Society. One could also be content with the limited Citizen responsibilities, otherwise serve occasionally, and enjoy greater free time. If a Citizen finds even those responsibilities to be too much, he or she can again become a resident.

In a Celebration Society, every person can serve a vision or purpose of their choice after exploring a multitude of possibilities, either by leading or supporting those in leadership, as the individual may prefer. Every person can serve other people, whether through invention or cleaning restrooms. In an Abundance Game, service differs from the work of today in that there is no coercion to serve, it also being understood that our capacity to serve requires taking good care of ourselves as well, and that there is no limit to the amount of service we can render to one another.

Leadership will not be based on hierarchical power structures of how many people are obligated to follow your orders, but rather on a collaborative model of how many people are willing to follow your vision.

I believe that a different nomenclature will be best, since "prince", "princess", "king", "queen", and so forth carry baggage from the past. I envision a meritocratic royalty as having three tiers based on accomplishment. For the leader of the Royalty, I like the Sanskrit word *Sarvay* meaning, "for all," and for the other two tiers I like *Mahana Sevaka*, or "great servant" and *Sevaka* or "servant". But it will be a community decision.

I don't mean to imply that every resident or even every Citizen must be an outstanding exemplar of compassion and other virtues. Citizens will pass through a rigorous qualification process, after which they will swear an oath to uphold the Charter and be both responsible and accountable for doing so.

Permanent residents will, like guests, be accountable to respect the Charter but not responsible for the government. That will be a function limited to the Citizens, with additional responsibilities bequeathed upon joining the Royalty.

Other aspects of life will be transformed as well. Traditionally, the selection of mates has generally been based on economic and genetic considerations. (It appears that in most cultures women tend to select men based on a sense of feeling "protected", while men tend to select women based on concepts of beauty that roughly correspond to healthy fertility.) Since the Celebration Society will meet all of one's basic needs for physical support and safety, and VR will meet one's desires for sexual excitement, future selection of mates will likely be based on who is the best provider of emotional support, shared vision, and who has earned the most respect and admiration from society.

Even the sociopath may prove to have a useful role in society, once more fully understood. Recent research indicates that they may not lack the *capacity* for empathy, as had been long supposed, but rather the *motivation.*

Said the authors of a recent study, "When the others were described as in-group members, participants higher in psychopathy showed greater concern for those others."[502] This distinction, should it be well-corroborated, would make them useful in certain professions and, potentially, even service-oriented. Though generally portrayed in fiction as vicious, the truth is that they simply lack common morality or emotional connection, instead gaining their only satisfaction in life from winning at games of their choosing. Regarding another person or animal as no different from a chair, they may devise games causing great harm.[503] Some, however, offer great service.

Statuses of People in a Celebration Society

I foresee three basic statuses of people in a Celebration Society: guests, residents, and Citizens. Each status will carry with it enumerated privileges and responsibilities. (Among Citizens, further statuses will exist carrying with them added responsibilities of service, but they will not affect the person's privileges.)

Whatever benefits the society offers in the form of general welfare, such as guaranteed food, shelter, clothing, and health care, will always flow first to Citizens. Once basic Citizen needs have been met, the government may extend such benefits to residents.

Guests will mostly be tourists or friends and relatives of existing residents and Citizens. They will pay national money in exchange for the privilege of visiting the Celebration Society, and for the products and services consumed. Guests will have a time-limited visa, based upon prepayment of their total daily admission fees.

---

[502] http://socialneuro.psych.utoronto.ca/understanding%20everyday%20 psychopathy.pdf

[503] *The Sociopath Next Door*, Martha Stout

Guests will be responsible for respecting the laws and customs of the city-state. (They will be provided with information before entering.) Guests will be entitled to fair treatment under the laws, with restitution required for any damage done. Most ambassadorial visitors are accustomed to enjoying special immunity. Those unwilling to waive such rights will be denied entrance.

There will be significant logistical issues with creating and maintaining the city-state's Guest List. For example, I anticipate that a waiting list for guests to visit a city-state will quickly develop as the society matures into one that offers multiple attractions. At some point, continuing demand will outstrip the number of visitor slots allocated by the government. This will create unfulfilled tourism demand that can be used to help make the business case for additional Celebration Societies.[504]

Once there are multiple Celebration Societies, Citizens of one such society could gain privileged guest status in other such societies. The rules of such privilege would be set by the individual city-states, but in general could mean higher placement in the guest list than guests not affiliated with a Celebration Society, with reasonable respect for the advance planning requirements of all guests.

There should be a limited Government Class of guests, with persons placed at the top of the list by approval of the appropriate Ministry. There would be no admission fee for these guests. These would include ambassadors and temporary representatives of governments who are visiting for a specific reason. (There could also conceivably be a Business Class of guests, with a limited number of slots that can bump people at the bottom of the guest list upon demand, with a higher admission fee paid by the host business.) I'd suggest that the bottom group of persons of the guest list who are

---

[504] Tourism employs 1 out of every 16 workers in the world, and represents the second or third largest industry in almost every nation.
(http://citeseerx.ist.psu.edu/viewdoc/download?doi=10.1.1.121.4818&rep=rep1&type=pdf)

slotted for the next available opening be classified as Standby and be occupied by people who have no special privilege to visit but are willing to be flexible about when they can come. They move ahead of a limited number of those who lack such flexibility.

One serious challenge will arise in the form of guests whom Citizens want to have permanently join them as residents (i.e., existing family or desire to create a family). While such events are certain to happen, unless the government finds a way to sustain a stable population with some accommodation of this, I can see only two solutions: either the Citizens and their proposed co-residents can gain preferred status for joining a new Celebration Society being formed elsewhere, or they can persuade some other person(s) to do so in their stead.

In the first case, during the capitalist transitional period, the Citizens would likely enjoy a much higher property value in the first city-state home than the second, allowing them to sell and emigrate with significant assets. In the second case, they would offer a mutually agreeable incentive to someone else to do this in their stead. (Even in a full celebrationist system, certain assets will have unique value in trade or loan. That value could be measured in a mutually agreeable form of money or via a simple exchange.)

Additionally, there is the obvious matter of family growth due to births. One solution here would be a policy that persons born in a city-state must relocate elsewhere upon attaining adulthood, unless another agrees to do so in their stead. I would suggest that a newly formed Celebration Society include in its planning some room for population growth and also develop clear, impartial rules to accommodate these situations.

Residents will have the right to live in the Celebration Society for life, provided they commit no acts that qualify for eviction. Residents will have limited responsibilities and privileges. Any resident may pursue the path of citizenship until successful, upon which success he or she will assume the responsibilities and rewards of Citizenship. Any Citizen no longer willing to bear the responsibilities of Citizenship may elect to revoke that status and become a Resident.

Citizens are people who have demonstrated real character, through acts that express the capability to live in community with other Citizens. Citizens will have to demonstrate courage, open-mindedness, fairness, an orientation towards service, and other specific virtues. (I expect that there will be an arduous and formal Rite of Passage.) In a Celebration Society, all Citizens will know the basic principles and laws that govern the society. This will be made easier by simplicity of laws since, in a highly interactive, networked and transparent system of governance, citizen watchfulness will substitute for much of the bureaucracy and law that is required in huge nation-states with a disempowered citizenry.

All citizens become members of the government. This means, with few exceptions, that any Citizen may be:

- Given the opportunity to vote on matters in which voting is called for. Non-citizens may not vote.
- Called upon at any time to serve a fixed, single term in parliament. As was the case in the Venetian Republic, such selection is by lottery, and terms are staggered to avert political parties. Citizens serving in another branch of government are exempt. Each such term should be followed by a period during which the person cannot be called into service again.
- Selected by lottery to serve on a jury. Only Citizens may serve. (There are issues with manipulation of the jury system by selection consultants. It seems that random selection without a vetting process would address those issues.)[505]
- Able to propose an Initiative which, upon attaining a threshold percentage of Citizens' approval, is placed on an electronic ballot. Specifics of how this works will need to be determined. An informed electorate who are actively involved in their society and government will help to assure that the Initiative process is not cluttered with frivolous or poorly worded offerings.

---

[505] http://www.theatlantic.com/politics/archive/2015/06/how-bias-shapes-juries/395957/

- Invited to serve a term as a judge, in a judicial support role, as a minister on the Administration Council, or to serve in another administration role. I see these as being non-mandatory positions, limited to Citizens.
- Invited for induction into the Royalty. (The proposed royalty, discussed elsewhere, should specify an induction process of its own design, which I suggest be subject to majority Citizen approval.)

With very limited exceptions, no person may serve in more than one branch of government at any time. There may be additional roles to be filled by Citizens, according to the Charter and parliamentary decisions. I would recommend that there be term limits for all positions without exception, so that the government is always one of laws and never of specific men or women.

Support Staff

Until full celebrationist production systems are in place, there will be a need for people to do many jobs. Some of these jobs will be professional and well-paid. Others will be less-skilled services such as gardening, cooking, and cleaning. It would be unacceptable to allow a two-class system to arise in a Celebration Society.

Less-skilled workers are unlikely to have the money necessary to buy land and build homes of their own. They will either work for the society as a whole or for private Citizens or residents. One solution is to include a certain number of condominium residences for society support staff in the central city construction plan, with the option of additional residences on private land.

Alternatively, residents and Citizens who wish to hire workers for their private use can donate one of their city or village residences for the workers to live in, or pool residences with another hiring resident or Citizen so that workers sponsored by someone living in a village could also live in that village, and workers sponsored by someone living in the downtown area could also live in the downtown area.

This, however, does not fully address the situation. I would favor passage of a law in the first Celebration Society specifying treatment of such workers. Such a law would serve as a moral precedent for future Celebration Societies. This law would designate such workers as provisional residents.

Additionally, the law would assure that they had all of the rights and privileges of residents (for so long as they were employed), as well as stipulating a model employment contract addressing wages, work hours, medical care, educational opportunities, and a severance package (including transportation to country of origin) at the end of employment. The terms of every employment contract would be a matter of public record, preventing Citizens and residents from taking advantage of people desperate to live in a Celebration Society.

I would further place such persons at or near the top of the list of persons given the option of purchasing their own home and becoming permanent residents in that particular Celebration Society or in another Celebration Society.

Once fully automated celebrationist systems of production are available to build housing and other infrastructure, means of payment will cease to matter. Until then, provisional residents who become candidate citizens can be given loans to acquire land and build homes, either in their current society or as part of the financial sponsorship of a new Celebration Society. (Such lending would need to be limited to what is practicable. Perhaps a certain percentage of new residencies could be earmarked this way.)

In this manner, I am hopeful that the issue of a two-tier society can be averted and those who commit themselves to serving as lesser-paid helpers can foresee a beautiful future for themselves and their children.

Although private employers of support staff may have their own preferences for hiring, I see the national support staff and perhaps others being hired through something different. A reality television program could be created in which the prize is the opportunity to live and work in a Celebration Society. This should serve not only to attract the best candidates, but also to widen global awareness of Celebration Societies and stimulate excitement about living there.

Intimacy in a Celebration Society

You can discover more about a person in an hour of
play than in a year of conversation.

~Plato

A concern one might have about a Celebration Society is that if non-Citizen residents are freed from social obligations or perhaps even the need for human company, whither intimacy?

It is, I will admit, disturbing to my early 21st century mindset to imagine a person sitting in a chair, doing nothing but playing in VR all day long; perhaps not even taking time to eat, excrete, exercise, monitor health, shower, or sleep. After all, computer gaming addiction is such a widespread phenomenon in China that the government is seriously concerned about how to handle it.[506] It seems likely that VR will have even more potential for addiction—though, as was established in the *Rat Park* experiments (discussed elsewhere) addiction needs to be reconsidered in light of societal influences.

Even so, such people will arguably be happier than they are today. Most currently have unfulfilled desires for sexual and other intimate companionship, which will be met at least in part via realistic experiences delivered in VR, via robotic "sex bots", or some combination of the two.[507] This is also true of people who are poor, lack social skills, or are deemed unattractive; not just VR addicts.

I do not want people to live this way. However, I recognize my prejudice and do not hold it as some sanctified truth merely because I prefer it so. (Neither do I regard my personal spiritual beliefs as valid to impose on others. If I have that

---

[506] http://www.telegraph.co.uk/news/health/11345412/Inside-the-Chinese-boot-camp-treating-Internet-addiction.html

[507] http://www.iflscience.com/technology/defence-sex-machines-why-trying-ban-sex-robots-wrong

power over them, then at another time they might have that power over me.) Objectively, if this person does no harm to others, preferring this "lifestyle" to others more engaged with the world, who am I to judge?

As for the rest of us, the possibilities open very wide indeed...

I have long felt that each person is like a world seen through a telescope. We can discern only the tiniest details; far more will await us through patient exploration. We have few opportunities for such relationships in one evanescent human lifetime. If we are lucky, this will include a spouse, parents, siblings, and perhaps children. Some of us find this with our closest friends.

Why is it so rare? I believe there are several reasons:

- Limited available time each day. This is the fraction of that 24 hours we can actually with discretion apply to our social desires. At best, for an independently wealthy individual this will be perhaps 16 hours not spent in sleep. It has been estimated that most people may have but a few hours each day for social interactions.
- Poor tools for selection of candidates. We have 7+ billion fellow travelers on this blue spaceship. Traditionally, people were limited to their own village and a few neighboring ones. As we moved to cities, the potential grew. Today, the internet gives us the illusion of still greater connectivity, and in a sense it is true. But ask yourself: how many of your "Facebook friends" are comparable in depth of intimacy to the friends whom you see regularly?
- Linear exchange of information. We meet. We exchange pleasant banter. We exchange basic information. All going well, our knowledge of each other deepens over time, a process that takes months or even years—and we still only scratch the surface.

In a Celebration Society, all of these problems can be successfully addressed:

- Everyone will have available most of the hours in a day other than time not spent sleeping.

- With our AI Butlers helping and, for those who choose it, our coming ability to download memories almost immediately, it will be possible to know quite a lot about someone[508] in minutes that would usually take hours or even years to replicate.

- Intimacy depends not only on knowledge of another person but, even more significantly, shared meaningful experiences. Since celebrations evoke strong emotions and a sense of meaning, the common bond of celebrating together often and richly will greatly enable intimacy amongst those who live in a Celebration Society.

One of the most precious sources of intimacy is family. Family has evolved over the millennia from societies in which parents owned children or husbands owned wives (often, plural) to the diversity of today. The concept of family diversity extends well beyond today's "hot-button" issue of same-sex marriages. It includes biological as well as adopted relatives who may reside together or they may not. It may include dear friends whom one regards as family.

In my view, the best way to support family in a Celebration Society is to make it a private matter among the persons involved. I would advocate the creation of a special kind of legal entity, the family corporation. Just as societal laws will protect all individuals within the society, so too they will enforce honest contracts. Family corporations would be special in that there would be default provisions protecting the rights of children and other family members, with some of those provisions being non-optional.

---

[508] I assume this would be a mutual "opt-in" situation.

In this manner, much as was the case in ancient societies where families existed as Houses with a life and purpose far beyond any individuals, people may be inducted into a family by mutual consent and there can be a specific process for separation as well. Ownership of assets is likewise specified, and a newly inducted member might vest a share of ownership over time.

With our needs for intimacy well met, what might we become?

Tony Schwartz of the Energy Project says that people have four core needs: meaning, security, self-expression, and serving a larger purpose in life. I believe that the structure of a Celebration Society simultaneously fulfills all of these needs. It does so in two ways. First, by creating a strong foundation for one's life, secure in one's basic needs, it supports full self-expression (either in reality or virtually), and the chance to create meaning and serve a larger purpose in the manner most dear to one's heart. Second, by cultivating a culture of service, where those who exemplify virtues are cherished and admired, it will inspire others to rise up as well. Larger purpose will be all around; it will be unmistakable and constantly available. The individual need only choose which such purpose he or she most resonates with as a personal focus of service.

Getting Started

There are multiple paths to a first model of a Celebration Society. Easiest, perhaps, is to create a virtual world in the form of a massive online simulation, wherein the participants co-create a model Celebration Society or even multiple such societies—perhaps competing in teams to see which model works best. Once such a model works sufficiently well, there are several paths to physical implementation.

Under international law, there are two bases for creation of a nation-state: the Constitutive and Declarative theories. Either is sufficient. When two existing nation-states both recognize the Celebration Society as a nation-state, the Constitutive theory is fulfilled. The Declaratory theory requires a defined territory, permanent population, a government, and lastly the capacity to enter into relations with other nation-states non-coercively.

Alternately, an existing nation-state could commit to transitioning from its current system to celebrationism in an orderly process. This transition would take longer than creating a new society and system from scratch, because entrenched interests will oppose some of the changes. I envision this happening after a model Celebration Society has been created and is thriving.

Some nation-state seeking additional revenue could charter a Special Development Zone, capable of following this vision during a 100 year lease, like Hong Kong was leased to Britain by China. (Unlike that lease, I would envision this one being renewable or even including a purchase option so as to assure legal status as a nation.) The chartered territory would have its own legal system and develop its own culture.

I envision tourism as the major industry of a Celebration Society. Apart from the novel entertainment options made possible in a place where immense celebrations are a frequent if not daily occurrence and all manner of exotic experiences are available, consider medical tourism. In 2014, Frost & Sullivan estimated this market at $50 - $65 billion, growing at 20 percent annually. Of the top 14 destination countries, only four of them are at first-world status.[509]

Second and third world countries offer medical procedures at lower cost than first world countries. That's the primary appeal, though occasionally they also offer advanced procedures not yet available in first world countries due to US FDA regulations, which can delay availability a decade or more. (Most countries outside Europe follow the FDA's regulations. Europe's regulations are in some ways more tolerant and in some ways stricter than those in the US.)

In addition to care, medical tourists will want high quality meals, accommodations, and entertainment. A Celebration

---

[509] http://www.forbes.com/sites/reenitadas/2014/08/19/medical-tourism-gets-a-facelift-and-perhaps-a-pacemaker/

Society will offer a tourism experience without graft or crime, with clear laws that offer unparalleled freedom, first-world amenities, and unique entertainment options. (Realistically, due to limits in facilities each society will need to specialize in the treatment of certain conditions and not others. I also envision the possibility of eldercare and hospice care at a level not available elsewhere, including the full range of palliative, therapeutic, and even restorative care options.)

Further, in a Celebration Society, the medical care will equal that of top first world facilities because its unique lifestyle and professional benefits will attract top personnel. Unlike other first world medical care, there will be no cumbersome regulatory apparatus nor burdensome costs due to byzantine insurance and adversarial litigation. (In the US, the average physician spends over 10% of their professional career dealing with malpractice claims, as well as significant time and energy practicing "defensive medicine"—which limits the treatment options they can offer and also raises costs.)[510]

This will allow superb medical professionals to offer the most leading edge treatments coming out of research facilities worldwide, with informed patient consent about risk/reward tradeoffs. This will be done in a non-adversarial environment, with straightforward pricing and an emphasis on less invasive or risky procedures whenever practical.

Revenues from tourism and other sources will be shared with the "host" country, and the host along with a carefully selected third nation will together recognize the Celebration Society as a new nation-state.

Other possible approaches include forming a legal entity that:

- Purchases a territory such as a large island from an existing nation and declares a new nation-state under international law.
- Reconstitutes a defunct nation already recognized under international law.

---

[510] http://www.forbes.com/sites/robertglatter/2013/02/06/medical-malpractice-broken-beyond-repair/

267

- Buys out an existing micro-nation, offering the existing residents many advantages including residency with a guaranteed income and a path to Citizenship.

The creation of Celebration Societies is not a zero-sum game. I anticipate that it will quickly lift the residents in measurable qualities of life such that it will quickly become the "new gold standard" for first-world living, and many visitors will leave with the desire to create the same in their own nations.

This gift and these blessings will be richest when shared. Abundance, the presence of sufficiency that is known to be permanent, is easily shared. The sharing enriches relationships, society and culture.

All understandings of quality of life aside, no one will have real, lasting abundance without a deep sense of security.

The Questions of Security and Surveillance

I am under no illusions about the kind of world in which we presently live. Barbarism, magnified by modern weaponry, is an ever-present threat in much of the world, whether it takes the form of war crimes, other state violence, gang violence, or terrorism.

It is almost inevitable that, once a Celebration Society is extant and thriving, some fanatic will envision its destruction as a great victory. Until some future time, likely a century or more after poverty has been eradicated and cultures that embrace revenge and violence have been transformed, security will be necessary. A reputation as a peaceful society offers no inherent protection. For example, Canada has been attacked by Muslim extremists.[511]

While perfect security may be impossible, at least until a future time of well-established AI's supported by very wide-spread multimodal sensors with robotic defense and peace

---

[511] http://www.theatlantic.com/international/archive/2014/10/radical-islam-canada-parliament-shooting/381873/

officers, there is a real-world model that works reasonably well. In Israel, successful ground-based terror attacks are relatively infrequent and the loss of life, while tragic, is small. Israeli deaths from terrorism in 2013 were low enough that the country did not register on the list of most-affected nations.[512] Even rockets have been largely rendered ineffective by its Iron Dome antimissile system.

Israel exists in the most precarious condition of any modern nation. Surrounded by hostiles, even in countries with which it is nominally at peace, it has no choice but to maximize the *intelligence* of its security. Equipped with the most modern security technologies and knowledge, Israel does not use intrusive screening lines in its airports. Instead, it has a multi-tiered approach with "rings" of security. I believe that a similar system can be implemented in a Celebration Society city-state without causing the Citizens undue hardship.

Further and of great importance, I anticipate that the initial Celebration Societies will happen in relatively tranquil locations. If not entire nation-states, then leased land in places such as Iceland, British Columbia, Australia, New Zealand, or the Mediterranean could serve. Since the Celebration Society will not be perceived as foreign occupiers but rather as offering a huge upgrade in lifestyle to the few existing residents, and will further offer a significant increase in tourism and other revenues to the "sponsor" government(s), it seems unlikely to face the extreme threats experienced by Israel.

Also, the open source and non-imperial nature of a Celebration Society, coupled with its commitment to "pay it forward" through service outreach and open source sharing of societal knowledge will help to ease perceptions of "us vs. them" and consequent jealousy.

In addition, I propose something radically new as part of Celebration Society design. I call it bimodal surveillance. In such a system, privacy within the home is absolute, except upon a particular warrant issued by a judge for probable

---

[512] http://www.theatlantic.com/international/archive/2014/11/the-geography-of-terrorism/382915/

cause. Even then, there would be no military-style raids into residences but carefully measured and cautiously deployed use of force only as necessary.

All activities outside the home would be under constant surveillance and recorded—but with a huge difference. Any Citizen would have the authority to examine any of this footage at any time. While some may find such a concept disturbing, this offers the following benefits:

- Children and other vulnerable persons may travel alone anywhere in the city-state at any time, in safety.
- In conjunction with other measures suggested by the Rat Park experiments, violent crime is generally eliminated.
- Contracts are greatly simplified.
- Government accountability is greatly increased. The government IS the Citizens.
- Abuses of power by police will become very rare.

A new technology called Black Lantern, now in use by the Estonian government, makes it very difficult if not impossible for insiders to tamper with government records.[513] Likewise, the migration of *blockchain* technology (notably used for Bitcoin) to other societal transactions, may decentralize power while increasing accountability.[514]

Modern communications technologies make possible quick and effective legislative participation without antiquated limitations. Likewise, when government officers know that their actions are being recorded and may be viewed at any time by any Citizen, they will comport themselves respectfully and carefully.

Regardless of whether one likes it or not, advances in micro- and nano-miniaturization assure us that universal sensing is coming. Costs are plummeting and, when wireless sensors cost little and are tiny, they will be widely deployed.

---

[513] http://www.wired.com/2015/06/tech-behind-bitcoin-stop-next-snowden/
[514] https://www.newscientist.com/article/mg22730384-100-blockchain-startups-promises-a-world-where-no-one-is-in-charge/

Likewise, proliferation of drones—even drones the size of insects—assures that sensors can be deployed everywhere. Universal sensing will, in turn, enable universal surveillance.

To prevent surveillance inside the home, Celebration Society Citizens may sweep to find any invasive electronics. However, I expect that in a future culture where there is no economic advantage to be gained from surveillance and unauthorized surveillance is a serious offense, it will not happen often.

To prevent "back room dealings" between members of the government and others, it may be the case that seated members of the government either forego some of these rights of privacy or are limited to gatherings that occur in public places for the duration of their term.

As to privacy in businesses, it seems to me that a middle ground between homes and public places will need to be established. Perhaps each business will make a choice as to security protocols, with color-coded marks on their signs of business to indicate the type of security in effect therein. Or, there may be specific conference rooms or offices designated the business' "home" where trade secrets are discussed but the rest of the business is designated "public".

Since one cannot stop the flow of a river, the wise will seek to guide its flow in the most beneficial direction.

Physical Imagery—Some Possibilities

I have tried to imagine how a Celebration Society might physically look. At the entrance, I picture a great archway of white stone or durable concrete (Roman or ceramic) through which all must pass to enter the city. Incised into the top of the arch and embossed in gold leaf are the words, "The Systems Serve the People. The People Serve Each Other." These words, conceived by my wife, to me embody the crowning principle of a Celebration Society city-state.

I see such a city-state as having a great dome in the center, perhaps at the base of soaring towers of offices and residences for those who seek the most "urban" of experiences. All would be able to quickly traverse the distance between any two points in the city through a combination of light rail "spokes" radiating outward from the center, and also be able to travel either clockwise or counterclockwise via ring rails or possibly (and more beautifully) via canals from any rail exit point to within a few blocks of any location in the city, with organically designed and aesthetic eddy points. There would be no need for internal combustion engines or anything noisy. Unless the entire city is domed, heavy cargo could be silently delivered via blimps, which could also be used in construction as necessary. The rights to quiet and privacy would be respected.

The dome would contain a Great Hall of Celebration—a place where the entire population of the city could gather, should they choose, for sporting events, concerts, exhibitions—and celebrations. I see there being a celebration of something inspirational on most if not all nights: a revolutionary scientific discovery or invention, the unveiling of a musical composition by a master, a visiting troupe of performing artists, and so forth. I see celebration of many holidays including what may well become the prime holiday of a Celebration Society, Mother's Day—the time when we should honor all mothers.

It doesn't matter so much *what* a society celebrates as that it does so, regularly and with enthusiasm. This brings forth the finest values of joy, wonder, appreciation, and communion. It inspires and uplifts, and can evoke precious awe. Done on a regular basis, it will help to assure the continuity of culture in a Celebration Society. It may even provide a non-sectarian element of spirituality, to be shared by various faiths.

I see the outskirts of the city comprised of villages, each with its own sub-culture and emphasizing local events and celebrations. Each would foster intimacy among neighbors by virtue of its design structures and systems. Within villages, I see individual homes being both condominium structures and stand-alone houses, none so much emphasizing external ostentation as comfort, beauty and usefulness. I also see these homes largely occluded from each other by trees, even if they are in fact close.

Beyond the villages, I see multi-story buildings in which huge quantities of vegetables and fruits are grown under artificial sunlight, mostly tended by robotic gardeners. When someone wants a particular item of produce or needs the ingredients for a recipe, they request it of their AI Butler, which routes the request to the gardeners. Ripe produce is then picked and placed onto the conveyor system (underground tunnels, leading in a network from any structure in the city to any other, used for transportation of products and foods, electrical wiring, internet cabling, plumbing, waste disposal and maintenance robot access), and quickly routed to a home or a restaurant.

This is but a superficial vision of possibilities. I expect that an actual design will be developed collaboratively within an on-line simulation, with guidance from panels of experts in various disciplines. That may lead us to something like Dogun...[515]

The Story of Dogun

It would be irresponsible to lay out a vision of a Celebration Society without offering a path from here to there. Information imparted in stories can be 22 times more influential than when stated as mere facts.[516] Here, then, is one such story, of a possible first Celebration Society that repurposes largely uninhabited land in Iceland.

Why Iceland? Iceland has one of the longest-lasting constitutional parliamentary systems in the world; its *Alþingi* (Althingi) was established over 1,000 years ago. This demonstrates that governments by and for the people and their associated institutions can have very long survival, at least in conditions where there is a homogeneous population with shared values, culture and heritage.

As Celebration Societies will be intentional, with shared values, culture and eventually a shared heritage as well, it

---

[515] Icelandic for Dawn.

[516] http://www.theatlantic.com/health/archive/2014/11/the-psychological-comforts-of-storytelling/381964/2/

seems to me that they will have certain things in common with Iceland. Further, my study of Iceland leads me to believe that their culture would be the most comfortable with a Celebrationist Charter of any modern nation. We would not ask that they change anything other than grant us sovereignty over a body of land. That said, compatibility of cultures makes for good neighbors. Consider the USA and Canada.

Iceland has the highest per-capita literacy rate in the world. I expect many Icelanders to discuss and debate this book! It is important that the populace of a host country be generally comfortable with celebrationism, and I believe this is likely to happen in Iceland faster than elsewhere. Icelanders prize their revelry and celebration.

Though founded by aggressive Vikings, Iceland is today a peaceful nation with high regard for individual rights and acceptance of differences. The sexes are perhaps more equal in Iceland than anywhere else on Earth. In 2009, Iceland elected the world's first openly lesbian prime minister. Iceland has a rich heritage of respect for the natural environment, including a widely held belief in spirit beings tied to the land; the *Huldufólk*. (Iceland has four holidays connected to them.[517])

Recently, Iceland has positioned itself as providing the strongest protections for freedom of the press of any nation on Earth. Nevertheless, Iceland has not been accorded the respect among nations that its cultural leadership would seem to warrant. Hosting the world's first Celebration Society would surely change this, forever. Such a society, structured to operate in a harmonious economic and political alliance with Iceland, would meaningfully enhance Iceland's revenues in a sustainable manner not correlated to Iceland's existing industries, thereby helping to shield it from the vagaries of the unstable world financial system—which severely stung Icelanders recently.

A Celebration Society would respect Icelandic customs and culture, while protecting and enhancing the natural

---

[517] *Parallel Worlds: Fieldwork with Elves, Icelanders and Academics*, Katrin Sontag

environment. That said, in considering such a possibility I can see Icelanders being concerned about several matters. Would the new residents and visitors overwhelm the existing culture? Would the new population and economic growth damage existing ecosystems or infrastructure? Iceland recently rejected a Chinese billionaire's overture to acquire 0.3% of its land for a resort development. As I understand it, this was due to cultural concerns. I believe that we can, through patient and respectful collaboration, address such concerns to assure mutual comfort.

This section includes many assumptions and financial forecasts. Those are for illustrative purposes only. Actual numbers will follow the input of experts and, in all likelihood, a massive online simulation in which everything is put to the test and refined.

That said, imagine with me ...

On Mother's Day, in the year 2025, many of the 250,000 Citizens, residents, and guests of the city-state of Dogun gathered in its Great Hall of Celebration at the heart of the city. Also in attendance were millions of others through VR and other internet connections. The lighting illuminated in softly shifting pastel colors the woman at center stage. She sat in deep meditation. Also on stage, in shadows, sat a full orchestra and dance troupe, awaiting later festivities. Despite the vast attendance, the people also sat in silence, reverently awaiting her words. At 8 PM she rose, raised her hands in acknowledgement, and began to speak.

"Many have called our accomplishments here revolutionary," said the Mistress of Ceremonies with a bright smile, "but I think it is better instead to think of them as evolutionary. We have brought together in a new way many established systems[518] and technologies, some of them not previously well-known but all of them well-researched. None of this is regarded as permanent. Instead, we are continuously experimenting and improving.

"Dogun is a place where people gather and live to celebrate, to explore, to learn, to create, to play—and, temporarily, to work. We do so on a foundation of orderly, well-functioning systems that allow us ample free time and provide for our needs. We commune with our neighbors. We live in clean, attractive villages in carefully planned harmony with nature. Each village has its own cultural preferences, consistent with the Dogun Charter. We eat healthy, fresh food. We work with nature and science for our medical care.

"Children are guided and supported to pursue their passions which eventually include, almost without exception, learning the skills necessary to function as Citizens of Dogun. We assign responsibility based on proven competency and willingness to assume it, and we give recognition based on service to the community. Each adult is sovereign over his or her own body, and each individual is expected to know and respect the Charter and the laws."

The Mistress of Ceremonies paused and adjusted her shimmering robe. Its beautiful overlaid sashes—the wider one purple; the narrower one silver—signified her royal status as a Great Servant, or Mahana Sevaka. She took a deep breath.

"Our goal has been to bring the best of humanity's accumulated wisdom together in one place, in service of our common set of values, as expressed in our Charter.

"It has been five years since we broke ground. We were pleased that some of the Icelandic *berdreymin* (dream seers) foresaw Dogun. Our Icelandic friends assure us that we have in our behavior respected all Icelandic customs, including our

---

[518] It will be far easier to establish such a fresh network of systems in a brand-new Celebration Society than in an existing society wishing to become a Celebration Society. The reason is that existing societies tend to have adequate though not great systems. (http://www.theatlantic.com/business/archive/2015/01/when-good-enough-holds-back-new-inventions/384248/)

treatment of lands and monuments believed to be important to Huldufolk, and that we are indeed the good neighbors they hoped we would become. Those Icelanders who graciously gave up their lands to allow the building of Dogun chose to take generous compensation and relocation, or to become residents of Dogun.

"We are gathered here with representatives of Iceland, Britain, and other friendly nations on this most joyous occasion to review and celebrate how we got from there to here. First, I will offer a brief review of our history. Then the celebrations will commence."

The Mistress of Ceremonies paused as a smattering or applause rippled through the assembly. Smiling and upholding a hand, she said: "Please, as is our custom, refrain from any applause until the end. If you wish to show your enthusiasm, I believe each of you has been provided with a colorful streamer that can be waved, yes?

"Six years ago, negotiations commenced between our sponsor state of Iceland, our founders, and our co-sponsor state of Britain. It was established that Iceland would lease to Dogun for 100 years the land we presently occupy, with a purchase option, in consideration of Dogun providing to Iceland 2.5% of all national revenues, public and private.[519]

---

[519] It was further agreed that Dogun could after 100 years achieve permanent sovereignty and independence from Iceland by making a one-time payment of $10 billion. With this stipulation, Sovereignty is asserted per international law under both the Constitutive and Declaratory theories of statehood as follows: (1) Iceland and Britain both recognize Dogun as a sovereign state, fulfilling the Constitutive theory and, (2) Dogun qualifies under the Declaratory theory because it has: (a) a defined territory, (b) a permanent population, (c) a government, and (d) the capacity to enter into relations with other sovereign states non-coercively, as evidenced by the Treaty of Dogun signed with Iceland and Britain and further actions and relations pertaining to the treaty.

Should Dogun's statehood be challenged in future by a competent party under international law on the grounds that its statehood is conditional, it is further

"Further, Iceland agreed to pay to Britain 1/3 of those revenues to a total matching the funds lost by British subjects and institutions when the Icelandic banking system collapsed, plus their lost interest.[520] In exchange for these promises, Britain and Iceland agreed by treaty to recognize Dogun as a nation state and all three nation states agreed to form a mutual defense and economic cooperation treaty. Iceland also committed to a major improvement of its national airport and to the creation of a second airport and port near Dogun.

"Dogun needed approximately $20 billion US to move from an idea of a city-state with a land lease to a functioning entity with basic infrastructure.[521] This funding was achieved in several ways. 100,000 would-be Citizens, excited by the vision they had come to experience through *Celebrationism: the Simulation* as well as their participation in the website www.aCelebrationSociety.com, committed into escrow an average of $100,000 US to the purchase of home lots under condominium design in the city-state. That represented $10 billion of the necessary funding. The money was escrowed according to a process that assured its disposition in a well-ordered legal manner.

"The additional $10 billion was secured in the form of investment by private entities that obtained valuable concessions on the underground communications/ delivery/ waste management system, the above-ground transportation system

---

agreed that Dogun shall have the option at any time of raising its payment to Iceland from 2.5% to 3.5% in exchange for permanence of lease, with the option remaining to eliminate this payment and all conditional aspects of its status at any time in exchange for the one-time $10 billion payment.

[520] Many numbers in this section are estimates.

[521] Masdar, a high-tech sustainable city, is being built in the UAE with an estimated construction budget of $20 billion. Unlike Dogun, Masdar envisions a permanent population of only 45 - 50,000 with that figure approximately doubled by commuting workers. However, it is not structured as a tourist destination, nor does it have the full advantage of breakthrough technologies. (https://en.wikipedia.org/wiki/Masdar_City)

including light rail and tourism management[522]—with the requirement that the operators maintain certain standards of operation and respect the laws and culture of Dogun. Payment on this investment was assured by our promise that 2.5% of the 15% in sales taxes[523] would be allocated to ROI.

"Given that 2.5% of the sales revenues were already allocated to payment for the land lease, this deduction of 5% left 10% for other Dogun needs. While a flat 15% sales tax might not seem substantial compared to the much higher income tax rates common in other nations, economists[524] had already determined that such a flat tax, free of all deductions and exemptions, would in fact offer very significant revenues.[525]

"Our business plan projected that tourism would be the major source of revenues,[526] and that the average visitor would stay 3 days and spend $1,300. In fact, we have found that the average visitor stays 4 days and spends $1,790 apart from their admission fees and taxes. Since Dogun's hostelry,

---

[522] Needed investment may come from *impact investing,* a type of investment wherein the investors seek both a healthy return on investment (ROI) and a positive social impact. Such funds are expected to total $500 billion by 2020, and Dogun's needs would represent 2% of this total. (http://en.wikipedia.org/wiki/Impact_investing)

[523] The exact structure of this tax will have to be carefully considered. It should meet Adam Smith's four criteria for sound taxation expressed in *The Wealth of Nations* as well as more current thinking such as Dan Pilla's ten principles. The tax must neither favor nor discourage particular activities, thereby never using taxation as social engineering. (Complementary currencies, rather than the main national currency, will serve that purpose.)

[524] Notably, Milton Friedman in consultations with the presidential campaign of Jerry Brown.

[525] http://www.commdiginews.com/politics-2/reigniting-the-flat-tax-debate-why-is-this-solution-repeatedly-ignored-20095/

[526] Venice shows that a city that is beautiful enough, with enough unique architectural features, can essentially function as a tourist destination. Venice also shows the need to balance tourism and residential needs, as tourism is overwhelming that city's residential functions. (http://www.csmonitor.com/World/Europe/2012/1031/Is-Venice-being-loved-to-death)

restaurant and other tourist facilities are always filled to capacity with the 50,000 visitors continuously allowed[527]— and with a waiting list of 3 years now!—our total revenues from tourism have been a solid $8.15 billion annually; much of it providing a healthy income to our residents and Citizens.[528]

"Dogun keeps the $125 daily admission fee[529] charged to visitors. It charges a 15% tax on all other expenditures by visitors. Therefore, the average 4-day visitor provides to Dogun's government $500 in fee revenues ($125 x 4) and $269 in sales tax revenues ($1,790 x 0.15), for a total of $769. This gives the government $3.5 billion in annual tourism-related revenues, apart from donations by Citizens and residents. Of this, 1/3 goes to service our debt.[530]

"These revenues have served to cover not only the operating costs of Dogun's government but also provide us with ample funds for the general welfare of Dogun's Citizens, including basic medical care, education, housing and food. While the average Citizen of Dogun is a highly productive and successful person, it was inevitable that some would exper- ience hardship, and covering this was one purpose of the General Welfare Fund.[531] On the other hand, as research has suggested, the complete social safety net of Dogun encourages our Citizens to take risks. We have a higher rate of business

---

[527] Venice's tourism has been estimated at 30 million annually, or about 82,000 persons per day. (http://www.spiegel.de/international/europe/death-of-german-tourist-prompts-venice-to-consider-limits-a-921845.html)

[528] $8.16 BB = 50,000 x 91 turns (4 days/turn) annually yielding 4.5 MM visitors x $1,790.

[529] Comparable to Disney World.

[530] $769 per 4-day visit x 50,000 visitors x 91 visitation cycles annually.

[531] Dogun was not the first nation to provide such an income to citizens. It was established in Norway, Kuwait, the Canadian province of Alberta, and the US state of Alaska as well. Switzerland has considered this. (Economists ranging from Friedrich Hayek to Milton Friedman to Paul Samuelson as well as Martin Luther King and Richard Nixon have advocated it.) http://www.theatlantic.com/national/archive/2014/10/alaska-paid-its-citizens-1884-last-week-no-strings-attached/381108/

startups per capita than anyplace on Earth, excepting Silicon Valley and Israel.[532]

"A secondary purpose of the Dogun General Welfare Fund is to provide for beautification and other enhancements to Dogun, including public works and monuments, as might be approved by the parliament. This has been made easier by our custom of "tipping it forward" instituted by the founders. Each owner of a business is encouraged to donate 10% of the shares to the Fund. Though non-compulsory, the transparent nature of financial activities in Dogun has assured a very high rate of participation. The market value of the Fund recently surpassed $8 billion."

The Mistress of Ceremonies paused again as ribbons fluttered wildly in the audience, creating a flowing rainbow of colors panoramically televised worldwide. "I should mention as an aside that some visitors expect to see a full celebrationist system of production and are surprised that we have a modified capitalist system with elements of celebrationism. We never promised a direct transition from capitalism to full celebrationism, and in fact we expect the complete transition to take decades. Thanks to our hemp production for biodiesel, along with geothermal, solar and other energy technologies, we already have all of the energy we need and our organizing intelligence systems are working well.

"Our complementary currency systems assure that unmet needs are constantly being matched with underutilized resources, creating alongside our conventional national money an effective financial system for sustainable growth, without booms or busts. Studies of our financial system are underway at universities including Minerva, Harvard, RPI, ASU and MIT.

"We are, as I speak, in discussions with Planetary Resources to begin establishing an off-world mining and manufacturing consortium within the next 5 years, in partnership with other aligned societies. Once that is fully operational, we will have functioning all three pillars of celebrationism.

---

[532] http://www.theatlantic.com/politics/archive/2015/03/welfare-makes-america-more-entrepreneurial/388598/

"Many visitors remark on the general happiness level of Dogun residents. With happiness generally regarded as a desirable attainment both individually and as a society, they seem surprised that we have for the most part attained it. In this as in all other areas, we have built our society on the foundation of science. The recently emergent science of positive psychology has determined that specific practices and values serve to promote happiness, and that happiness in turn massively promotes success.[533]

"Given that this research works so well on the individual level, and that a society is a collection of individuals, I believe that a typical Dogun resident when asked about our prevalent level of happiness would smile and say, "It's not living in Dogun that makes us happy. One could be happy anywhere. Rather, Dogun reinforces everything supportive of happiness such that one would have to work to be unhappy here." Happiness is not effective as a goal; it comes as a byproduct of living in a state of curiosity coupled to passionate, playful pursuit of that which means most to us—one's purpose.[534] Also, one must learn how to deal with pain,[535] which is distinct from suffering."

Many ribbons fluttered. "One of the things that promotes happiness is service to others in a way that the individual finds meaningful,[536] and perhaps the greatest of these is what some have called "paying it forward" as a whole society. We have chosen to call what we do *tipping it forward,* because of the entendres embedded in that phrase.

---

[533] https://www.youtube.com/watch?v=GXy__kBVq1M

[534] https://www.youtube.com/watch?v=vVsXO9brK7M

[535] https://www.youtube.com/watch?v=UunaTEpWrME

[536] In his legendary book, *Man's Search for Meaning,* psychiatrist Viktor Frankl recounted his experience living in a concentration camp and how he found meaning and happiness there. In *Shantaram,* author Gregory David Roberts described the happiness prevalent in a filth-infested slum of Mumbai, where caring for others was commonplace.

"As the years have passed, I am pleased to report that the value of 'tipping it forward' ownership positions along with the annual $3 billion in government revenues has enabled Dogun to begin fulfilling its third financial obligation: that of providing support for the creation of two additional Celebration Societies. This financial support has been, of course, in addition to the personal services rendered by Dogun Candidate Citizens who are seeking full, permanent Citizenship—and other volunteers.

"We are today a thriving small nation,[537] and as predicted in our business plan we have indeed become the world's premier tourist destination at least on a per capita basis. Most of those who visit do not want to leave, or wish to create their own Celebration Society elsewhere.

"We are only too glad to help them.

"Of course, a city such as this requires support services. Let's take a moment to look at how that works.

"Each lot purchased is structured as condominium space, with homeowners' association fees that cover basic support services as well as common usage of facilities at both the village and city levels. Each lot owner has both the opportunity to build a home on their lot and ownership of a condominium unit in the city center.[538] We have centers of learning, sports and exercise facilities, gaming centers, museums and wellness centers. We have parks, beautiful walkways, well-maintained bodies of water, and botanical and coral gardens. We have administrative offices, a parliament, judicial centers, and other facilities common to all civilized societies.

---

[537]Concerns about the viability of a tiny city-state such as Dogun can be at least partially addressed by considering the Republic of San Marino. The oldest nation in Europe (founded in 301 AD), it is completely enclosed within Italy. The "Most Serene Republic of San Marino" has no army and maintains neutrality. According to the CIA Factbook, it occupies 23 square miles with a population of about 32,000. It has taxes about 1/3 the average for the EU, of which it is not a member, and a per capita GDP of about $55,000 per year. In addition, the state of Monaco is only about 1 square mile.

[538] This then allows the owner to either rent out one of the residences to visitors or to house support staff who will provide services such as gardening, cooking and cleaning.

"Home construction is required to meet village and city level covenants. It must meet community aesthetic requirements as well as being quantifiably carbon neutral or negative. At first, most of our structures were built from imported materials. However, as our hemp and bamboo fields and processing facilities have ramped up, much construction has shifted to use of these extraordinary materials whose usefulness is starting to be appreciated worldwide."

The Mahana Sevaka held up her hands and laughed. "I believe I have heard all of the jokes about growing bamboo in Iceland. We have also begun to explore the manufacture of so-called Roman concrete—which can last thousands of years. Being 85% volcanic ash, such concrete is a natural product for this volcanic area.

"Physically, Dogun can be seen as four directionally oriented concentric rectangles, with extensive use of the Golden Ratio—a number found to accentuate the experience of beauty in architecture and music.[539] Innermost is the city center. Around that are the villages, comprising the second rectangle.[540] Together, these are the populated areas. Around the villages is the third rectangle, including the hemp and bamboo greenhouses and the automated vegetable and fruit farms as well as meat cultivation—which, excepting eggs, involves no living animals. All of these complement permaculture and aquaponics gardens that permeate the residential areas.

---

[539] http://freshome.com/2014/10/29/how-architects-take-advantage-of-the-golden-ratio/

[540] Each village is comprised of a set of hamlets, each of which is comprised of neighborhoods, each neighborhood with a population of approximately 150. This respects Dunbar's Number, which was discovered by evolutionary anthropologist Robin Dunbar. This number has been confirmed as the optimum size for a self-organizing group and was likely the normal size of human tribes during ancient times.

"The fourth and final rectangle consists of the great forest which is rapidly growing thanks to permaculture and which supports a variety of trees and synergistic plants and animals. This is a place where wild animals, including wolves and deer, roam freely. The great road into Dogun is elevated through the fourth rectangle, allowing people and wild animals to appreciate each other from a distance. We have created a complete ecology there, and we respect it.[541]

"Construction in Dogun is a mixture of locally occurring resources and grown and imported resources. The guadua bamboo is like flexible steel, and with our groves of bamboo grasses we have also added pandas; a popular tourist attraction. Structures that might otherwise be built of stone for great durability, such as the wall around the villages, are typically made of concrete. So are walkways, monuments and many buildings. However, a significant portion of the construction materials are hemp products—pressed blocks as well as plastics—grown on our own farms and processed in our factories. Hemp is a prolific crop; it is not for nothing that it was called a "weed"." She laughed and streamers fluttered.

"Medical care in Dogun has a heavy emphasis on prevention, with medical personnel acknowledged and rewarded for success at sustaining the health of their patients. Corrective care is rare and minimalist, being regarded as a failure of either our preventive health care systems or the city's safety systems, which are continuously monitored and improved. Of course, with all high speed transportation being automated, accidents are very rare.

"Internal combustion engines, being a source of pollution and noise, are banned except by special exemption. In general, noise regulations restrict potentially disturbing sounds to special indoor venues because peace and quiet are greatly valued in Dogun.

---

[541] In future, diverse Celebration Societies may create and sustain ecosystems that support local wildlife as part of their tourism appeal. This might be a way to preserve species.

"Construction is generally much quieter and faster than elsewhere because of our emphasis on modular methods and the fact that heavy objects and structures are hoisted into place via silent blimp. We have also instituted the use of 3-D printing for some structures.

"Security is another thing people wonder about, mainly because they see so little of it. While we do have a small force of Peace Officers, security in Dogun is generally automated, hidden and unobtrusive. It begins at the outskirts of the city in the forest and continues throughout into all public places. Everyone is advised that all public activities are subject to monitoring and recording. While some have complained about this "Orwellian" surveillance,[542] when it is pointed out that we turn that concept upside down by making all public surveillance footage available to all Citizens at all times, and that this system makes Dogun safe for everyone, they tend to relax.

"The greatest threat to Dogun has come from infection. Three years ago, a man who had been infected with Bas-Congo virus but was not yet showing symptoms sought to enter the city. Fortunately, our medical AI's, which track all known infectious disease outbreaks worldwide in real time, coordinating with the US Centers for Disease Control and other agencies, determined that he had recently visited an area with several known cases. Based upon a lab-on-a-chip on-the-spot diagnosis, he was quarantined and spread was prevented. Several less extreme infectious threats have also been identified and deterred.

"Still, we acknowledge that outbreaks are not fully preventable. At some future time, a serious pathogen outbreak will likely happen in Dogun. Therefore, we maintain ample

---

[542] This is a serious matter in other societies such as the USA, where law enforcement has actively pursued the use of "RAT software" to take control of citizens' PC webcams and internals.
(http://www.theatlantic.com/technology/archive/2014/12/the-webcam-hacking-epidemic/383998/). When tiny drones can peer inside windows or fly or crawl into private places like insects, those too will be used for surveillance.

stocks of all known immune-boosting as well as antiviral and antibacterial substances alongside a trained rapid response hazmat team with biosafety level 4 certified suits, protocols and containment facilities, along with lab-on-a-chip devices; at minimum one per neighborhood. Also, by tightly restricting entry into the city, we maintain maximum ability to monitor for symptoms and other indications that someone may pose a health risk.

"We submit that a city-state design such as ours offers a society the best chance of avoiding pandemic.[543] OK, I think that's enough disturbing information. Let's return to more pleasant topics.

"Many visitors marvel at how even small children are allowed to go where they please in Dogun without adult supervision. However, when we combine the universal open surveillance of public spaces with the ability to monitor children's whereabouts at all times, it is a natural way to live. Also, I believe it is accurate to say that we have established a culture in which adults tend to feel protective towards the children, as has prevailed in villages and small communities throughout most of human history.

"Side benefits of our system have included an almost total elimination of bullying, and so we have little concern that children with brains susceptible to damage from violence and other destructive behaviors will ever manifest the consequences of such damage. In fact, building on the successful life of Dr. James Fallon, it has been suggested that even non-abused sociopaths may become valued and contributing Citizens, since they live only to win games of their own choosing and most of the games here have to do with service.

"We have achieved a society in which the basic right to be left alone is considered sacrosanct. In our view, this is

---

[543] Also, a new kind of antibiotic works on a different principle than others and bacteria have, so far, not been able to mutate to resist it.
(http://www.theatlantic.com/health/archive/2015/01/ a-new-drug-in-the-age-of-antibiotic-resistance/384291/)

essential if people holding significantly differing beliefs are to harmoniously coexist. We have, by last count, 18 religions represented in Dogun.

"Participation in civil and social activities is very high. Since each Citizen is subject to serve by lottery selection as a member of parliament or juror, interest in governance is almost universal and laws are kept simple and clear.

"Because our laws are streamlined such that any Citizen can understand all of them without need for a lawyer except under extraordinary circumstances, and because laws only exist if they have a high level of acceptance amongst Citizens, civic compliance with law is nearly universal. Also, the opportunity to air grievances is easy and straightforward. Due to all of this, instead of the alienation from government which is sadly common elsewhere, we find almost universal support for the system among the Citizens.

"In fact, what the past five years have taught us is that our greatest legal problem is visitors wanting to overstay their welcome. While understandable, this particular civil violation—we do not call it a crime—is easily rectified by virtue of the fact that the locations of all persons are continuously known.

"Speaking of crime, it shocks some to learn that we have no prisons. We do have holding facilities for persons who have committed violent offenses or are otherwise deemed a threat to others' safety. These, however, are used only until they receive a judicial hearing and decision, always within a week of the offense being committed. We do not use the word 'sentencing'.

"Guests who commit minor offenses are remanded to their own countries and charged all costs of restoration. Guests who commit serious offenses have their home countries notified and are banned from returning. Residents and Citizens who commit serious offenses (or demonstrate mental illness that makes them dangerous) are given therapy and, if necessary, segregated from the general population until they are well again. If they have caused harm, they are then responsible for restoring what they have damaged to whatever extent possible.

It is a system based on prevention, restoration, and atonement, rather than punishment.

"AI's pervade our lives, with most of us interacting with the City's systems and much of the rest of our lives through personal AI Butlers. These tools, while optional, make the routine aspects of life automatic and help us to filter out any unwanted information or communications while opting into whatever is wanted. For most of us, these tools enable us to discover opportunities for play, learning, friendship and exploration that might otherwise have been missed.

"In addition to the triple redundancy that's built into all of the mission-critical systems in Dogun, we also have AI's focused on making sure that nothing important, as defined by the administration or the Citizens, ever goes wrong. I am pleased to report that, while we have had some glitches, notably the power outage of three years ago that lasted for two days and which led to the spontaneous candlelight celebrations that have continued on occasion to this day, most glitches do not seem to repeat themselves.

"To sum up, by any reasonable standard we have achieved a successful society that in many ways is leading the world. We can all be proud of our contributions to this, and can look forward together to further successes as Dogun continues to pioneer a new way of being and living in the world.

"Thank you for joining us today! Let the celebrations begin."

Towards a World of Celebration Societies

Open Source is not just software. It is a philosophy. It's the idea that sharing is better than secrecy. It's the proof that cooperation is more effective than ruthless competition; and that by opening up the blueprints, the development of science, culture, the arts, and everything that is positive accelerates.

~Federico Pistono

We can create a model society of prosperity, of flourishing arts and sciences that many who visit will want to call home. Such a place will be an open source model community, the first of many, and when duplicated again and again on a "pay it forward" model, can lead us to a truly new world.

To understand how this could happen, consider the following scenario. One Celebration Society is started in 2020. It commits to sponsor two additional societies within 5 years. In exchange for receiving that support, each of the new Celebration Societies would make the same commitment to sponsor two others. (The following assumes that each Celebration Society continues to sponsor two additional ones every 5 years, and that multitudes of people desire to live this way.)

This becomes an exponential expansion. If the average peak population of a Celebration Society is half a million residents, here is how the math works:

- By 2040, 40 million people will live in 81 Celebration Societies.
- By 2055, over 1 billion people will live in more than 2,000 Celebration Societies.
- By 2065, the entire population of Earth will live in Celebration Societies—if they so choose.[544]

While a 5 year plan of duplication is highly aggressive, certain factors make it more plausible. First, the initial Celebration Societies can be inhabited by people capable of paying their own way. If 200,000 adults escrow $100,000 each that is $20 billion; the amount that was needed to build the new city of Masdar. (While the population will be higher than Masdar's 40,000, advanced technologies should slash infrastructure and housing construction costs.)

Assuming the early cities do not need financial sponsorship but only the expert mentorship of their sponsor cities, that can be more quickly provided than billions of

---

[544] See spreadsheet, "Prospective Growth of CS Populations", at www.aCelebrationSociety.com.

dollars. Further, the early city-states will have a clear path to revenue from medical tourism and as unique entertainment destinations. This revenue should fund the bridge from capitalism to celebrationism.

As some of the early Celebration Societies make the successful transition to fully celebrationist systems of production, they will be in a position to gift those systems to future Celebration Societies and money will cease to matter. (In this manner, all sorts of impoverished societies can bootstrap into abundance.)

Finally, it is likely that once several successful Celebration Societies exist in disparate environments some existing nation states will seek to make the conversion. Once such an existing society has successfully converted, the rate of conversion should greatly accelerate as citizens of many nations demand this quality of life.

Based on such considerations, it is possible that the entire world (estimated peak population: 8.7 billion)[545] will have the option of converting to celebrationism much sooner than 2065.

Even with a more conservative scenario where the first sponsorships are delayed 5 years to prove viability, and each Celebration Society "only" sponsors two others and then stops, we reach 1 billion people living this way by 2075.

I have discussed how medical tourism could provide a substantial revenue source. Let's now consider more deeply what medical care might look like.

Health Care in a Celebration Society

Among the various systems of a Celebration Society, few will be more different from current standards than that of health care. A comparison is appropriate.

---

[545] http://www.cnbc.com/id/101018722

A Broken System

It is generally recognized that the US healthcare system is broken. It has been called an "illness-profit" model, which I find to be generally accurate. Far more can be charged to cure someone than to keep them healthy. Nearly all medical practices must be vetted by the US Food and Drug Administration (FDA) before they may be deployed and this process is rife with politics. In general, only those procedures that are expected to make a profit are performed.

Examples of FDA failures include:

- Against the effective consensus of the world medical community, the FDA opposed for years recommending a folic acid supplement to women of childbearing age, resulting in thousands of babies being born with the crippling disease spina bifida. In the Appellate Court case of Pearson v. Shalala, the Court found that, "the FDA's decision to classify Plaintiffs' Folic Acid Claim as 'inherently misleading' was arbitrary, capricious, and an abuse of discretion."[546]

- Based upon one bad batch of tryptophan from one of multiple manufacturers, the FDA banned *all* sales of this normally safe and effective sleep aid naturally found in milk and turkey. Millions were thereby forced to use drugs such as Xanax, which is highly addictive, and Ambien, which can cause dangerous "sleep driving".[547]

- The FDA has raided publishers of medical advice and providers of products with which it disagreed, deploying military-style police tactics to seize records and shut down businesses.[548]

---

[546] http://www.emord.com/Emord%20&%20Associates,%20Pearson%20v.%20Shalala%20II.pdf

[547] http://www.huffingtonpost.com/2014/01/15/ambien-side-effect-sleepwalking-sleep-aid_n_4589743.html

[548] http://www.naturalnews.com/021791.html

- An FDA research scientist whom I know informed me privately that he and his colleagues have repeatedly been offered bribes by representatives of pharmaceutical companies seeking favorable outcomes from research then underway. To his knowledge, no one had been punished.

- In 2000, a friend and I opened a business in Thailand offering a rapid self-test for HIV. It was based on a strip made by Abbott Laboratories, a major medical products manufacturer, and relied on a drop of blood. In 2014, the FDA finally approved such a test for use in the US.[549] Such delays are not uncommon.

- The political nature of FDA decisions has never been clearer than with the new "female viagra". It was twice rejected by FDA due to lack of efficacy and dangerous side effects. In particular, FDA determined that a mere 8-13% of users will enjoy any improvement in their sex life. This is a drug to be taken daily yet users must completely abstain from alcohol or hormonal birth control to avoid a dangerous loss of blood pressure. Nevertheless, following an aggressive marketing campaign in which FDA was accused of sexism, it approved the third application *without a change in the data*. Said Dr. Adriane Fugh-Berman of Georgetown University, "(this is) a mediocre aphrodisiac with scary side effects..."[550]

More such examples could be added. The FDA charges pharmaceutical companies enormous fees to run investigational new drug trials. These are vital to winning approval for distribution. It is an incestuous situation wherein pharmaceutical companies are sometimes viewed as "clients" and they pay a significant part of the FDA budget.[551]

---

[549] http://www.fda.gov/ForConsumers/ConsumerUpdates/ucm310545.htm
[550] http://www.naturalnews.com/051048_female_viagra_side_effects_FDA.html
[551] http://www.pbs.org/wgbh/pages/frontline/shows/prescription/hazard/independent.html

The FDA may have originally been chartered with the intention of serving as a way to assure that "snake oil" was not provided to unwary patients in lieu of valid evidence-based medicine. It *has* provided for a standardized system of care that is *generally* evidence-based and is often effective. FDA's limitations notwithstanding, it retains the respect of much of the medical community. Indeed, doctors will point out that a small clinical study of a few dozen patients, as is commonly cited by supplement manufacturers, has far less validity than a "gold standard" study including thousands of patients.

However, the system has huge shortcomings in that such tests are absurdly expensive. An effective drug or non-prescription medicine that cannot be patented will never win FDA approval because such approval requires a process taking years and generally costing hundreds of millions of dollars.

Without protected opportunities to collect revenue and recoup those costs, no one will pay such fees for something that, even if it wins approval, can be copied by other drug companies who did not bear the costs of getting it approved. (Even when the system works, a single pill may cost $1,000 in the US while being far cheaper elsewhere—hardly equitable from the standpoint of those users who must, in effect, subsidize other users.[552])

A prescription medication that has been approved by FDA for one condition may never be re-tested when discovered to have promise for treating another condition. One example is Fosamax, which was approved to treat Paget's disease of bone and osteoporosis, and later recommended (with FDA consent) to treat osteopenia, a slight thinning of the bones that occurs naturally as women get older. Osteopenia is very widespread among mature women, but:

> "There was no difference in the number of [nonspine] fractures you had, whether you took

---

[552] http://www.npr.org/sections/health-shots/2014/02/06/272519954/maker-of-1-000-hepatitis-c-pill-looks-to-cut-its-cost-overseas

the medicine or a placebo," says [Susan Ott, an associate professor in the department of medicine at the University of Washington]. "It does make your bone density go up higher, but the number of fractures is what really matters, and that didn't really change."

There are no long-term studies that look at what happens to women with osteopenia who start Fosamax in their 50s and continue treatment long-term in the hopes of preventing old-age fractures. *And none are planned.* [emphasis added]

Ott worries that taking (Fosamax) long-term — over 10 years or more — might actually make bones brittle.[553]

Much of the world follows the US FDA's lead. Why not? FDA funnels billions of dollars into research studies annually, and it would be irrational to repeat this process. But at what general cost?

The system in the US and in most developed countries favors rigid approaches to medical care that may serve many but do not support testing and approval of promising therapies such as the above examples, as well as private trials by physicians and informed patients. Some such therapies may be quite simple.

The rigidities of top-down, command-and-control medicine were designed to prevent quack therapies from achieving mainstream status, as well as to incentivize companies to invest in the huge costs of medical research. They are less and less effective at doing so as patients:

- Increasingly choose complementary and alternative medical approaches, such as chiropractic, acupuncture, dietary supplements and even more exotic

---

[553] http://www.npr.org/2009/12/21/121609815/how-a-bone-disease-grew-to-fit-the-prescription

therapies, some of which have recently achieved significant acceptance in the medical community. (The US National Institutes of Health includes Complementary and Alternative Medicine Funding, which totaled $367 million across agencies in 2014.)[554]

- Increasingly seek their own health care advice and practices on the internet, with no good way to differentiate valid claims from those of hucksters promoting a specific product.

- Increasingly monitor and control their own health care through wearable computers that can indicate when treatment is warranted. (In future, such monitoring will enable people to determine in real time the effects a therapy is having, which is significant not only for complementary and alternative medicine therapies but also for prescription drugs, whose effects can vary dramatically from patient to patient.)

Patients who could benefit from conventional medicine delay using it at great personal cost, while others continue to use it as a first course of treatment when something far less risky or expensive might have sufficed. Evidence shows the illness profit model is broken.[555]

While other nations have universal health care based on what is called a *single payer* model, this too has issues. When there is a single payer, that payer has the power to decide which forms of care will be approved and which will be denied.

Further, while there is considerable interest in "pay for performance" schemes in which doctors are paid more for improved patient outcomes, the research to date does not offer clear evidence of efficacy or lack thereof.[556]

---

[554] https://nccih.nih.gov/about/budget/institute-center.htm

[555] http://www.economist.com/news/international/21660974-global-rise-caesarean-sections-being-driven-not-medical-necessity

[556] http://www.cochrane.org/CD008451/EPOC_the-effect-of-financial-incentives-on-the-quality-of-health-care-provided-by-primary-care-physicians

A Different System of Care

Now let's consider how medical care might work in a Celebration Society.

In a Celebration Society, medical care will be a decision made by an adult patient or parent under advice of his or her physician. The patient will have full authority over his or her own body, since this will be viewed as an inalienable right for a responsible adult. Children will be protected from harm, either via commission or omission, but with a bias that parents may choose various therapies that are physician-approved provided neither the child's welfare nor general health is endangered. What would this mean in practice?

There would be universal health care for all Citizens of a Celebration Society. (Access to and payment for health care for residents and visitors might well vary among different societies.) The focus of this health care would be not on allopathic treatment of symptoms, often in crisis mode, but rather on regular preventive practices and medical attention at the first sign that something was wrong. It would embody the old adage, "an ounce of prevention is worth a pound of cure."

This will be a program that moves from diagnosis of a problem to therapy that carries minimal risk of harm, consistent with the appropriate time-frame for treatment. It will advance to options such as drugs, radiation and surgery only after less risky and less costly options deemed appropriate by doctor and patient have been exhausted or found inadequate due to the urgency of the situation. In short, it will be rational—influenced by neither profit nor politics.

Such an approach will protect many from ever experiencing chronic health problems, such as BPH, cancer, or Type II diabetes. By emphasizing prevention over cure, this will also enable a reduction in medical personnel since the treatment of crises necessitates huge arrays of equipment and staff. Doctors may actually be able to work fewer hours per week, primarily helping patients to stay healthy and enjoy life.

Professional licensing would also be voluntary, and available through professional associations for limited areas, so that a health practitioner would not be required to learn everything in a medical school curriculum but rather could focus on their areas of interest and take qualifying exams as appropriate for those specific areas. (Such associations would have significant influence but no legal authority.)

While some may fear that charismatic quacks will endanger public health, this is already true in the illness profit model. For example, the hospital in my wife's former small town was forced to make public radio and television announcements informing people who'd had prostate cancer surgery performed by a specific doctor that he had lost his license due to malpractice and that those patients needed to come in and make sure their surgeries were effective.

In a Celebration Society, where information flow is high and transparent, and physician ratings will carry great significance, the quacks should rapidly be exposed. (I suspect that most patients would still choose licensed physicians over the unlicensed, since the implied peer approval would offer reassurance, as would transparency and accountability.)

Further, advanced and exotic medical technologies that are not generally accepted or have no established place in current western allopathic medicine will have an active role. Among these will almost surely be, by way of examples:

- EMDR, a technologically assisted method to enhance talk therapy that can rapidly produce intense, transformative experiences. It has become widely accepted among counselors over several decades of use.[557]
- Pulsed electromagnetic fields (PEMF), researched by NASA and others, and found to significantly improve certain conditions.[558]

---

[557] http://www.theatlantic.com/health/archive/2015/07/emdr-trauma/399650/
[558] http://research.jsc.nasa.gov/PDF/SLiSci-12.pdf

- Cold lasers, widely used in veterinary practice to accelerate healing.[559]
- Fasting, which can cause dormant stem cells to awaken, renewing the immune system.[560]
- Alcoholism treatment via naltrexone, Antabuse[561] and ibogaine.[562]
- Self-compassion and mindfulness education.[563]
- Alternative, evidence-based approaches to managing pain, depression, anxiety, and insomnia such as the Fisher Wallace Stimulator.[564]
- Methods of replacing tooth decay with new, healthy enamel, as are being developed in Britain and elsewhere.[565]
- Advanced forms of colloidal silver with nanometer-sized particles, which have shown promise against certain difficult to treat pathogens.[566]

Many folk and other remedies await scientific evaluation. It is possible that some of our most intractable and dangerous

---

[559] http://www.ncbi.nlm.nih.gov/pmc/articles/PMC3065857/

[560] Prolonged Fasting Reduces IGF-1/PKA to Promote Hematopoietic-Stem-Cell-Based Regeneration and Reverse Immunosuppression. Cell Stem Cell , Volume 14 , Issue 6 , 810 – 823

[561] http://www.theatlantic.com/features/archive/2015/03/the-irrationality-of-alcoholics-anonymous/386255/

[562] https://www.ucsf.edu/news/2005/01/5247/controversial-drug-shown-act-brain-protein-cut-alcohol-use

[563] http://mindfulnessyautocompasion.org/resources/Neff+$26+Germer+MSC+RCT+2012.pdf

[564] http://www.fisherwallace.com/pages/published-research

[565] http://www.theguardian.com/business/2014/oct/12/tooth-decay-dentists-remineralisation-the-innovators

[566] HIV: http://www.ncbi.nlm.nih.gov/pmc/articles/PMC1190212/, http://www.jnanobiotechnology.com/content/8/1/19, http://www.jnanobiotechnology.com/content/3/1/6, http://www.riskscience.umich.edu/nano-silver-used-treat-ebola-victims-nigeria/

modern medical threats may fall to some of these, once properly tested. For example, hundreds of thousands of people suffer or even die annually from infections contracted during hospital stays. (MRSA and XRSA are bacterial infections that have become immune to conventional antibiotics.) It is obviously unacceptable that this is so.

An extract from chestnut leaves appears to offer a non-toxic way to deal with antibiotic-resistant skin infections. While FDA will take years to approve an extract—if it ever does—those with loved ones in hospital can make a tea from these leaves and give the hospitalized person a sponge bath.[567] (Further research to confirm efficacy is needed, but this preventive remedy has no risk.)

Will some persons use ineffective therapies, perhaps endangering their health and even their lives, under such a system? Almost certainly. But this is, in my view, an acceptable price to pay for acknowledging their adult informed freedom of choice about their own bodies that is presumed to be an inalienable right of a Citizen in a Celebration Society. It is also the price of allowing people the opportunity to effect a cure at far less cost, risk and discomfort than a mainstream approach. It concedes the absence of infallible medical knowledge.

Further, it is almost certain that many of these persons will enjoy health benefits that are not available to persons living in tightly controlled regimes such as the US. For example, it is hard to see why a man diagnosed with BPH but with no urgent problems should not try PEMF before embarking on costly, painful, and dangerous surgery. If, in three weeks, it fails he can always take surgery with his doctor's consent. How, exactly, is it beneficial to "protect" this man from a promising therapy whose only "harm" is that using it has the potential to briefly delay a more dangerous choice?

A more invasive but still far less dangerous than mainstream protocol called prostate artery embolization is starting

---

[567] http://www.sciencedaily.com/releases/2015/08/150821164150.htm

to win converts in the medical community for treating BPH. As of 2014, following years of testing, it remains "experimental" in the US even though unlike the current gold standard treatment not a single patient has been documented to suffer acute, lasting negative consequences, and the published research shows 87% efficacy in reversing BPH. Patients being "protected" by the FDA must either fly to Portugal for this therapy or find a clinical trial in the US which, if they are lucky enough to qualify, will cost them about $15,000 out of pocket.

There are numerous other such examples in the annals of medical practice. Such therapies may not be available in so-called advanced countries for years or even decades, depending on FDA politics, cost/benefit analysis of clinical trials and so forth. Meanwhile, patients who could benefit at little risk from these therapies are suffering.

To sum up, in a Celebration Society there will be a consensual commitment to rational, evidence-based therapies, untainted by large monied interests and bureaucracies that may serve as stepping stones for those seeking lucrative corporate sinecures. While this culture will have its failings, I submit that, on balance, it will lead to a far higher standard of preventive care as well as availability of some truly promising curative modalities—all in a more patient-centered healthcare system than prevails today.

A Scientific Society

As stated previously, a Celebration Society will have a culture that respects the scientific method, with the best available evidence guiding decisions and laws, consistent with the values of the Charter. All empirically testable phenomena, including repeating and repeatable patterns in various domains not commonly considered "scientific", could be candidates for scientific inquiry.

Ecological systems science, in particular, has much to offer societal designers. It has been found that sustainable systems balance efficiency with resiliency, with more resiliency than efficiency typically present.[568] This is an entirely different way of looking at systems than the present-day focus on efficiency at all costs.

While many are concerned that achieving sustainability comes at the cost of quality of life, recent modeling of the Canadian economy has found that a switch to such practices would only reduce Canadian growth by 0.14% (far less than 1%) annually.[569]

One major challenge is our predilection as a species for irrational behavior, as documented in Dan Arielly's book *Predictably Irrational*, and more generally in the field of behavioral economics. An indication of how pervasive this challenge is can be found in our reaction to faces.[570]

We all have innate tendencies toward irrationality, hard-wired into us by evolution. For example, research is finding that feeling empathy for those harmed can lead us to want harsher punishment for others not part of the harm.[571] Awareness of these tendencies and cultural support for countering them could help.[572] Public policy needs to acknowledge and correct for bias-related phenomena whenever possible.[573] Science, as both a system of knowledge that yields technology and a systematic approach to acquiring knowledge, will serve the society and the people—never the reverse, except by individual decision.

---

[568] http://capitalinstitute.org/wp-content/uploads/2014/12/Quantifying-Ecosystems-Sustainability-Ulan-Eco-Complexity-Publ-Mar-2009.pdf

[569] http://degrowth.org/wp-content/uploads/2011/05/Victor_Growth-Degrowth-and-Climate-Change.pdf, http://stirling-westrup-tt.blogspot.com/2014/07/tt-ns-2976-we-can-build-sustainable.html

[570] http://www.theatlantic.com/health/archive/2014/10/the-introverted-face/381697/2/

[571] http://www.theatlantic.com/science/archive/2015/09/the-violence-of-empathy/407155/

[572] https://www.newscientist.com/article/mg22730400-700-morality-2-0-how-manipulating-our-minds-could-save-the-world

[573] http://www.fastcompany.com/3049022/the-future-of-work/3-lessons-ibms-watson-can-teach-us-about-our-brains-biases

While some critics of science like to cite isolated incidents of scientists falsifying data, this criticism is valid for all other human endeavors as well. Further, in science it is weak. While journal retractions have been rising recently, even today, "fewer than 0.02 percent of publications are retracted annually." The overall state of science is excellent[574] and science is responsible for the discoveries that are enabling an Abundance Game. Technology is rooted in science and is by far the dominant force on the planet today.

The major advantage of science is that it is a system for deriving *testable, repeatable knowledge.* No other system of knowledge can lay claim to this; direct revelation may be real or it may be delusion. Scientific knowledge can be codified and it can be tested and shared with predictable results. Further, genuine scientists remain open to new ideas, evidence, and discoveries; remaining ever aware that their understandings are based on the best available evidence and assumptions that are believed to comport with reality. The spirit of inquiry that motivates scientists was perhaps best expressed by Harvard physicist Lisa Randall, "Science is a living entity that continues to evolve. Not only the answers, but also the games and riddles and participation make it interesting."[575]

There is no finality in scientific knowledge—but is there ever really finality in any knowledge? Religions evolve and die over millennia, and believers change beliefs and even sometimes religions. Science is therefore as solid a basis for a new civilization as we are likely to find. Codified into open-source technology, science will allow us to rapidly prototype and improve new social systems and even societies. And, vitally, it allows room for diverse belief systems to coexist.

---

[574] http://fivethirtyeight.com/features/science-isnt-broken/
[575] *Warped Passages*, Lisa Randall

A Government Worth Celebrating

Democracy is the worst form of government, except
for all the others that have been tried.

~Winston Churchill

According to Pew Research, public trust in the US
government is at or near historic lows.[576] For a nation that is
organized upon the principle of government by the people and
for the people, there is a clear disconnection between purpose
and performance. Trust is falling elsewhere as well.[577]

This is not hard to understand. Thanks to the internet,
there is a rising awareness of the lies, manipulations, and
abuses committed by those who "serve" us.[578]

Present-day governments tend to call themselves repub-
lics, social democracies, constitutional monarchies or even
communist. In actuality, the systems these governments
profess to follow have little to do with their actual practice of
governing. Most practice some form of capitalism, though
always including elements of other systems.

Issues and Trends in Present-day Governments

There is an old saying, "if you want to understand
something the government is doing that seems absurd, follow
the money." While cynical, it is hard to dispute—and indicates
the central role money plays in Scarcity Game societies and
their governments.

Fine-sounding labels and noble ideals aside, present-day
governments primarily exist to protect the interests of those
who control money and other property. This is largely a matter

---

[576] http://www.people-press.org/2014/11/13/public-trust-in-government/
[577] http://www.pewresearch.org/fact-tank/2013/11/21/confidence-in-government-
falls-in-much-of-the-developed-world/
[578] Many such abuses are well documented, in each case from multiple mainstream
sources, at www.WantToKnow.info.

of allocating scarcity so that the less fortunate do not complain too much or too loudly.

Although the allocation of scarcity throughout history has led to endless wars and losses of life, dignity, and the other finer values, this allocation has always been limited—for better or worse—by the capabilities of those doing the allocating. I doubt that anyone who really thinks about it will want limited resources allocated by superhuman AI's without absolute, irrevocable innate sympathy for humans.

Those who control, those who rule, those who are "masters of the universe", tend to believe that it's due to their innate superiority. Said former Fed Chair Ben Bernanke in his Princeton commencement address of June 2013, "A meritocracy is a system in which the people who are the luckiest in their health and genetic endowment; luckiest in terms of family support, encouragement, and, probably, income; luckiest in their educational and career opportunities; and luckiest in so many other ways difficult to enumerate — these are the folks who reap the largest rewards."[579]

One of the most powerful forces in governance today is *devolution*; the breaking up of long-standing yet often artificial national boundaries, with the new nation-states often based on tribal alignment. Since the founding of the United Nations, the number of such states has roughly tripled. The process continues: Scottish independence was recently averted by Britain offering more sovereignty to the Scots. Similar movements and trends are lively elsewhere.[580]

Devolution need not be in opposition to continental or even planetary unions, as the European Union has demonstrated recently. People can simultaneously regard themselves as, for example, Czech, European and part of humanity.

On the other hand, there are economies of scale that smaller nation-states may not enjoy. This can, perhaps, be remedied through alliances with other states. I see such an

---

[579] http://www.federalreserve.gov/newsevents/speech/bernanke20130602a.htm
[580] http://www.theatlantic.com/international/archive/2014/09/stronger-than-democracy/380774/

alliance arising as multiple Celebration Societies come into existence. Since ties between nations tend to be strongest when cultures are similar (consider, for example, those between Britain, Canada, Australia, and New Zealand), I would expect a formal league of Celebration Societies to have great appeal once several exist, given that all Celebration Societies will be founded upon a common set of values and commitments.

Another major development is e-citizenship. As the functions of government move online, the concept of citizenship and even nationhood may shift from physical borders to voluntary affiliations. Estonia is pioneering this development.[581] All of this should serve to make it easier to establish a Celebration Society somewhere in the planet: the more diverse governments that exist, the more they will feel competitive pressures to create new value for their citizens—provided citizens remain free to emigrate.

These issues and trends are real and continuing. However, they are superficial compared to what is needed to address massive unemployment. In a fully developed Celebration Society, where non-employment is expected to be the norm, it will be necessary to change the incentives in a way more fundamental than anything that has been tried before. To accomplish this, the system will have to offer a purpose that is emotionally and spiritually captivating, and motivate people through something other than economic rewards.

Birth of the Servocracy

We make a living by what we get. We make a life by
what we give.

~Winston Churchill

---

[581] https://www.newscientist.com/article/mg22429913-400-estonias-e-citizen-test-is-a-test-for-us-all/

This section about government is speculative, and I believe that multiple structures of government could work in a Celebration Society. The concept that follows represents my best thinking as to what will work; however, it is by no means the final word. (This is a high-level explanation. More details are provided in the Appendix, A Possible Structure of Government.)

My wife coined the term *servocracy* to describe the "new" system of government that we expect to arise in a Celebration Society. It is actually a proposed system that rests upon and is informed by multiple established proposals and systems: The American Constitutional system, modern parliamentary democracy, the meritocratic approach historically favored in China, and the largely forgotten yet highly successful Venetian Republic.

Once the world's premier naval power, the Venetian Republic spanned the Mediterranean and lasted for many centuries. Visitors today marvel at Venetian architecture and art, its beauty, and its partially artificial construction. Sadly, few seem to consider what sort of society could have built all of this. In the Venetian Republic, the highest officials were unpaid servants. To be appointed the Doge—or head of state— was a great honor conferred upon one exemplary man. He had almost no power, but great influence.

A servocracy would be a system based on service. By this I mean that service is considered to be the noblest and highest good. People are recognized for their acts of service, be they performed over a long time in many small ways or instead acts of great service that may happen quickly, as for example throwing oneself in the path of danger to protect others. Such service must never be mandatory else it becomes something else: conscription or even slavery.

Among those who will likely reject this concept of servocracy are *objectivists*—followers of Ayn Rand, as well as others who exalt selfishness. In a world where human productivity will be separated from economic value, her principle of "To each according to his ability—period" will only apply to whatever game a person chooses to play, and not to the basic necessities of life. It is therefore interesting to consider her view that the "essence" of objectivism was "man as a heroic being" with "productive achievement as his noblest activity."[582]

If productive achievement is defined as that which is valued by one's fellow people, this essence would be compatible with celebrationism. If this concept is instead understood to be based solely on one's perception of self, then it makes no sense in light of heroism. Heroism, by its very nature, requires service to something greater than oneself. In Rand's view, the act of expressing one's individuality against the oppressive State was heroic because the actor risked loss of life and liberty. If the State is non-oppressive, the individual may find other ways to express heroism.

While some may consider such a notion as a servocracy fanciful and impractical, research is now establishing that the primary human drives are for sociability, attachment, affection, and companionship. It is only when the empathic drive is suppressed that secondary drives such as materialism, aggression, narcissism, and violence become dominant.[583] We are not primarily competitive creatures.

Further, having a supportive environment (including cooperation) is apparently vital for well-being.[584] People who demonstrate self-control and practice delayed gratification, both of which correlate to success, but do so in an environment without significant social support, do so at the expense of their health. However, when these qualities are demonstrated in a supportive environment, not only is there no toll on health but health is improved.[585]

I am not saying that competition is bad in moderation. Indeed, competition in games and for prizes can lead to great

---

[582] http://aynrandlexicon.com/lexicon/objectivism.html

[583] *The Empathic Civilization*, Jeremy Rifkin

[584] http://www.regent.edu/acad/global/publications/ijls/new/vol7iss1/ IJLS_Vol7Iss1_Gilbert_pp29-47.pdf

[585] http://www.economist.com/news/science-and-technology/21657768-self-control-improves-your-prospects-it-may-harm-your-health-no-good-deed

contributions; look at the X Prizes. Instead, I assert that our present society, in which competition is glorified above service and cooperation, is an aberration. It is an aberration caused by the Scarcity Game and, in particular, the artificially scarce money in use everywhere today.

If you think that people cannot be motivated to make offerings of service, consider volunteerism. In a recent study, over 26% of U.S. adults engaged in volunteer activities[586]—and this in a culture where leisure time is precious.

What motivates someone to give hours each week to their religious organization, to a chorale or other community performing arts group, or to simply caring for the needy? What motivates people to offer their service freely in support of cherished causes and businesses that stand for values those people support? What motivates someone to spend hundreds of dollars and precious vacation time caring for the needs of others in a venue such as Burning Man?

While critics argue that modern social networks are isolating rather than connecting people, there are some interesting counter examples. For example, Waze is a social network for traffic and driving control that relies in part upon the reporting of traffic conditions by unpaid users. Why do they do this? Selfishly speaking, there's no substantive benefit. People can use the reporting of others without any payment or obligation. Nevertheless, the system works very successfully.

It is clear that these volunteers are receiving something more precious to them than the time and money they sacrificed in order to volunteer—perhaps some sense of belonging, of contribution and self-worth. Research indicates that the happiness gained from volunteering (serving others) just once a week is equivalent to a rise in salary from $20,000 to $75,000.[587] When people are freed from the struggle to survive, they will also be freed to give more than the very few

---

[586] http://www.bc.edu/content/dam/files/research_sites/agingandwork/pdf/
publications/FS03_TrendsVolunteerism.pdf
[587] *Social: Why Our Brains Are Wired to Connect*, Matthew Lieberman

precious hours that are available for service today. This may blossom into a whole new basis for society.

Research is now establishing that service to others is good for us. Specifically, "Scientific evidence is in many ways ... showing that there are systematic changes in the brain associated with acts of generosity (that correlate to increased happiness, resiliency and health)."[588] Further, pleasurable activity devoid of meaning leads to unhealthy patterns of genetic expression similar to those of a stressed person. On the other hand, meaningful activity, particularly activity that serves others, leads to a healthy genetic expression. So, over the long term, a meaningful life of service will tend to be a healthier life than a self-centered one.[589]

There is a story told about Heaven and Hell. In Hell, the story goes, the people surround a banquet table laden with all kinds of delicacies. Each person has a 3 foot long fork strapped to one arm and a 3 foot long spoon strapped to the other arm. People are busy grasping food with the utensils, flinging it into the air and attempting to catch some of the food with their mouths. There is great waste and cries of frustration, with food splattered all over. Heaven, according to the story, is a place that's just the same, with one difference. The people are feeding each other.

If a Celebration Society is a place where great beauty is widely expressed, including monuments, works of art and the interweaving of natural beauty amongst dwelling and public places, then it has the potential to inspire the rare and precious feeling of awe. Awe is an experience that is not only deeply moving to the person having it, but also with substantial social benefits, making people more considerate and generous.[590]

---

[588] http://www.theatlantic.com/health/archive/2015/07/dalai-lama-neuroscience-compassion/397706/

[589] http://www.theatlantic.com/health/archive/2013/08/meaning-is-healthier-than-happiness/278250/

[590] http://www.newscientist.com/article/dn27612-seeing-aweinspiring-natural-sights-makes-you-a-better-person

Though awe is most commonly associated with spirituality, it can be evoked by majestic sights, sounds, and inspiring stories. While most of us experience it only rarely, there is no particular reason why it cannot become a frequent occurrence. I believe that would have profound positive consequences.

Citizenship in a Celebration Society

In at least one respect, I expect life in a Celebration Society to be far more challenging than life anywhere today. Citizenship will be neither a birthright nor will it be something easily attained. It will carry serious responsibilities.

To my knowledge, in today's societies citizens are treated without exception as at worst property and at best vassals by the states under whose forbearance they live. Even in America, founded on certain noble-sounding principles, citizens are hardly treated as full adults:

- Despite a Constitution dedicated to supporting each person's "pursuit of happiness", one's ability to choose what to do with one's own body or with other consenting adults is limited.
- Choice of medical care is restricted by the FDA.
- Entry into various professions is limited by licensing regulations which vary from essentially protectionist (taxi medallions) to arguably helpful in certain cases (for example, architects and doctors) although paternalistic.

These are but a few of many possible examples. The United States is actually better than most nations in how it treats its citizens. The idea of governmental powers emanating from the people is still taken seriously there in some respects though, sadly, fewer and fewer.

To be clear, when I use words such as "limited" and "restricted" above, I am speaking of *crimes* that generally carry harsh prison terms, and in a US prison one is offered little if any protection from indignities such as rape and beatings.

Part of the problem, some observers will argue, is that few people anywhere are informed enough to actually assume full responsibility for their own lives. There are admittedly some challenges in achieving rational governance. For example, people with strong beliefs who are presented with contradictory evidence tend to not only dismiss the evidence but actually cling tighter to those beliefs.[591]

This is either evidence of irrationality or that the person profoundly distrusts the motives of the authority presenting evidence. In the first case it is a failure of education to foster critical thinking skills; in the second, it is a result of such systematic government deceit that trust is broken. I fear that both are true. If so, the only solution may be starting society afresh.

In a Celebration Society, *Citizenship* will be earned through passing tests that demonstrate a firm understanding of Celebration Society principles, Charter and history. I would further advocate a specific Rite of Passage in which one would be placed with a group of fellow *candidate citizens* into a harsh environment for a week or so, with survival not guaranteed—unless people learned to cooperate and rely upon one another. The pursuit of Citizenship would be optional; no one would need to take those risks.

I envision the Rite of Passage coming at the end of a lengthy period during which the candidate citizen serves in helping with the creation of a new Celebration Society, or absent that opportunity by performing other service approved by parliament. (As mature persons know, words are cheap and actions dear. I think that such a period of service would address the societal need for Citizens to demonstrate their commitment to the betterment of society.) I see the Rite of Passage as a final qualification that one is trustworthy at a deep level of integrity and commitment.

At the end of the week, there might be a secret ballot process by which survivors (the vast majority of non-survivors would quit or be removed for health reasons) would determine who became Citizens by deciding whether this was someone

---

[591] Predictably Irrational, Dan Arielly

whom they would trust with their life as a fellow Citizen. (The actual process would arise from community deliberation and experimentation.)

The Rite of Passage would also help to assure that Citizens of a Celebration Society never forget the challenges and hardships endured by those who came before, those thousands of generations of humans who struggled for their existence and upon whose backs was hard won the knowledge that enables a Celebration Society to exist.

Citizenship, once voluntarily earned, will carry privileges including assurance that one's basic necessities of life will always be provided. It will also carry significant responsibilities. *This will be the primary social contract.*

Per the successful Venetian model, any Citizen will be on call at any time for being selected by lottery to serve in the legislature or on a jury, with a few particular and well-enumerated exceptions such as medical conditions. Also, a supermajority of Citizens could always change the Charter, thereby assuring that government "of, by, and for the people" remains a reality forever. Each Citizen, as the final act of attaining that status, will swear an Oath to uphold the Charter for so long as they remain a Citizen.

Venice also offers to us a cautionary note about Citizenship. It eventually limited the lottery for parliament to those with a hereditary claim of citizenship. In this way, the system was perverted to favor entrenched interests over newer ones. One has to wonder: had newcomers who fled Napoleon's conquests been welcome to serve in the Venetian parliament, might Venice have prepared itself to resist his invasion? Might Venice today remain a world power?

Perversion of a Servocracy

Any system, no matter how noble in intent, can be perverted. This observation led me to think about how that might happen in a Celebration Society.

In a Celebration Society, service is the highest virtue. Service can be perverted in several ways. First, one can serve others to the neglect of one's own happiness and needs. This is like draining a battery without recharging it. In the long run, the person will become unhappy or ill and be a drain upon others and the society.

Second, one can offer service that is unwanted for the sake of looking good. This is recognized over time by others as false and is not appreciated, nor is it truly service. Service is both intention and action, operating in unified purpose.

Third, one can choose martyrdom; actively damaging oneself in the hopes of looking heroic. Ironically, the service of others who recognize this is then to keep the person from being a martyr.

Finally, I think it important to state that we don't need (or probably even want) perfect people to serve in the Royalty or, potentially, the Council of Immortals. So far as I can discern, such people walk the Earth only rarely, if ever. Trying to found a society on such a basis would, in my view, create an automatic kind of hierarchy and a pressure for perfection that is unrealistic.

If, instead, we seek people for these roles who show a profound and genuine commitment to service combined with real wisdom; people who acknowledge that they have made and do make mistakes, then we will get "real" people to fill these roles—and there will be no mistaken desire to place them upon a pedestal.

In a Celebration Society, I would expect that significant research will be performed into the nature and expressions of service. Based on the flurry of recent positive psychology research, I expect this to be a fertile field of study.

Never a Utopia

With service enshrined as the most valued of activities in a Celebration Society, everything about the nature of society changes. I submit that these changes, coupled with the immense abundance a Celebration Society will generate, will eliminate many of the problems that plague societies today.

No Celebration Society will ever be a utopia. Utopia is a static, "perfect" vision—a fantasy. Instead, a Celebration Society will be based on science and technology. This is evolving knowledge, ever subject to improvement based on newer and better understandings. It will be a place of interlocking systems, and systems within systems.

There will be systems that do nothing but monitor other systems for compliance within acceptable tolerances (otherwise known as system governors), and all important systems will be triple-redundant. Triple redundancy means that when something goes awry—which will happen, again and again—it can be immediately flagged for attention, diagnosis and correction, because two of the three elements of the system will remain in agreement. This redundancy assures continuous function in nearly all cases.

I also see a Celebration Society as a place where reliance on authority figures dwindles upon reaching adulthood. The word "guru" will return to its original meaning of "teacher", and not some godlike authority figure who all too often displays feet of clay. Likewise, a spiritual leader will be a person who lives a life immersed in a spiritual tradition, offering wisdom from that tradition to those who seek it, but without any secular authority.

No one and no group will ever stand above the consensus of the Citizens. That said, I see nothing wrong with honoring those spiritual traditions that carry meaning for the Citizens of a particular society.

Also, every new Celebration Society will begin on the foundation of knowledge established by those that came before, and with the open source model all will be looking to each other for possible inspirations, improvements and experiments. When an experiment succeeds, it can in general be quickly adopted everywhere.

Part VII: The Road to Tomorrow

We will never make a journey of a thousand miles by
fretting about how long it will take or how hard it will
be. We make the journey by taking each day step by
step and then repeating it again and again until we
reach our destination.

~Joseph B. Wirthlin

The Foundation of Celebrationism

Celebrationism will be built on a foundation of awareness;
of understanding. Nothing more is needed than for large
numbers of people to become aware of and understand the
possibilities for a new world of universal abundance.

Already, most are aware of various dystopian futures that
could happen. These are not preferred or even welcomed, but
no clear, feasible, and attractive alternative has existed until,
perhaps, now.

We will not suddenly awaken into a celebrationist world.
Many beliefs and systems that are today obvious were, when
introduced, virulently opposed. I fully expect that persons
whose livelihoods depend on current systems will oppose
celebrationism with arguments that are sometimes clever and
sometimes specious. They will not want my reasoning to be
correct, and so they will find reasons to prove that it is not. (I
am reminded of the saying, *a man persuaded against his will
is of the same opinion still.* This can also be stated as: people
decide based on emotion and justify their decisions with
reasons.)

Substantive, rational arguments will, if offered, be
seriously considered and accommodated whenever possible.
Rational criticism makes new proposals stronger. Over time,
sometimes a long time, I believe that rationality will prevail
because it does a better job of explaining and predicting
reality.

Though I expect the first Celebration Societies to happen in bodies of sparsely inhabited land, one could also start within an existing society as an experiment. Some societies are better suited to such an experiment than others:

- Japan, which has an aging populace and no clear way to provide for them from the production of younger people, could designate a city as a test case, or allow the building of a floating city in its waters.
- Iceland, with a history of going its own way and a highly educated, tolerant, open-minded population, might designate an area of unused land for such a "new city" as an experiment.
- Any country with a devastated or underutilized area of land that's seeking a way forward from our present morass could designate that area as an autonomous Special Economic and Political Zone.

Many new societies have been successfully created in recent years. Arguably the one most similar to the society we wish to create is the city-state of Singapore, founded in 1819 and independent from Britain for 50 years. Its huge success has been due to a "best practices" model. When solving a problem, Singapore scours the world to see who has successfully addressed it and then chooses the most effective and suitable approach. We will do the same.

We have seen the emergence of 34 new nations since 1990 and, while 21 of them arose from the breakup of the USSR and Yugoslavia, 13 others also emerged. Nations will continue to break up in future—either in a planned and cooperative manner or in a fractious and potentially warlike manner.

Beyond restructuring an existing area of land into a celebrationist city-state, bolder possibilities exist. The base structure of an oceanic city-state could be literally created from "nothing". This would be based on generation of hexagonal floating concrete blocks from seawater via electrolysis, and their linkage into new land mass.[592] Alternately, it could possibly be based on materials that are strong yet float, such as aerogels.[593] Such "new lands" could be built in the open ocean outside of standard shipping lanes, or anchored to an uninhabited island.

Wherever we choose to build our first society, whether we are invited to help an existing country attain a more abundant future or strike out on our own to prove the viability of our design, the intended end result will eventually be the same: a model society that's duplicable, leading us towards a world of celebration and abundance.

Funding a Celebration Society

In today's world, and until the completion of capitalism, money will be required to accomplish anything on a large scale. Requirements for projects come in two categories: start-up capital to purchase or build assets, and ongoing expenses.

The startup capital requirements of a Celebration Society will be considerable, especially if it is created from scratch in a new location. Needed assets will include land, dwellings, and infrastructure.

The ongoing expenses of a Celebration Society can be funded through a combination of conventional and unconventional methods. The conventional methods may include taxation. The unconventional methods may include a culture of tithing, and what I call *tipping it forward.*

Tithing

Tithing is widely used today by religious organizations to fund themselves. However, it has not always been limited to religion. Adam Smith gave the example of Swiss cantons that trusted citizens to pay a certain percentage of their assets as taxation on good faith. His understanding was that this system worked well, without allegations of misconduct. He

---

[592] *The Millennial Project*, Marshall Savage
[593] http://www.shimz.co.jp/english/theme/dream/pdf/GF_last.pdf

also implied that these were tightly knit communities, with common values and government that was local and respected. 10% of income is a common value.

By emphasizing transparency and being built on a common set of values, I expect Celebration Societies to enjoy a much higher level of voluntary support for government expenditures than nations where secrecy, waste and a sense of separation prevails. This could go to a new level entirely; something extraordinary beyond the sharing of income.

Further, people could tithe to specific areas of government or pet projects, such as support for the arts, civic improvements, research institutes or others. Large charitable campaigns have found a significant increase in donations when they allowed donors to direct their pledges.[594]

Tipping it Forward

The founders of a Celebration Society, as I see it, could be people who commit part of the ownership in their enterprises to the City Development Fund. This would be a voluntary gift; there would be no penalty for not participating. But consider the pervasiveness of restaurant tipping in societies that embrace this practice. How much more powerful an influence would be something deemed central to the well-being of the society one had chosen to join?

As I see it, regardless of the source, money will pour like a waterfall or fountain into buckets, filling in turn:

1. Administrative and infrastructure needs of the City
2. Meeting the basic needs of Citizens
3. Meeting the basic needs of residents
4. Providing matching money to start two more Cities in turn
5. Public works, including beautification, monuments, etc.
6. Research institutes

---

[594] Personal conversation with IBM Charitable Contribution Campaign department fundraiser.

Taxation

Given the expected appeal of Celebration Societies as tourist destinations, it may be that simply taxing all tourism-related activities at a flat rate of 15% will be enough. If not, all economic activity within the Celebration Society could be so taxed on a value-added or consumption tax basis, with evasion essentially eliminated by making the entire monetary system electronic.

The definition of "fairness" in taxation seems subject to endless debate, from those who consider any taxation to be theft to those who favor "progressive" taxation in which the rich pay at higher rates than do the poor. However, a "regressive" system, such as the US has for hedge fund managers' compensation relative to others' earnings, or a "progressive" system rife with exemptions and exclusions, is clearly less "fair" than a flat (neither regressive nor progressive) system devoid of exemptions and exclusions.

Adam Smith articulated four maxims of taxation which remain valid today:

1. Citizens should financially support the state in proportion to their income earned under the protection of the state.
2. The tax required of each individual should be certain and not arbitrary.
3. Tax should be levied in a time and manner convenient for the taxpayer.
4. Every tax should be designed to minimize overhead costs and to avoid discouraging productivity.[595]

Any system of taxation, to be free from manipulation and resentment, must be transparent, simple, non-burdensome, and as unobtrusive as possible. In a Celebration Society, taxation needs to fund only activities that promote the general welfare. General welfare needs to be defined through consensus, so that resentment is minimized. When individuals are

---

[595] Adam Smith's Wealth of Nations, Jonathan Kolber

cared for, it needs to be understood that not caring for them would cause more damage to the society than doing so. Head Start and rehabilitation programs are prime examples.

The systems, as described in this book and those to be added or substituted in future with more and better knowledge, will serve to assure that each Citizen (and eventually resident) of the city-state has a healthy and diverse diet, decent housing, education in accord with one's interests and passions through whatever level is desired, adequate preventive and curative health care unencumbered by non-peer regulation or profit motive, and the opportunity to experience community with options for entertainment and companionship.

Eventually, once a Celebration Society has transitioned from capitalism to full celebrationism and money ceases to matter, taxation will also end. At that time, probably decades hence, the massive production of the automated systems will provide abundance for all.

I have laid out *a* possible path to celebrationism. I believe there are many other paths that wind around and through the great central road. There may be other roads entirely. Should we take this road, we will make many mistakes along the way. We will learn from them. The milestones and perhaps even the destination will likely differ in significant ways from what I have foreseen.

To take this road, we must first appreciate the crossroads at which we stand.

Standing At the Crossroads of Destiny (Reprise)

The only limits to creating a planet that future generations will be proud of are our imaginations and our social systems.

~Erle C. Ellis

321

As a species, we face massive challenges. We have the capacity to address these if we engineer social systems that use technology intelligently. Pessimists may call such confidence hubris and insist that advanced nations must greatly reduce consumption in order for humanity to survive. However, people in advanced nations have shown no willingness to make such reductions despite aggressive exhortations and "educational" campaigns. Instead, we need a different road forward that people will actually embrace.

Where we stand, there are three roads forward. One of these roads, the default road straight ahead, continues our onrush towards massive unemployment while we remain unable to systematically cope with the turbulent and accelerating changes now underway. Lacking an organizing vision, we will lurch from crisis to crisis until some great central authority assumes control over every human life—or we slip onto one of the other roads.

Taking this other road, we stumble so colossally that the human era on Earth ends. The final road, at least one form of it, has been the subject of this book.

In times to come, Celebration Societies could proliferate across the Earth; each a dynamic, thriving oasis where residents and visitors enjoy lush, sustainable living in peace, prosperity and wonder. Each would offer unique cultural experiences and physical attractions. Art, nature and technology would fuse in ways we can only begin to imagine, yielding an amazing variety of expressions.[596] Various experiments in government would also be tried and evolve. Continuous improvement would become a way of life, with city-states sharing amongst themselves and others their best practices and discoveries.

---

[596] One can visit places such as Masdar, Venice, and Burning Man to get a sense of possibilities

Such societies might extend into the oceans, built on interlinked blocks of "seacrete" or other floating materials, offering homes to sea dwelling organisms as well as to people, plants, and animals.[597]

Celebration Societies could eventually be built in space as majestic, crystalline space colonies, sparkling in the ocean of night. In these O'Neills, residents would enjoy complete environmental control, with some choosing to create perfect ski conditions and others tropical paradises. Idealized forms of ancient societies and even extinct flora and fauna such as mammoths or dinosaurs might come to life—safely quarantined from Earth's modern culture and ecology. All would surely have the chance to become tourist destinations.

Unique new forms of entertainment possible only in O'Neills would proliferate. Some people would strap on gossamer wings in low gravity (at the central axis of a great, rotating cylinder) and fly through clouds like birds; swooping and soaring in games and other self-expression. Others would choreograph and perform new forms of dance, art, and sports that use three dimensions rather than two, making controlled use of variable gravity and zero gravity.

After terraforming, Celebration Societies could proliferate on Mars as well, and eventually on other planets or even moons.

Fanciful this may seem, but all of it is grounded in known and emerging science and technology. All of this is possible, if *we* choose it.

However...

No matter how compelling may be the arguments for a Celebration Society, no matter how self-evidently necessary it may be to meeting the needs of vast numbers of people, several mindsets will surely oppose it, in whole or in part.

First, there will be those who legitimately question the viability of this solution, considering it impractical or incomplete. Such evidence-based objections must be met with

---

[597] *The Millennial Project*, by Marshall Savage.

thoughtful consideration and correction of my and others' inevitable mistakes. The distinction between such critics and those who criticize on an irrational basis will be clear from the quality of evidence mustered and the logic with which it is presented.

Second is the cynicism of oligarchy. Oligarchs can use their wealth and influence to protect and enhance what they have. This is often—though not always—done without regard for the larger social consequences. It includes manipulating public opinion. Recent examples have included cannabis prohibition, climate change distortion,[598] and promoting war with a hidden agenda.[599]

Some would say that oligarchs have prevented the emergence of advanced energy technologies and that they will stifle an emergent Celebration Society as well. Perhaps. However, I note that cannabis prohibition is ending, the world is actually safer on a per capita basis than at any time in history,[600] and various advanced energy technologies are now approaching deployment.

Third, people crave stability. As discussed by David Brin, the majority of the population is fearful of sudden extreme change and can become violent against proponents or causes of such change. He points out that it is necessary to learn to enroll those who might wish to stop constructive change, even at the cost of civilization itself.[601]

Finally, there is extremist ideology. This includes certain types of fundamentalists and cults who brook no opposition to their worldview.

---

[598] http://www.scientificamerican.com/article/exxon-knew-about-climate-change-almost-40-years-ago/

[599] *War is a Racket*, by US Marine Corps General and Medal of Honor winner Smedley Butler.

[600] http://www.salon.com/2013/04/23/the_world_is_actually_safer_than_ever/

[601] http://futurism.com/videos/david-brin-on-so-you-want-to-make-gods-now-why-would-that-bother-anybody/

One of the most prominent current examples is ISIS. In addition to brutal punishment of those who disobey its edicts, ISIS promises some of what makes a Celebration Society so attractive: food, health care, housing and clothing for all its people.[602] (The reality can be quite different than the promises.)[603]

According to the International Centre for the Study of Radicalisation and Political Violence, ISIS has attracted over 20,000 jihad fighters as immigrants to its self-declared Islamic State. Says John Horgan, director of the Center for Terrorism and Security Studies, "people who join groups like ISIS are trying to find a path, to answer a call to something, to right some perceived wrong, to do something truly meaningful with their lives."[604]

In this world of accelerating change, people will be increasingly desperate for certainty and for meaning; a calling. If they cannot find these in a positive focus for their lives, many will instead take a dark course. In this respect, ISIS and others like it are but the tip of a very dangerous spear pointed at the heart of civilization.

We can offer to the people the needed positive focus; a beacon of light and a mighty shield against negativity. We can offer them a new, brighter world. Will we do it?

---

[602] http://www.theatlantic.com/features/archive/2015/02/what-isis-really-wants/384980/

[603] http://www.theatlantic.com/international/archive/2015/09/isis-territory-taxes-recruitment-syria/403426/

[604] http://www.theatlantic.com/international/archive/2015/03/why-its-so-hard-to-stop-isis-propaganda/386216/

Call to Action

> There are those who look at things the way they are,
> and ask why... I dream of things that never were, and
> ask why not?

> ~*Robert F. Kennedy*

This section is only for those who wish to help with the establishment of a Celebration Society. It seems that, no matter the worthiness of the cause, only a minority will arise from the shadows to stand as champions. As in the fable of *The Little Red Hen*, the others will wait to enjoy the benefits without taking any risk—or actively oppose that which could nourish the ground upon which they stand. So be it. As discussed below, 10% of the population—fully committed—is enough to do everything that matters.

This book should not be the *final* word on a Celebration Society; far from it. It is only the beginning. I dream with every fiber of my being that this is but the initial exploration of something that will rise from these bare-bones musings by a single thinker and become a movement. I invite you to participate and help to "flesh out the bones", as it were:

- Visit the website: www.aCelebrationSociety.com. Join. Core membership is free. You will be notified of important developments, and receive access to new information on a regular basis.
- Join the threaded discussion forum, offering your own views. (This will be moderated and civility will be enforced. Trolls will be tracked and banned. Honest, evidence-based debate will be encouraged.)
- Donate funds or services. There will be need for ongoing services (web hosting, book marketing, etc.) All such donations can be made to a 501 (C) 3 nonprofit organization, to be formed as soon as feasible. All cash in and out will be transparently recorded at this website. (Until that time, donations are welcome but will not be tax deductible.)

- If you wish to volunteer services, please let us know your special passion and talents and your availability, including a resume.
- Consider helping to organize a local, grassroots campaign to create awareness and change minds. Research has shown that, "Sharing, listening and showing vulnerability can change beliefs about public policy."[605]
- All going well, I intend that this present book will be followed by a multi-author book or symposium series called, *Building a Celebration Society.* Those with relevant expertise who wish to volunteer their services will be invited to participate. (This will not substitute for collaborative development by all, but rather will provide us with grounding in reality on matters of civil engineering, architecture, and so forth where most of us—myself certainly included—know little.) In effect, these experts will inform us about the physical requirements for building a viable city-state based upon present-day technical knowledge.
- Contribute to the *third culture*, a movement now afoot in which empirically based thinking prevails that deeply and freshly considers great issues of the day.[606]
- Participate in the development of a virtual Celebration Society, with the intent to move it to a physical instantiation:
    - Create an immersive simulation that enables the co-creation of a Celebration Society in a virtual Earth.[607] It is now becoming possible to create

---

[605] http://www.nytimes.com/2014/12/19/upshot/how-same-sex-marriage-effort-found-a-way-around-polarization.html

[606] http://edge.org/conversation/the-third-culture

[607] http://www.theatlantic.com/technology/archive/2015/03/video-games-are-better-without-characters/387556/

realistic simulations of complex physical systems such as cities.[608]

- o Play and design will go on for several years as a testing period, refining and perhaps rebooting—until there is a consensus that, "this is it." This will be a viable design; one that can work well and reliably once instantiated. It will be continuously improved.

- o Use instantiation methods and plans developed in parallel with the above testing period to transfer the Celebration Society from the virtual world to the actual world.

- o More details about how you can participate, as well as requirements for experts, can be found online at www.aCelebrationSociety.com.

- I expect that other and better ideas for achieving a Celebration Society than those in this book are waiting to be discovered. How would *you* move us toward celebrationism?

Finally, THANK YOU—for reading, for being open-minded, for being willing to participate in this, which I believe to be the greatest game in history, the forging of the brightest possible future for all who choose to play in it: the co-creation of a Celebration Society.

There is a concept in physics called *phase transition.* It is the point when a seemingly stable system suddenly transforms into something very different; when (for example) ignition happens or water turns to ice. Research into political and ecological systems suggests that similar mechanisms may exist in realms of human society as well.[609]

As Malcolm Gladwell popularized the concept in *The Tipping Point,* it is never knowable in advance which incremental change will transform a system from one state to another. We

---

[608] http://www.newscientist.com/article/mg22630223.000-virtual-worlds-so-good-theyll-change-our-grasp-on-real-life.html#.VWFL8U_BzGc

[609] http://news.rpi.edu/luwakkey/2902

may not know how we will convince people of the value and viability of celebrationism; we do however know how many we need to convince. In particular, "Scientists at Rensselaer Polytechnic Institute have found that *when just 10 percent of the population holds an unshakable belief, their belief will always be adopted by the majority of the society.*"[610] (Emphasis added.)

We live in a time when attractive ideas can spread virally over the internet, becoming *memes*, reaching millions and even billions. By continuing to grow, one person at a time, we will reach that critical mass.

The world hungers for a better approach to production and a more humane way to organize society. We have a unique chance, together, to deliver it.

---

[610] ibid.

Appendix: A Possible Government Structure

I have hinted at the overall structure of a celebrationist government elsewhere in this book, but did not want to let the vision get bogged down in the details. Here, for those who want them, are the details.

This proposed possible system of government is designed to address specific deficiencies of modern systems, including the formation of political parties with attendant conflict, gridlock, campaigns for office and political influence; the disconnection of citizens from their government; and the conflation of a ceremonial leadership role with the executive.

This system has four branches of government initially, with a fifth to be added when and if feasible. The four original branches are: parliament, judiciary, administration, and royalty. All act in service to the Charter.

The Charter

The Charter is a statement of principles to which all Citizens swear an Oath of support upon becoming Citizens. It is not a statement of good wishes that is then ignored whenever the government finds it to be inconvenient. It is instead explicitly treated as the highest law of the land.

Any law passed by parliament or by Citizen Initiative that in any way conflicts with the Charter is to be declared entirely null and void by the Supreme Court and must be passed again in compliant form. Any legislator, administrator, judge, or royal who willfully violates the Charter without extraordinary need (as determined by an appropriate court) may be removed from office by Citizen or appropriate Branch supermajority vote and held to the highest standard of responsibility for such actions or omissions.

The Charter may be changed in the following ways:

- Upon consensus of all the four or five branches of government.
- Upon Citizen Initiative, properly started by Citizens and receiving a specified supermajority of votes.
- Once there are multiple such cities, a League of Celebration Societies may be established amongst them

to address common concerns and opportunities. Such a league may have the power to change the *model* charter but, in my view, should not have the power to enforce change upon a preexisting society's Charter.

However the Charter is changed, I would suggest that there be an automatic review process one year after adoption before the change becomes permanent. (This would borrow from Iceland's history in which, "It was specified that every new enactment should be subject to a probationary period of 3 years before ... becoming permanent."[611]) I think this would be a good idea for laws in general—there are often unintended consequences that can only been seen after the passage of time.

I would favor a system in which each branch of government, to the extent practicable, conducts its own affairs, filling vacancies and making promotions based on a system that is transparent and deemed acceptable amongst its members and the Citizens.

I would also favor a system wherein voting, to the extent used in a Celebration Society, involves consensus-building *ranking* of one's choices rather than simply selecting one option. In this manner, a widely favored second or third choice might win rather than a first choice that fails to garner an absolute majority, thereby eliminating the need for multiple votes (i.e. runoffs).

Parliament

Parliament works much as it did in the Venetian system. Any Citizen, at any time (barring incapacity) may be called through the periodic lottery to serve in parliament for a single term. Parliamentary terms are staggered to prevent the emergence of parties, with terms varying from, for example, 3 months to 3 years. Openings occur upon completion of term, death, incapacity or resignation. There are no elections of members; each Citizen is presumed competent to serve.

---

[611] *A History of the Old Icelandic Commonwealth*, Jón Jóhannesson.

Parliament elects its own leadership and sets its own rules of operation. It also selects the members of the Administration Council, preferably through consensus and secondarily through election.

Parliament may have a physical place of meeting and/or support virtual meetings. Voting need not require physical presence; only a secure means of sharing communications.

By eliminating the corrupting influence of election campaigns and political parties, lobbying will return to its original function of providing information and arguments to decision-makers rather than buying their cooperation.

Judiciary

In modern America, as in much of the world today, the independence and integrity of the judicial system is in danger. Much of this danger, at least in America, comes from the politicization of all aspects of government in thralldom to money. Increasingly, judges are being elected.[612]

By eliminating the election of judges and changing the society's relationship with money, independence and integrity will have a better chance.

Private influence of friends upon friends will of course remain. However, a monetary system in which all transactions are electronic allows for easy auditing to reduce the chance of large-scale bribes and conspiracies.

I envision the judiciary having three levels: Adjudicating Courts, Appellate Courts and the Supreme Court. Seats on the adjudicating courts *could* be assigned to Citizens selected randomly by lottery, or who volunteer for the post. Given that the legal system will be clear, simple and intelligible to an average Citizen, this is plausible. (Indeed, I would argue that a system in which a Citizen requires a lawyer to understand the law is excessively complex.)

---

[612] http://www.theatlantic.com/politics/archive/2014/10/courting-corruption-the-auctioning-of-the-judicial-system/381524/2/

However, even with a streamlined and rational legal system[613] and assistive AI's there will still be a need for familiarity with bodies of law and, possibly, precedent. I would see random selection, if adopted, as limited to Adjudicating Courts.

Appellate judges should be persons with significant experience in and understanding of the law. Their selection could be by consensus of serving adjudicating judges. Another option would be for the Court senior to that court where a judge is needed to put forth a list of candidates it deems suitable, with Citizen voting then choosing from amongst those candidates. For example, upon an Appellate opening, the Supreme Court could produce a list of candidates, likely from among serving Adjudicating judges. The Citizens would then vote their selection from this list.

Supreme Court Justices could be selected and serve as follows: upon an opening, Justices are chosen by consensus of the currently serving judges. There are 9 Justices, with terms staggered annually. Each Justice serves a single 9 year term. In the 9th and final year, that Justice serves as Chief Justice, having the most experience of anyone serving on the court. She or he sets the agenda, participates in discussion and debates, but votes only to break ties.[614] As a check upon judicial power, I would advocate that Citizen Initiative be able to remove a sitting Supreme Court justice by supermajority vote.

There is also a question as to whether the legal system should be adversarial. This approach is prized in America. In nations such as Costa Rica and Japan that do not have an adversarial legal system, lawsuits are few and lawyers are modestly paid.

I expect that the profession of lawyer will change to something new, and it may split into different functions. For

---

[613] Model legal systems have been devised and proposed by researchers, and should be considered as starting points.

[614] The Chief Justice, then, would have a function in the court system similar to that of the Sarvay in the administrative system.

example, In Britain, the American concept of lawyer is broken into two different positions, barrister and solicitor.

Any ambiguity in the Charter, as determined by the Supreme Court, would require immediate rectification either by consensus of the branches of government or by a supermajority vote of the Citizens. If a law is ambiguous in any particular, the Supreme Court would void it. Such voiding could happen quickly, but I expect very rarely as this requirement will necessitate great care in the wording of proposed laws. I would anticipate that laws would never be passed without being read by all voting members of parliament.

All laws must be brief and intelligible to an average citizen. While this reposes more powers in the judicial system than may be customary today, it also keeps government simple and avoids bureaucracy.

Civil disagreements will ordinarily be resolved through mediation and arbitration, based upon standard forms of agreement that can be modified by the parties. In addition, recordings of communications, whether public, or if private with mutual consent to the recording, are also admissible as evidence.

Per the Venetian model, alleged non-civil offenses may be reported via a secret but not anonymous complaint. Anyone who suspects a crime may submit a secret written complaint to the appropriate Court. It must be signed and witnessed by at least one Citizen in addition to the complainant. If the offense is charged and convicted or if it is determined to be groundless after investigation but a reasonable person could have inferred an offense from the evidence that was available, the reporting note is kept secret. However, if the court determines that the charges were both unwarranted and malicious, the penalty for the offense(s) alleged falls upon the complainant.

There are no "crimes" per se. There are "intentional offenses" and "accidental offenses", with the understanding that negligence is presumed to be negative intent. The whole system is oriented towards restoration and protection against future offenses. It is only punitive to the extent that such is required to enforce these purposes.[615]

As an example of the legal system's workings, with a culture that emphasizes safety, transparency and rationality there will likely not be a need for rigid building codes. However, certain practices such as standard wiring will be highly recommended, and most likely qualify the owner for lower insurance rates. Further, when it comes time to sell such a building, the one that can certify compliance with the recommended practices will be easier to sell at a higher price. As part of the transparency, the Celebration Society will require full documentation of everything done to the building from initial construction to present circumstances.

Contracts become simpler as well. For example, suppose that John and Sally orally make a contract. Sally agrees to invest certain assets into a corporation that John is forming in exchange for certain ownership. They agree to later finalize the details in writing. John does not follow through in a reasonable time. Sally may enter the matter into mediation, which will automatically become arbitration if the mediation fails. Sally and John may enter into evidence third party testimony, but the strongest evidence will be recordings of their conversations about the matter—made automatically in public or, if in private, by recorded mutual consent.

Another and perhaps more common conflict might arise when some people have a party in a public park, creating noise that upsets a neighbor. In current societies, where there is no recording of public communications and noises, the concept of "too loud" is subjective and much debated. In a Celebration Society, a decibel threshold could be specified in law and recordings would determine compliance.

If a person who is mentally ill commits an offence, they are isolated as necessary to protect others and themselves. The

---

[615] Some believe that only execution assures an offender cannot again commit a heinous crime. Others argue that innocent persons are sometimes executed. Segregation without sentences of dangerous offenders, with continuous monitoring until brain normalization, assures that both concerns are addressed.

isolation is not punitive, and continues until they are deemed cured by the best available scientific psychological testing. Complaint may be made and a court may decide to isolate or supervise this person even prior to an offense being committed. For example, a person suffering from dementia might be declared no longer competent to function as a Citizen and, following exhaustion of appeals (if any), placed into protective care.

Administration

The Administration Council oversees the administrative duties of the government and society. There are a fixed number of ministers, perhaps 10. Each minister has a portfolio, similar to such in other parliamentary systems. They head the major areas of administration, potentially including education, health, infrastructure, foreign relations, banking/money, and others.

The Administration Council hires a paid, professional city or national administrator to manage the general administrative functions, particularly in those areas where Ministries overlap. (There may be subsidiary levels of administration, as appropriate.) Each ministry may hire its own administrator and staff as appropriate and as funded by parliament.

Administration administers. It does not lead. There is no prime minister nor is there a president. The Sarvay may represent the government in discussions with other government leaders, but cannot make decisions. Instead, decisions are made by the Administration Council or, as appropriate, by the Branches working together. The Administration Council may send other representatives to accompany the Sarvay in such discussions, preceding a vote.

Ministers are appointed by parliament for fixed, non-renewable terms of service, which may or may not be staggered as decided by parliament. Upon completion of a term of service, an ex-minister is customarily expected to mentor her or his replacement. These ministers will, ideally, be persons of impeccable morality and wisdom. They can be removed by vote of parliament or by Citizen initiative.

All administrative and parliamentary positions are unpaid if the person has passive income exceeding a comfortable predetermined threshold such as US $100,000 per year. When the occupant earns less than that threshold, the government will make up the difference to assure that financial concerns never color a leader's judgment. (Singapore has achieved a high level of professionalism and non-corruption among government workers by making the positions highly paid and respected.) There will be no revolving door between government and industry, perhaps assured by a multi-year delay in any appointments of former officials to activities they formerly supervised.

Ministers must refrain from all active business interests and investments, placing such into blind trusts while on the Council. The Ministers come together to decide matters that extend beyond an individual minister's portfolio, and they may collectively review any individual minister's actions.

Royalty

Royalty serves, at its best, to inspire and uplift society. It serves in pageantry, ceremony and celebration. It provides a focus and a model to emulate. It is not about entitlement.

This will be a royalty unlike any the world has known since the Doge of the Venetian Republic. It will have no power, except as an equal branch of the government in instances where agreement among multiple branches of government is required or, in one particular function discussed below, as a tiebreaker. Therefore, it is in no way a monarchy. It is a *meritocratic royalty.*

This royalty serves two functions: to exemplify the highest values of the Charter and to preside at ceremonial events. (These would include celebrations, weddings, speeches, commencement of great projects or organizations, inaugurations, VIP visits, etc.) They may also serve in ambassadorial, emissary and plenipotentiary capacities. Some of these functions will necessitate long periods apart from their home, living in significantly less desirable conditions. Therefore ambassadorial service, in whatever capacity of title or support, would be a high form of service.

People are inducted into the Royalty by invitation of the Royalty itself, and must first be Citizens. Royalty is a lifetime appointment, absent egregious misconduct. This is not an office but an honorific with responsibilities.

Though tied to a particular Celebration Society, royalty will have no geographic authority or power. Therefore, I consider the traditional titles to be inadequate.

I envision three tiers and titles within the Royalty: Servant, Great Servant and *Sarvay*. None of these titles carries with it any power except for the Sarvay who has a tie-breaking vote on the Administration Council. Therefore Sarvay should be time-limited, perhaps with an honorific title afterwards of Sarvay Emeritus.

The Sarvay (a Sanskrit word meaning, "for all") will serve as a leading exemplar of the society's values—similar to the Doge of the Venetian Republic. The Royalty chooses the Sarvay. This person walks, talks, and lives service to the society. This person serves as "head of state"—though only in a ceremonial capacity of service rather than one of power.

A handful of royals, possibly three, are designated Great Servant, or *Mahana Sevaka*. Upon the retirement from office, completion of term, death, or incapacitation of the Sarvay, one of them is appointed as his or her successor by consensus of the Royalty. Another possibility is that, upon constitution of a new Celebration Society, a Mahana Sevaka from an existing Celebration Society would be invited to assume the role of Sarvay in the new Celebration Society, helping the Citizens there to build their own royalty.

Induction into the Royalty would carry with it additional responsibilities but no additional privileges. This would help to assure that royals are truly motivated by desire to serve rather than the pursuit of some sort of personal gain.

A Possible Fifth Branch of Government

Wisdom, it turns out, is measurable and cross-cultural. Dilip Jeste has made a study of it and found that:

> The traits of the wise tend to include compassion and empathy, good social reasoning and decision making, equanimity, tolerance of

divergent values, comfort with uncertainty and ambiguity. And the whole package is more than the sum of the parts, because these traits work together to improve life not only for the wise but also for their communities. Wisdom is pro-social.[616]

Although people often talk wistfully about the need for wisdom of elders guiding society, it remains elusive. There are several reasons. Elders are often compromised by infirmities. Also, with the rate of change now being so rapid, much of elders' perspective seems dated. However, when in the future elders remain in good health for centuries or longer, they will have the long vantage point that such lifespans in good health will afford them. Remaining aware of recent developments in society and technology, I expect that their views will be much more highly regarded.

As discussed elsewhere, by the mid to late 21st century physical immortality may become an option, either in a biological body immunized against decay and disease, or by the downloading of memories and personality into a computer. This will not necessarily *be* the person but, from the standpoint of contributions to society, that may make no difference.

Immortality, in whatever form, would enable an important fifth branch of government. I call it the *Council of Immortals*.

In his *Republic*, Plato described how a society will decay over time, as more enlightened rulers would inevitably be replaced by those less enlightened. Errors of judgment would compound, and the decay would continue until the society would eventually devolve into tyranny.

The problem is how to ensure continuity of wisdom. Essentially, for any civilization to endure while remaining true to its values, it needs for those values to be explicitly codified. However, that is not enough. The world is full of nations with high-minded principles codified in their founding constitutions; principles routinely ignored in practice. Also, the

---

[616] http://www.theatlantic.com/magazine/archive/2014/12/the-real-roots-of-midlife-crisis/382235/

meanings of words and phrases changes with context, time and advancements in society.

What is needed are not just wise people to guide the society, but a vigilant, informed citizenry (as demanded by Thomas Jefferson); ideally supported (not ruled) by wise *immortals*. We stand at the threshold of this possibility.

As Aubrey de Grey has pointed out, all that is needed to achieve immortality is to gain at least one day of life for each day lived. The kind of regeneration required is now being researched by scientists, and some exciting tools are already at hand. When nanotechnology can monitor and repair all cellular damage, immortality may be achieved. Biological repair may also suffice.

Regardless of the method ultimately used, I expect that persons whose wisdom has guided a Celebration Society for a long time will desire to continue to do so. What could be more satisfying, more joyful? Whether they remain human or become something else, I envision such a Council of Immortals providing a long-range perspective not inherent to the other four branches of government.

While this would be only one of the five branches, I expect that the other branches would rarely if ever vote against this council. (For that reason, it might vote only in the event of a tie amongst the other four branches.) It seems likely that this council would run numerous simulations of every proposed major change to the society and share the results with the rest of the branches and the Citizens.

If the entire society eventually becomes one of immortals, the need for this council may fade away. But even then it might continue as a body expressly constituted to assure continuity of the society's values; a body whose members have taken upon themselves the ultimate level of service.